LEADING FROM THE HEART

LEADING FROM THE HEART

AN EDUCATIVE PREVENTIVE APPROACH

ALEJANDRO RODRIGUEZ

INSTITUTE OF SALESIAN STUDIES
BERKELEY, CA.

Copyright © 2020 Alejandro Rodriguez

All rights reserved. This book or parts thereof may not be reproduced in any form, stored in any retrieval system, or transmitted in any form by any means—electronic, mechanical, photocopy, recording, or otherwise—without prior written permission of the publisher, except as provided by United States of America copyright law. For permission requests, write to the publisher, at "Attention: Permissions Coordinator," at the address below.

arrsdb@gmail.com

ISBN: 978-1-7354283-4-5

Front cover by Alejandro Rodriguez.
Book design by Alejandro Rodriguez.

Visit the author´s website at https://www.liderazgo-preventivo.org

First edition 2020.

To Paula (†) and Severiano.

To Checo, Toyo, Rafa, Chano, Valdo and Yola.

You are my lived experience of Don Bosco´s Oratory.

You are my Valdocco experience.

The foundation of all education is a matter of the Heart.

Don Bosco

Contents

1. CURRENT ENVIRONMENT — 15
2. SELF-APPROPRIATION — 51
3. SCAFFOLDING FOR AN EDUCATIONAL MODEL — 73
4. LEADERS AND LEADERSHIP DEVELOPMENT — 111
5. SALESIAN PREVENTIVE LEADERSHIP — 163
   - AN ATTEMPT AT DEFINITION — 163
   - SALESIAN PREVENTION — 164
   - SALESIAN PREVENTIVE LEADERSHIP — 168
   - SALESIAN PREVENTIVE LEADER — 171
   - BE BENEVOLENT (AMOREVOLEZZA, LOVING KINDNESS) — 179
   - BE REASONABLE — 187
   - BE AN EDUCATOR WITH TRANSCENDENT INTENT — 191
   - BE A PERSON OF REFLECTION AND SELF-AWARENESS — 195
   - BE THE SALESIAN ORATORY ANYWHERE, ANYTIME — 197
   - BE A BUILDER OF A FAMILY ENVIRONMENT, IN CONFIDENCE AND JOY — 202
   - BE A PROMOTER OF INTEGRAL AND PERSONAL DEVELOPMENT — 205
   - BE A PROMOTER OF AN ACCOMPANYING COMMUNITY — 208
   - BE A CONSTANT PRESENCE WITH AN ACTIVE AND FOCUSED ACCOMPANIMENT — 212
   - BE A GENERATOR OF A PEDAGOGY OF POSSIBILITY — 216
   - BE A PROMOTER OF DISCERNMENT — 219
   - BE A PROMOTER OF A CULTURE OF ENCOUNTER AND DIALOGUE — 222
   - BE SUPPORTIVE IN SOLIDARITY — 226
   - SELF-REFLECTION OF CHAPTER V — 228
6. EFFECTS OF THE PREVENTIVE LEADERSHIP — 231

POSSIBLE FACTORS OF LEADERSHIP DEVELOPMENT WITH PREVENTIVE TRAITS: CONVERGENCE PARADIGM	231
THE GRACE OF UNITY	234
INLO AS A FRAMEWORK FOR THE DEVELOPMENT OF THE PREVENTIVE EDUCATIONAL LEADER	238
INLO AS A FRAMEWORK FOR THE DEVELOPMENT OF ORGANIZATIONAL PREVENTIVE LEADERSHIP	240
FLO FOR THE DEVELOPMENT OF PREVENTIVE EDUCATIONAL LEADERS	242
FLO AS A FRAMEWORK FOR THE DEVELOPMENT OF ORGANIZATIONAL PREVENTIVE LEADERSHIP	245
POSSIBLE INDICATORS OF THE DEVELOPMENT OF A PREVENTIVE LEADER	246
POSSIBLE INDICATORS OF THE DEVELOPMENT OF PREVENTIVE LEADERSHIP	248
SELF-REFLECTION OF CHAPTER VI	249
FINAL THOUGHTS	**251**
REFERENCES	**257**

List of Tables and Figures

Tables

TABLE 1 SOME GUIDELINES FOR THE CLASSROOM	42
TABLE 2 LONERGANIAN FUNDAMENTAL PRECEPTS AND FUNCTIONS	55
TABLE 3 LONERGAN IMPERATIVES	56
TABLE 4 DIMENSIONS/APPROACHES TO CONSTRUCTIVIST PEDAGOGIES	76
TABLE 5 ELEMENTS THAT INTERVENE IN THE KNOWLEDGE CONSTRUCTION PROCESS	79
TABLE 6 KEY ELEMENTS FOR A POSITIVE SCHOOL CLIMATE	84
TABLE 7 KEY ELEMENTS FOR A HIGHLY EFFECTIVE LEARNING ENVIRONMENT	85
TABLE 8 CONSTRUCTIVIST THEORETICAL FOUNDATION WITH EXAMPLES	97
TABLE 9 PRINCIPLES FOR A THEORY OF LEARNING WHOSE KEY FACTOR IS ACTIVITY	106
TABLE 10 TRAIT FOCUS LEADERSHIP THEORY	120
TABLE 11 SKILL APPROACH LEADERSHIP THEORY	122
TABLE 12 STYLE APPROACH LEADERSHIP THEORY	123
TABLE 13 CONTINGENCY LEADERSHIP THEORY	124
TABLE 14 SITUATIONAL LEADERSHIP THEORY	125
TABLE 15 PATH-GOAL LEADERSHIP THEORY	126
TABLE 16 LEADER–MEMBER EXCHANGE (LMX) THEORY	127
TABLE 17 CHARISMATIC LEADERSHIP THEORY	128
TABLE 18 SERVANT LEADERSHIP THEORY	130
TABLE 19 AUTHENTIC LEADERSHIP THEORY	132
TABLE 20 ADAPTATIVE LEADERSHIP THEORY	134
TABLE 21 ETHICAL LEADERSHIP THEORY	135
TABLE 22 PSYCHODYNAMIC ORGANIZATIONAL AND LEADERSHIP PERSPECTIVE	136
TABLE 23 SPIRITUALITY AND LEADERSHIP	137
TABLE 24 TRANSFORMATIONAL LEADERSHIP THEORY	138

TABLE 25 TRANSACTIONAL LEADERSHIP THEORY	139
TABLE 26 PRAGMATIC LEADERSHIP THEORY	139
TABLE 27 SYMBOLIC LEADERSHIP THEORY	140
TABLE 28 COMPLEX LEADERSHIP THEORY	141
TABLE 29 SHARED LEADERSHIP THEORY	142
TABLE 30 DISTRIBUTED LEADERSHIP THEORY	143
TABLE 31 RELATIONAL LEADERSHIP THEORY	143
TABLE 32 COLLECTIVE LEADERSHIP THEORY	144
TABLE 33 CROSS-CULTURAL LEADERSHIP THEORY	144
TABLE 34 E-LEADERSHIP	145
TABLE 35 IMPLICIT LEADERSHIP THEORIES	146
TABLE 36 MULTI-LEVEL THEORY AND METHODS IN ORGANIZATIONS	147
TABLE 37 LEADERSHIP AFFECT AND EMOTIONS	148
TABLE 38 BASES OF POWER	150
TABLE 39 KEY ELEMENTS FOR A LEADERSHIP IN HIGH DEMANDING ENVIRONMENTS	152
TABLE 40 SALESIAN PREVENTIVE SYSTEM READING ON ORGANIZATIONAL PERSPECTIVE	167
TABLE 41 NEW CONCEPTUALIZATION OF PREVENTIVE SYSTEM ACCORDING TO THE PREVENTIVE LEADERSHIP	173
TABLE 42 FIRST NON-NEGOTIABLE CONDITION IN PREVENTIVE LEADERSHIP®	185
TABLE 43 SECOND NON-NEGOTIABLE CONDITION IN PREVENTIVE LEADERSHIP®	188
TABLE 44 THIRD NON-NEGOTIABLE CONDITION IN THE PREVENTIVE LEADER EDUCATOR	193

Figures

FIGURE 1 UTRU WORLD	27
FIGURE 2 TOUCH SCREEN GENERATION ENVIRONMENT	34
FIGURE 3 KEY ELEMENTS FOR FUTURE EDUCATION	35
FIGURE 4 SOME SYMBIOTIC SCENARIOS OF THE GENERATION TS	40
FIGURE 5 CORE SOCIO-EMOTIONAL SKILLS	44
FIGURE 6 DYNAMIC STRUCTURE OF THE CONSCIOUS INTENTIONALITY	52

FIGURE 7 DELIBERATION PROCESS	59
FIGURE 8 INTENTIONALITY	65
FIGURE 9 INTENTIONALITY IN A WIDE SENSE	65
FIGURE 10 SELF-APPROPRIATION LOOP	66
FIGURE 11 THE INQUIRY LEARNING COMMUNITY	74
FIGURE 12 DOUBLE LOOP LEARNING MATRIX	80
FIGURE 13 LEARNING ENVIRONMENT DESIGN	81
FIGURE 14 LEARNING THEORIES	83
FIGURE 15 SOCIO-CONSTRUCTIVIST LEARNING TOOLS	86
FIGURE 16 TOOLS FOR THE LEARNING PROCESS	88
FIGURE 17 NEW SYMBOLS AND LANGUAGES	89
FIGURE 18 DEEP REFLECTIVE THINKING	90
FIGURE 19 REFLECTIVE CYCLE ACCORDING TO GIBBS	91
FIGURE 20 KOLBE´S MODEL OF THE PROCESS OF LEARNING	93
FIGURE 21 THE STUDENT LEARNING SPIRAL	94
FIGURE 22 ZPD	95
FIGURE 23 MEANING AND KNOWLEDGE	96
FIGURE 24 SOCIO EMOTIONAL LEARNING	98
FIGURE 25 PEDAGOGICAL AND TECHNOLOGICAL CONTEXTS	99
FIGURE 26 COGNITIVE STRUCTURES	100
FIGURE 27 RESPONSIBLE DECISION-MAKING	102
FIGURE 28 COMMUNITY OF INQUIRY IN THE CLASSROOM	103
FIGURE 29 COMPETENCIES ON EDUCATION	104
FIGURE 30 COMMON ELEMENTS FOR A LEADERSHIP THEORY	117
FIGURE 31 THINGS THAT LEARNERS PAY ATTENTION TO	157
FIGURE 32 DISRUPTIVE EDUCATION MODEL	158
FIGURE 33 EFFECTIVE EDUCATIVE LEADER	160
FIGURE 34 SALESIAN PREVENTIVE SYSTEM NEW APPROACH MODEL	170
FIGURE 35 EMPATHY	183
FIGURE 36 BE THE SALESIAN ORATORY	200
FIGURE 37 LEARNING COMMUNITY	210
FIGURE 38 LOOP LEARNING	235
FIGURE 39 INLO & FLO	236
FIGURE 40 INLO & FLO AS DOUBLE LOOP PROCESS	238

Acknowledgments

To the Director and to the Staff members of the Institute of Salesian Studies (ISS) in Don Bosco Hall who have supported me with their Salesian presence, who have edited my text, and have encouraged me to publish this material.

My gratitude to Kathia Rodriguez who translated parts of this book.

My gratitude to Fr. Jesse Montes, SDB, who copy edited this book.

INTRODUCTION

Education is an art. Educational work, today, is considered a delicate task of accompaniment, a shared life project, intentionally proposed goals, and values assimilated by those who facilitate the educational experience itself: educators. Vitally linked to the educator is the student, the center of all educational action in his own social context, in his personal dynamism, in his generational sensitivity, in his dreams, and in his aspirations.

The educator and the student are key factors in the learning experience. Both are an essential element in the educational universe. Both are, metaphorically speaking, a binary star: two bodies with similar mass orbiting around a center of mass in elliptical orbits. In the absence, or loss of one of them, in the relationship or in their own individuality, the educational experience itself is destroyed. Both must fluctuate in the role of each other, linked, but not assimilated.

In this book, education is an art that touches the most sensitive fibers of the whole student: the heart. The heart is understood as the center of decision-making, as the place where affections are clearly present, as the meeting point where will and reason converge, like the horizon in which educational love meets and intertwines with reason and openness to transcendence.

Education is an art that requires expertise and experience to discover the best in each person. It asks for patience and hope to accompany and see the fruitful seed of good in every human being.

The person of the educator is an essential piece, a key factor, because he or she is an essential trigger for all educational goals.

Educators, your point of departure for your students is decisive because the way you perceive the person will be your way of interacting with him or her.

An educator who is a leader requires a process of self-knowledge (discernment), self-appropriation (judgment), and self-determination (decision). To become an artisan the educator and the unrepeatable originality of the student, are the key variables combined in each educational intervention. The "material" in the hands of the artisan-educator is unique and valuable: the student's life, dreams, aspirations, and goals.

The educative preventive approach aims at a multidisciplinary and systemic convergence of humanism and leadership, socio-constructivism and intentionality, benevolence and self-appropriation, preventive conditions and educative success.

Every leader embodies a peculiar form of leadership, this book enriches that leadership experience by proposing the Salesian Preventive Leadership approach. Educative leader will benefit from the richness of the Salesian Educative Preventive System. An Educative System that has developed generations of leaders worldwide for over 100 years and does so by educating from the heart.

1. Current Environment

Educators know that it is of little use to raise learning goals of the pedagogy implemented in the school if it is not improved in its aims and its processes. It is not enough to answer who the learning subjects are. It is obvious, the educator and student. A challenge for educators arises from the interest in answering the question about what students learn in a digital universe where the information they receive is almost infinite. It is not enough to focus on how both educator and student learn. I am convinced that we must consider the answers of whom we educate, how they learn, what they learn, where they learn it, and if what they learn is relevant and accurate. Because education is always intentional. Intentionality in education means to be a better human being assuming their life as a project. A project that involves the search for the common good, taking care of themselves, others and the humanity´s *common house*.

The complexity of the human being in his self-understanding, in his internal structure, and in his motivations is a common starting point to attempt any accompanying and significant educative intervention. The complexity of the educational practice is also palpable in the virtual classroom. In all educational systems, this complexity is greater by involving socio-emotional issues because the motivation, feelings, and emotions of the student and the educator are an indispensable part of every successful learning process (Starr, 2019). But, a lack of a broadly accepted definition, an object of study with blur boundaries, an extreme individualized way of dealing with some socio-emotional issues make urged to embrace an education from the heart.

The heart, in this book, is understood as the center of decision-making, the place where human affections are clearly present, the point where personal will and reason converge, the horizon in which educational love meets and intertwines with transcendence.

The specific contexts in which people and societies interact are convulsed with ambiguities, uncertainties, and paradoxes. Those factors condition the educational practice in its very inner essence: the complete development of the human being. The formal educational proposal is at risks by shrinking curriculums to some abilities for job but not for life, or for social agents, neither for an active citizenship. Hence, the necessary versatility to touch the heart, the brain, and the will of every student with the help of technology and much personal accompaniment in school learning environments (Andere, 2015).

Society of knowledge

The world currently presents itself as convulsed in many of its aspects: zones of armed conflict, forced migration, xenophobic speeches and practices, legislations in struggle of interests, fragile interpersonal relationships, lack of dialogue between parties in conflict, fear or rejection of the diverse, greater absence of ethical criteria in the public and private spheres, to name a few (Esguerra, 2017).

Previously, a formal education process was considered as the springboard that catapulted students to better opportunities, to better succeed in life. The *society of knowledge* was the proposal that stated that knowledge would be the key to success. That is, the one who possessed more knowledge would be more successful in everything, would have better job promotions and would live a happier life. However, in recent decades this "society" have shown the evolution to a neoliberal capitalism that seems to favor results with a lack of ethics rather than educative processes.

Also it favors the standardization of tests more than the personalization of learning experiences, the legislation and monetization of teaching more than the inspiration and joy of learning, skills for a job more than skills for life. Moreover, the debt at the end of college is bigger than the opportunities for a job, a better life or a decent success.

The *society of knowledge* has become commercialized. This society seeks out those who have more economic means to access better sources and stimuli of knowledge, thus generating a new mode of exploitation of those who have less access, because the education market ignores the subtle difference between how to learn and what they need to know. Whoever has more resources has access to a better education, period. (Montero & Gewerc, 2018).

The society of knowledge is twisted to an *economy of knowledge* according to Cochran-Smith and Villegas (2016). The "economy of knowledge" is perceived as one deepening the gap between those not favored in access to knowledge-generation experiences and those that are. Those not favored know less, accomplish less, and get low expectations compared to those who can accomplish, expect, and aspire to more knowledge. Thereby, the product "knowledge" gives them an advantage in all professional and social fields.

Quality education is a universal right, but it is not possible for developing countries to provide this right to all and in all contexts because the globalization of our days "has witnessed increasing prosperity and at the same time as increasing inequality" (Deaton, 2015, p. 21).

Globalize the economy, not citizenship

The globalized economy makes the borders of nation-states a space for negotiation of free flows of capital and swallow investments, but where the free mobility of people is becoming less easy and with restrictions that have clear signs of exclusion of many. This economy justifies any xenophobic discourse of social security and welfare of the few (chosen by skin color, religion, social status, economic level, political party, etc.) excluding the many. Finances, investment capitals, labor markets, and the movement of goods override the powers and scope of governments, which cannot, therefore, determine the rules and ethical boundaries for the greedy of corporations, stock markets, and wealthy individuals (Bauman & Bordoni, 2016).

Mediation

Less and less hidden in the *society of the image* is the situation of rampant corruption of the ruling classes and those in power, coupled with the wave of violence, mostly, although not exclusively, in countries considered as developing is a reality that modifies the practice of values in education.

The individual is willing to sacrifice the privacy and the personal for the momentary fame in the "society of image" by appearing with "originality" exposed on the networks with the ephemeral minute of fame and the number of virtual followers. The price is the annulment of those who are not popular or "famous" in the networks. For many young people and adolescents today, it is a way to understand themselves and relate to them (Vargas Llosa, 2012). Sexting, packing, cyberbullying, etc., those are situations that occurs continuously and at increasingly younger ages. The minute of fame is a situation that hides the inability of adequate socialization of the person. Although it seeks high levels of socialization. The on-line socialization is an intrinsically self-referential reality, where the world of their own experience provides authenticity by being "true to himself," putting brackets, suspending, removing or wiping out any "strange" fragment that the individual recognizes as imported from outside of him (Bauman, 2006a).

A volatile, uncertain, complex and ambiguous world (VUCA)

The world seen from the perspective of Johansen (2012) uses four convergent perspectives and is a world composed of volatility, uncertainty, complexity and ambiguity (VUCA). It seems to me that these four categories of interpretation regarding the current context should be considered by every educational leader, in every organization and in every social entity that tries to live, survive, and have an impact on current and future societies. It should be highly valued for those who have decision-making power in the various educational institutions to become familiar with sociological perspectives in order to help form better leaders in the communities that they serve. A global perception of the current cultural context and the dynamics of society can place any leader in macro and micro cultures and understand that both are co-constitutive.

A *volatile* society where the structures that were socially solid –State, Church, Family– today are questioned, devalued, or pointed out as rigid, stifled or diachronic to contemporary axiological sensitivity. The volatility of financial markets today is perceived at the level of interpersonal relationships: butterfly capitals that seek only the maximum profit without social, moral, fiscal obligations. Also, relationships between boys and girls seem little committed to each other or only exist for enjoyment without obligations of any kind.

Volatility affects the internal life of individuals. The emotions lived on the surface, the necessary communication between people to achieve common goals, currently also seem to be affected by volatility. More emotions per day, it would seem a life with more meaning or at least more fun, but it gives the impression of become a life transformed into a game of power or a search for mutual benefits. Any decision and objective are based more on emotions than on ethical principles or moral norms. Social situations where the achievement of the common good is involved and dialogue is necessary, individualized desires look stronger in life than values (Bauman, 2008). In a volatile world, there is little security to remain until retirement in a current job because for many qualified people, the labor market dynamics teaches them that they can be replaced at any time and for the profit of the company.

Uncertainty of an individual who lives and develops before the fragility in time and form of ways of interacting with others, of types and levels of relationships in all areas, both private and public. The individual lives a reality of possibilities because if "I can," then "I must" (Bauman & Donskis, 2015, p. 15). The strength of the various institutions is no longer presented as such: the family is diverse in its conformation and divergent in its ways and motives of organizing. The truths that guided decisions and ways of living together are now presented as fragmented and vulnerable. The knowledge about the human being that allowed us to better understand our reality today is relativized, temporary, and comes with an expiration date. This reality makes our environment something uncertain and everything one get produces an experience of anxiety, discontent, fragmentation, hopelessness. The goals for studies, life, job, cultural immersion, seem clear and correctly verbalized, but the strategies seem to be emotional, that is, with high intensity content, but with a short duration in time and consistency (Stein, 2013).

The "ethical radar" is the new GPS for young people. This way of navigation avoids any compromised and compromising stance in decision-making, with the intention of keeping away unnecessary collisions with other individual ethical systems (Lanz, 2012; Bauman, 2006b). Human relationships appear as an experience of "navigation" where the subject is surfing among the avalanche of information that changes constantly and on a whom, sometimes external to the subject itself.

Leihan (2011) considers that globalization, new technologies, education, travel, and immigration are dissolving many of the ties that united the societies. Leihan points out that volatility fragments points of view and makes public opinion easily manipulated. Any information considered as true and solid today, tomorrow is questioned and, in many cases, weakened.

A *complex* reality makes dialogue between disciplines something that borders on the impossible where the excess of information for decision-making and the possible consequences or the specialization at the end of any field of knowledge. Paradoxically, the individual is shaped by globalization and its market forces, but he or she cannot respond in a viable and sufficient way to the social and political challenges that are part of their lives, not by conscious decision but by extrinsic imposition. The results of globalization in all spheres of life is a complex horizon of possibilities (Bauman & Donskis, 2015). In all the moments that make up human history, humanity has found itself as a complex reality in its social structure.

The criteria of social and private organization are complex. Social, political, economic, religious complexity is lived by the individual in his innermost level because his emotions, feelings or thoughts are complex issues to deal with. Apparently, there are no rules that apply to everyone as each one is unique, and it is not possible to think or speak of universal morality against people who want to radically live their being within themselves.

A complex society defends the position of uncommon criteria on decisions or personal and collective actions. If all the paths are equally true, what results is perplexity, not the commitment to make one of them, paralyzing any long-term decision, commitment, and attachment (Barrios, 2008).

The past, the present, and the future are perceived with confusion, but at the same time, extremely interconnected (Johansen, 2012). Any decision is intertwined with many consequences that make life something that is not easy to live. The clarity to make an internal process or to make any decision is not a common product today; Clarity is not easily gained with thousands of data to digest every day. Personal responsibility is diluted by the impossibility of assuming responsibility for someone or something in the sphere of the social.

Today, the hypersensitivity of the educational reality makes the learning experience seen as a tense act between two parties that avoid getting hurt and take care to get involved in actions that can be legal consequences of demand or counterclaim.

The spontaneity of learning is measured by the benefit received to a paid service. Today, the vocation to educate is more concerned about legislation than about learning, more profits rather than more ethics, more budget rather than more education itself. The virtual world seems simpler, but it is more complex and with more edges than the palpable reality.

Education has always been complex. Currently virtual educative practice is overly complicated.

Ambiguity is experienced in the educative, axiological, moral, social, and relational levels. Coupled with it, there is a prevalent relativism, not rarely, radical and closed in itself, because although connected to social networks, these levels present an essential distinction: the "right" of the individual to unilateral interruption in any forum or cyber space when she or he wants to do it with just one click. Because, unlike communities in the real world, networks are individually configured and "are individually remodeled and dismantled and base their persistence on individual will as the sole foundation" (Bauman & Donskis, 2015, p. 187). The singularity of the individual are intense punctual actions enclosed in themselves without connection with the rest and assumed in all decisions that involve long term and sustained commitment (Kinnaman, 2011; Rodríguez, 2017). Any decision that involves long-term commitments is considered rigid and difficult to maintain because it implies an ethical position to maintain, a religious belief to practice or a political option to support.

Especially present from the perspective of ethics and decision making, ambiguity creates confusion and uncertainty. The wide range of options before any decision affects the ethics of the individual, the core values of the organization, and the way in which each member and group perform in society.

Today, each decision made presents a series of ambiguous dilemmas (Johansen, 2012), say in politics, economics, finance or business ethics, to name a few. The good seems to live in the shadow of suspicion for hidden intentions. The bad seems to be diluted in the right to be wrong. Errors are not accepted, because that requires the experimentation of anything. Values seem to be emotional and individual appreciations without something to do with regulations or ways of acting. The rules seem to be unsolicited and sometimes invasive advice.

Good customs are a reminder of generations that have left their bad taste in the past because the struggles raised by better social benefits, housing, job security, development, and quality of life, social mobility and improvements to public services, to name a few today, are considered almost as fossils of a frustrated past.

The intricate VUCA world is affecting and shaping criteria in the detection, training and accompaniment of leaders at all levels of social reality including education. According to De Déa Roglio and Ligth (2009), volatility, uncertainty, complexity, and ambiguity cause relativism among members of our educational communities. This generates a weak identity, without strong cohesion of fundamental values in organizations and companies. In addition to a strong sense of individualism that manifests itself as the sole criterion for decision-making, an absence of ethical considerations where others are also the responsibility of those who are in a position to exercise decisions that affect others.

This ethical and social situation has mitigated the weight and the role of educational institutions in the most varied areas:

a) the absence of impact in the field of public policies is perceived as schools are not social agents involved in it;

b) in economic policies because market dynamics seems to only affect the pocket of those who must pay tuition and not in the life of wealthy class;

c) in government organizations, because politicians many are corrupt and in whom any citizen should not trust;

d) in non-governmental groups (NGOs), because their presence in schools is almost nil, reducing sensitivity to nature and random human action on the planet, to recycling, dental hygiene or care and cleaning campaigns not relate to each other neither social justice issues.

The school is perceived more than an island than a space for debate and the search for the common good. Some educators forget that the classroom is society as a whole and not just a reflection of family life or society. Citizens nowadays understand and interpret less and less frequently a community as a place of belonging and a place to live. Community as the experience to configure a social ethic concomitant to individuals. Even less the social institutions from the past are perceived today as an authority capable of guaranteeing equitable access to the resources and services of an institutional proposal that benefits the common good. Rather, the suspicion is evident in political parties, religious associations, government agencies, financial institutions, established companies or groups. The feeling, and not infrequently the evidence, that members of these institutions pursue their own benefits by forgetting the citizen they should serve, ignoring the legitimate aspirations of those who are today considered the landless, the voiceless, the unrepresented. They forget the great masses of those who know and feel without aspirations, without work, without creed or hope or desire to be part of the established as normal citizenship.

Virtual movements, such Anonymous, Wikileaks, etc., are more real and binding hopes of change, although they are individualizing in their persistence. Young generations persist on the idea that "likes" or the number of virtual followers, are real people and political agents. Becoming an "influencer" on the social webpage, maintaining the fans subscribe to their channels, exhorting to get involved on social justice the strength of the movements they "lead," can change reality. It seems that virtual reality is as simple as maximize or minimize a screen's window. Leadership for a great number of teenagers is related solely to relevance on the virtual world. Relevance linked to the number of "likes" and fan followers. Such numbers express the engagement of individuals with the "stuff" an influencer holds on his own channel.

A volatile, uncertain, complex, and ambiguous world just outlined above, confronts each individual with precarious situations in all areas of the person, at all educational levels and in the most varied circumstances. An educator who pretends to be promoted as a leader to impact on the society that has had to live, must face this complex world, and should be relevant on the virtual reality in which he/she exists, lives, and relates as stated by Rodríguez & Rodríguez (2015).

Unprecedented Transformation and Radical Uncertainties (UTRU)

An innovative attempt to understand current trends is to use unprecedented transformation parameters and radical uncertainties (UTRU).

Humanity at the beginning of the 21st century is discovered in a new, disruptive, different environment and with an uncertain future and different society from what has been known for hundreds of years (Fig. 1). Advances, scopes, fears and possibilities of biotechnology, Artificial Intelligence, human migration, climate change, pandemics, economic systems in a globalized world are volatile opportunities and complex challenges. The borders between the physical and the virtual reality are increasingly blurred on ethical, emotional and social topics.

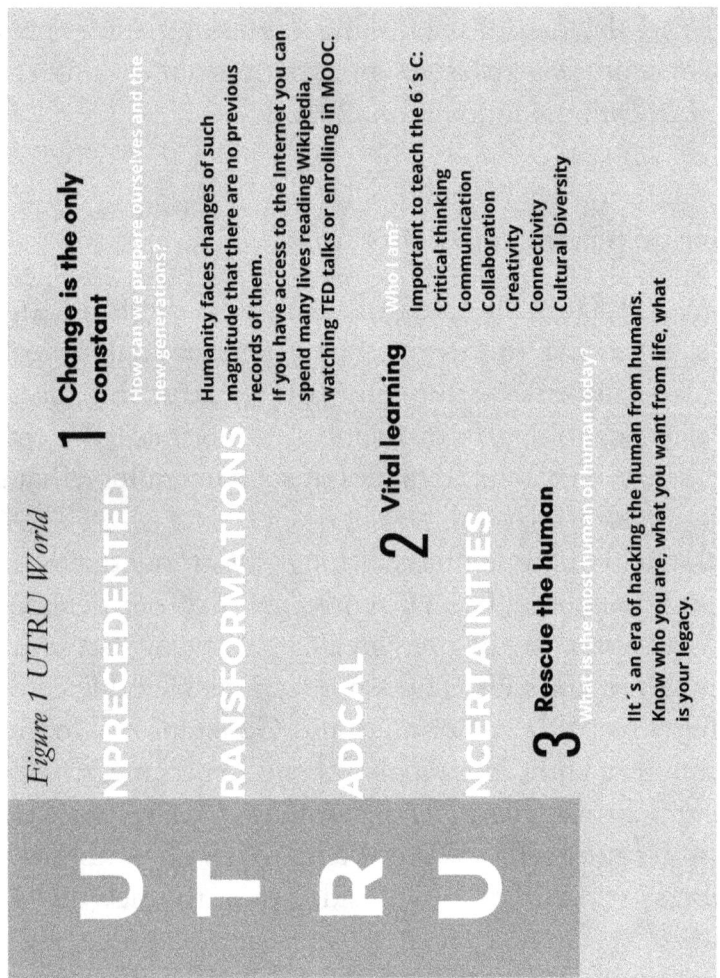

Figure 1 UTRU World

A metaphor about the UTRU world and related to education is that humanity is not facing a subject of more and better applications —pedagogical innovations—, even in the face of the need for new adaptations and updates —Artificial Intelligence, e-learning Connectivity.— It is a matter of a new "operating system." A "new paradigm" of learning and education. Youngest generations get with a finger and a touchscreen device the complete access to what the humanity knows about the universe, the information about us as specie and the nature itself, the human artistic expression through centuries, massive information about almost anything (Educational innovation, 2018).

Change permeates reality

Humanity faces all kinds of changes at all times. In fact, change is part of the essence of a species that never fully adapts to its given environment. It is also true that, given advances in technology, in medicine, in economics, the changes that will be seen will be advances of such magnitude that there are no previous records.

In the field of humanities, although postmodernism already foresaw it, it seems that, currently, most of our generational beliefs fall apart one by one: greater well-being, better quality of life, better paid jobs. These convictions sound like archeological myths of Baby Boomers and Generation X in the ears of Millennials and Centennials. At the same time, no new agglutinating history has emerged so far to replace those beliefs. Unless the number of "likes" and followers with bloggers, youtubers, or twitters are considered as the new history of humanity.

For educators, many pressing questions continue to arise. How can we prepare ourselves and prepare new generations for a world of unprecedented transformations and radical uncertainties? What should we teach a child that will help him survive and thrive in the world of the 21st century? What kind of skills will he or she need to get a job? What kind of skills will he or she need to understand what is going on around them and navigate safely in life?

Paradoxically, on this century it is possible to find huge amounts of information a click away, but that does not solve essential vital issues where feelings, people, decisions or own existence are involved. If you have a smartphone, you can spend countless hours reading Wikipedia, watching TED Talks or taking free online courses. Virtual environments are the window for a globalized identity where social status, place of residence or cultural environment are always in beta version.

Contrary to the past, are no one person try to block access to information in the network, but rather some people, political parties or corporations seem to focus their interest in spreading erroneous or distracting information as irrelevant, since it is very difficult to hide all the information that does not align with the political agenda of whomever holds the power. In addition, it is relatively and alarmingly easy to flood the Internet user with contradicted reports and false clues about any information: the famous fake news. Additionally, there are excess of information that is just a click away. This leads to make concentration difficult on the essential. When politics, social justice or science contents seem too complicated, it is tempting to switch to funny videos of cats, celebrity gossip, trendy music or Tik Tok.

In such a world, the last thing an educator needs to provide his students with is more information, since they are already saturated with images, data, videos on social networks. People need the ability to make sense of information, to differentiate between what is essential and what is not, and above all, to be able to combine many bits of information in a broad and coherent image of the world.

Many educators are currently required to be updated in the exchange of data, but they should focus on being relevant by encouraging students to "think for themselves," to be themselves. Educators are called to generate and/or disseminate narratives that provide human meaning to reality because they express the deepest and most genuine aspirations of the human being. Educators are required to provide learning experiences where students build their own image of the world by synthesizing data in a coherent and meaningful history of their reality.

Vital learning

Educational practice appears to be interested in information. Most schools also often focus on providing students with a set of predetermined skills, such as solving differential equations, writing computer codes, identifying chemicals and their reactions in a test tube, or conversing in Mandarin. Since we don't know what the world and the labor market will look like in 2050, we don't really know what particular skills people will need. Perhaps by 2050 Artificial Intelligence (AI) can code the software much better than humans, and a new application allows you to make a conversation in any language.

Maybe we should be teaching "the six Cs": Critical Thinking, Communication, Collaboration, Creativity, Connectivity, and Cultural Diversity (Rodríguez, 2020). In general schools should minimize technical skills and emphasize general-purpose life skills. It seems that the most important thing in the future will be the ability to deal with change, learn new things and preserve a mental balance in situations all of them uncharted.

Such a profound change is transforming the basic structure of life, making discontinuity its most prominent feature. From time immemorial, life was divided into two complementary parts: a period of learning followed by a period of work. In the first part of one´s life, information is accumulated, skills are developed, a worldview is developed, and a defined identity is amalgamated. In the second part one´s life, adults usually focus on accumulated skills to navigate the world, make a living, and contribute to society.

In a couple of decades, the dizzying pace of accelerated changes and the longer life span will make this traditional model obsolete. "Who am I?" It will be a more urgent and complicated question than ever. This is likely to involve immense levels of stress. Change is almost always stressful and, after a certain age, most people do not like to change. When you are fifteen years old, your whole life is change. Your body is growing, your mind is developing, your relationships are deepening. Everything is in flux, and everything is new. You are busy inventing yourself. Most teenagers find it scary, but at the same time, exciting. New perspectives open before them, and they have a whole world to conquer. When they are 50 years old, stability is usually preferred. Adults have invested so much in their skills, their career, their identity and their vision of the world that they don't want to start over. The harder adults have worked to build something, the harder it will be to leave it and leave room for something new. Adults may still appreciate new experiences and small adjustments, but most people in their fifties are not ready to review the deep structures of their identity and personality (Harari, 2018).

Human beings as individuals, and humanity in general, will have to deal more and more with things that were seen in movies: super intelligent machines, designed bodies, algorithms that can manipulate emotions with amazing precision, rapid cataclysms caused by human beings. What should be done when facing a completely unprecedented situation? How should you act when you are flooded by a huge amount of information and there is absolutely no way to absorb and analyze everything? How to live in a world where deep uncertainty is not a mistake but a characteristic?

To change profession every decade, to survive and flourish in such a world, to be yourself in a unknow future you will need mental flexibility and large reserves of emotional balance

You will undoubtedly have to repeatedly set aside some of what you know best, and feel at home with the unknown (Harari, 2018). Unfortunately, teaching students to embrace the unknown and maintain their mental balance is much more difficult than teaching them an equation in physics or the causes of World War I. You cannot learn resilience by reading a book or listening to a conference. Some teachers generally lack the mental flexibility demanded by the 21st century, since many of them are the product of the old educational system.

Rescue the human

The best advice that today may be appropriate to give a 15-year-old boy trapped in a traditional school somewhere in Mexico, India, Alabama, Dubai or China is: "Trust adults, but not too much because they do not know everything. Better, we learn together." Most adults have good intentions, but sometimes they do not understand the keys to interpretation and interrelation in which new generations develop. In the past, it was a relatively safe bet to follow adults because they knew the world well and the world was changing slowly. But the 21st century is different. Due to the growing pace of change, one can never be sure if what adults are telling the students is timeless wisdom or results from their own bias and personal development.

So what can you trust? The advances of technology? Technology can help a lot, but if it gains too much power over life, the human being could become a hostage of the technological advances themselves. Technology is neither good nor bad. If you know what you want in life, technology can help you achieve it. But if you don't know what you want in life, it will be very easy for technology to configure its goals for you and take control of your life. Today, we can see young people roaming the streets attached to their smartphones. We can see problems of addiction to technology. We can see screens configuring the younger minds.

Should you trust yourself then? To be successful you will have to work very hard to get to know the operating system better; to know what you are and what you want from life. It is the very old affirmation of "know yourself." It is the most important and urgent advice in the 21st century, because unlike the days of Socrates, it now has serious competition Google, Coca-Cola, Amazon, Facebook, Instagram, and government are all trying to hack the individual in the attempt to find himself. They use the smartphone. But that is not what they want to control. They can enter your computer, but it is not what they want.

They can know and block or empty your bank account, but it is not the most valuable thing. All big data manipulators are in a race to hack yourself, your organic operating system, your personal life project. We may hear that we live in the era of hacking, but that is not entirely true. We are living in the era of hacking the essence of humans: the ability to love, to self-determine, to freedom, to reason and to be surprised at the marvels in nature (Harari, 2018).

Generation Touch Screen (2010-2025)

The Touch Screen (TS) generation, also called 'technology generation' or 'alpha generation', is the demographic cohort that follows centennials (born around the year 2010 and are expected to end in 2025, although this date is only a reference). The TS are boys and girls who have been born digital. From an early age they are connected to the network, and this involves an adaptation effort when they have to perform daily tasks without an internet connection. Some authors consider that the TS, regarding interconnectivity and technology in their lives, are considered symbiotic (Braojos, 2018; Vallín, 2018; López, 2017). That is to say: the devices are ready to respond immediately to your requirements with more control than the body's own organs. The connection is vital as is the brain or the functioning of the bodily organs. Not having the internet is like not existing. The TS are accustomed to interacting with the devices as extensions of them, like orthopedic devices or a prosthesis: the devices are part of them with a replaceable character when they stop working.

Collaborative networking is a natural part of their socialization: they play with other interconnects, exchange information through the network, meet and evaluate each other on the network, and seem to replicate this behavior when they are in the disconnected world. In the virtual world they touch, hit, die, pinch, greet, enjoy, and suffer because the attachments connected to the virtual world allow them that (Fig. 2). It seems that boys and girls are sensitive in a slightly different way to Centennials. Privacy and confidentiality are valuable and delicate educational elements, because in networks they tend to socialize all aspects of their lives in public and private forums.

Figure 2 Touch Screen Generation environment

Like Millennials and Centennials, TS generation is a complex challenge for educators and educational systems that are not flexible and are focused on content and with traditional methods. The pedagogical transformation involved in the use of technology in the classroom, as well as the ease with which the children of this generation learn collaboratively through the network using digital tools, should stimulate many educators. Especially those who are still having difficulty the accompanying new learning environments (Fig. 3).

Figure 3 Key elements for future education

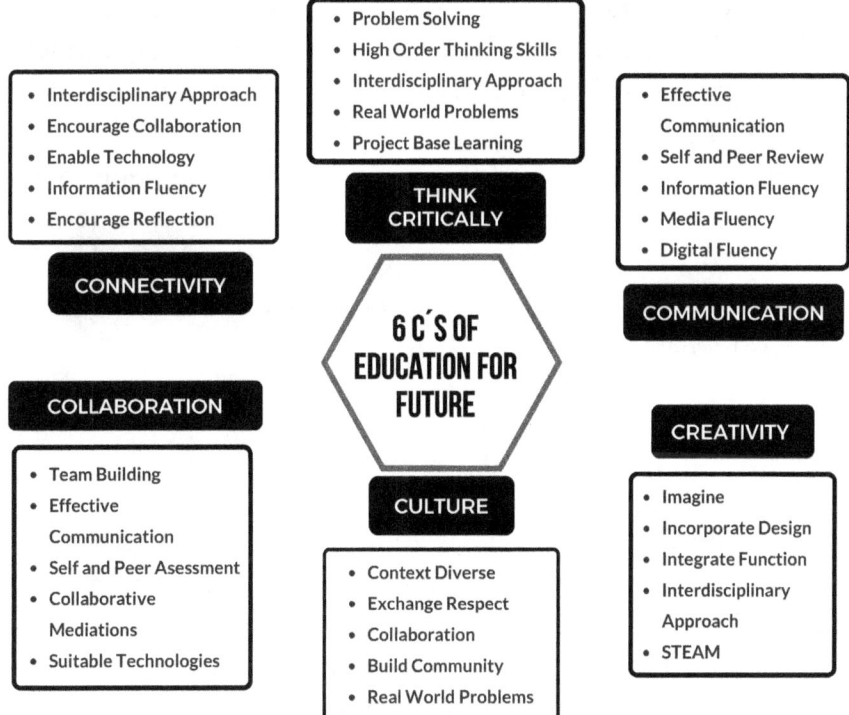

Touch devices connect with primitive learning processes and 3D experiences resemble a garden full of sensory stimuli. The logic is simple: drag your finger across the screen to move the objects up, down and sideways. They play and something happens immediately, without having to mediate in an process of abstraction as with the computer mouse, where one controls a device that directs a cursor on the screen.

TS approach to devices in an instinctive "let's see what happens" behavior. It's natural. It's easy, it's fast, it's not complex. And it seems to me, that therein lies the challenge for educational leaders and also, for parents so that to think about teaching from images, graphic or audiovisual material.

It is a paradigm shift, because it is teaching thinking from visual sensory experiences and not from concepts, ideas, abstractions or arguments. An observable consequence is the ability to displace a part of the body, a finger, in a certain way and, therefore, obtain overflowing information and access any part of the universe.

It should be considered that, together with the benefits reported by tactile dynamics in learning, there are also derived risks that do not depend on the model of the device but on its use. Many of these benefits and risks are cultural, not technological *per se* (González, 2013).

Centennials

The Centennial´s level of independence and self-sufficiency makes them require their own spaces rather than shared spaces in labor fields. In addition, that it is even easier for Millennials to approach reality as multitasking. Perhaps they share a high degree of dispersion which generally makes them superficially efficient but limited in levels that require greater depth of analysis. In addition to this, they tend to obtain credentials. They become more certified rather than obtain a university degree because a graduate degree takes too long and is expensive. They have learned that continuous training is essential to remain at work as an asset, and hard work is a possibility for permanence.

Centennials know how to work hard and entitled to demand their reward for it. Thus, many of them consider that the university is not the only nor the most valid source of knowledge acquisition and professionalization.

Faced with the uncertainty of the future that awaits them in the workplace, they are committed to solving the many realities in social networks. The digital linking platforms (Snapchat, FB, Twitter, Instagram, etc.) are the scenarios where a good part of their existence reaches certainty in the networks. They apply for new jobs, they can also generate experiences of friendship, or dating, or use the net to buy and sell and interact with suppliers, etc. The Centennial does not see an obvious dividing line between work and home because connectivity allows them to work in personalized schedules and in spaces they consider appropriate to continue their required work. They tend to feel comfortable with more autonomous work and projects that require short periods of intense demand (Vallín, 2018).

Centennials move from welfare society promised to the cruel reality of hopelessness, because the promises of professionalization for a better quality of life seem to be *flatus vocis*. Today, a university graduate must try to survive the uncertainty of the VUCA world, in the labor, professional, relational, moral and/or personal sphere. Youth generations many times are unable or unwilling to be part of a working world where employment is Darwinianly neo-liberal.

The terrible situation of children and youth in developing countries who are impoverished in all aspects of humanity occurs because opportunities for mobility and social improvement are minimal or inaccessible. Within a State concerned only with managing rather than resolving the global problems that exceed their local possibilities for improvement, causes a fragmented social fabric, with little responsibility and a reduced sense of participation and belonging.

Some features to consider

Centennials use their smartphones 30% more than other adults and spend up to 35% more time on their devices throughout the day. They usually spend an average of three hours a day connected on their smartphones compared to two millennial hours. A centennial would not use a mobile application or a web page that is difficult to navigate. They also use ad blockers on their mobile devices or computer if they find it invasive or irrelevant.

On average, social networks like Facebook are used for 11 minutes a day, Snap Chat for 30 minutes, Facebook Messenger for about 28 minutes, and Twitter for 22 minutes (FinancialFood.es, 2019). In addition to this, in the online field, Centennials have a greater propensity to identify with their profiles on social networks than other generations –61% admitted that the content they publish says a lot about themselves, compared to 56 % of Millennials– (López, 2017).

The Annual Study of Social Networks 2018 shows that a trend among young generations is to become an influencer. The current influencers use more Facebook and Instagram followed by YouTube and Twitter. Regarding the credibility that influencers have for users, it should be noted that the percentages are fairly matched: 38% consider that influencers as credible source of information, while another 38% consider what they propose is just scam (Braojos, 2018).

Communication is markedly visual. This allows them immediacy in the message as to compact the content without a major difference between concept or feeling, between argument or emotion —emoticon, meme, Snapchat, etc.– (Vallín, 2018).

The centennials are more politicized than the Generation X, but less than the Millennials, who were thrown into politics for the breach of the promises of prosperity caused by corruption, neoliberalism, social Darwinism, incessant migrations, etc. Centennials consider that positions of power are not occupied by those who should occupy them causing a great disidentification with political institutions.

They play video games naturally, although there is still a gender bias: men play more and longer than women. But for both, video games are no longer an exercise in solitary leisure: they usually play online with strangers, but more often with friends. Because of their dynamism, they are more likely to exchange ideas, identities, and make new friends. And they are the most prepared for the precariousness and volatility of the *Uberization* of the economy. They live in more democratic families than their elders (Generation X), in which their opinion has weight, so the image of the triangular family built from a strong father figure quickly loses its effect.

Climate change is no longer a matter of opinion: it is a reality. They undoubtedly prefer freedom to security, and do not fully accept the terrorist alarmism of their elders.

Centennials are young people whose lives are mediated naturally by digital technology. They were born between zeros and ones, carry pocket-size high-tech devices and conceive the world as in need of hyper-connection. They use technology more as a prosthesis than a symbiotic suit. They do not have the same problem as the Millennials with networking. They show and share only what they want, and they are "aware of their privacy" at the same time as multitasking. They can "spend more than four hours on at least
two platforms simultaneously, so they have more fragmented attention" (Vallejos, 2019).

Educational concerns

A question that is urgently asked today, is whether the educational leaders are training these citizens of the future with the skills that are required to respond to the challenges of the technological presence today. TS and Centennials are a prosthetic generation, in which technology is part of its organism. They are cyborgs in the intellectual sense and almost in the material (Vallín, 2018). Perhaps it would be better to say that the Smartphone is as part of them as their eyes or legs (Fig. 4).

Figure 4 Some symbiotic scenarios of the Generation TS

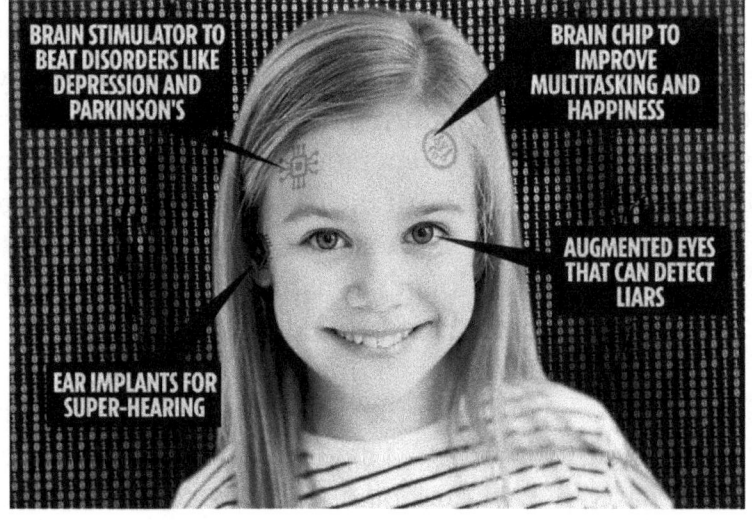

In the past, the request to provide the classroom with more technology was considered the best answer for a better learning experience. Now, with the presence of screens and uninterrupted access to social networks it does not seem to be the main problem. There is the paradox of having believed that technology would improve the learning experience.

Currently, however the presence of educators with educative intentionality begins to be value anew due to fear of the neutral nature and the disruptive possibility of technology.

Is school organization the best method to face the challenge of significant learning? Are we in a position to consider making educational systems more flexible? Will we be able to focus on students and their own learning processes assessing individual achievements more than standardized tests? Although knowing and mastering the technological language must be a code of common use for these generations, such as a second language or a list of competencies for working life, learning to live in a hyperconnected society requires other essential skills that allow developing new ideas; among them, a strongly trained attitude towards innovation, creativity, lifelong learning, collaboration, and critical thinking.

Therefore, contemporary scenarios request for an innovative school that identifies these challenges and trains TS and Centennials in the complexity of big data, artificial intelligence and digital technology with the will to lead with the ability to use these levers for social transformation. The following guidelines for the "regular" classroom, also could be applied for online school meetings. (Table 1)

Table 1 Some guidelines for the classroom

Strategies	Assumptions	Implications
Make right questions.	In terms of information, teachers have to manage abundance of online resources.	Ensure that students come up with the right information and in an attitude of renewal throughout life.
	The teacher needs to manage that overabundance to reach the contents intentionally.	Ask the right questions so the student finds his own answers. It is not about completing the sentence but to pose a challenge that can only be solved by consulting several correct sources.
		Do not plan all of the content. Sometimes it is convenient to come to the classroom with a question and be surprised by what students can find.
Prepare your class in beta version.	In computing, the software beta version is a complete version of a program or application, but it may still contain errors and needs adjustment. This is the world in which student function: a world where they can intervene and be part of the change.	Involve students in collaborative activities rather than in assigned material.
		Do hand out teachers notes so that students are the ones who prepare them collaboratively.
		Arrive with prepared goal objectives letting students discover them a new path each time.
Have a significant and demonstrable digital expertise and relevance	Achieve a reputation by being relevant in the digital contexts. Everyone can be on the web, but not everyone can be relevant (followers and likes) with a reputation that deserves respect.	Share interesting content and comments on it. Students want immediate feedback.

The School challenges

The challenge of updating the curriculum so that it aspires to be an instrument in the service of the student learning process individually more than standardized evaluation criteria. It requires a school that prepares for life and the reality that students will face from within the school classroom and school spaces, rather than simulate in the classroom what could happen outside of it. What is happening in society must be part of the classroom dynamic.

The relevance of what has been taught and the real implications of school teachings for life and society. The quality that is intended in the schools presents nuances emphasizing the transfer and standardized verification of knowledge; other educational centers focus on the technical skills that should be acquired; other schools place emphasis on skills related to socio-emotional aspects. A challenge to focus on personal achievements and learning pedagogy, considering the human being as a whole.

Parcel knowledge

The learning process, in many schools, mimics the trends that society presents in itself: a compartmentalization of knowledge in specialized fields within a knowledge area (Science, Technology, Engineering, Arts and Mathematics). This separation by specialization is sometimes unable to dialogue with the traditions of the community and with other areas of knowledge, such as the social sciences or the humanities.

Today, students live surrounded by information, almost drowning in a tsunami of data. But, there is no control over the incidence of comprehensive training, and even less is known what to do with it in the classroom. Big data advances by leaps and bounds in the business world and gradually enters the school. Unfortunately, educators seem not to have yet understood the reality of this new front. The flood of information makes students and educators feel a greater fragmentation as individuals and in the learning process, without having clarity on how to face these new scenarios.

A common situation in education is the use of powerful technological tools, which, in the absence of wise pedagogy and intelligent teaching, subtract more than they contribute to learning (Philip & Garcia, 2013). In addition, according to Petrie (2014), the understanding of the educational leader and leadership development in school environments is given as a "horizontal" process, focused more on job skills and the transmission of knowledge, competences and abilities to market demands, instead of orienting in a "vertical" direction, conceived in stages of development and whose growth requires a commitment to self-training in self-knowledge, self-awareness and issues of social relevance and community impact (Fig. 5).

Figure 5 Core socio-emotional skills

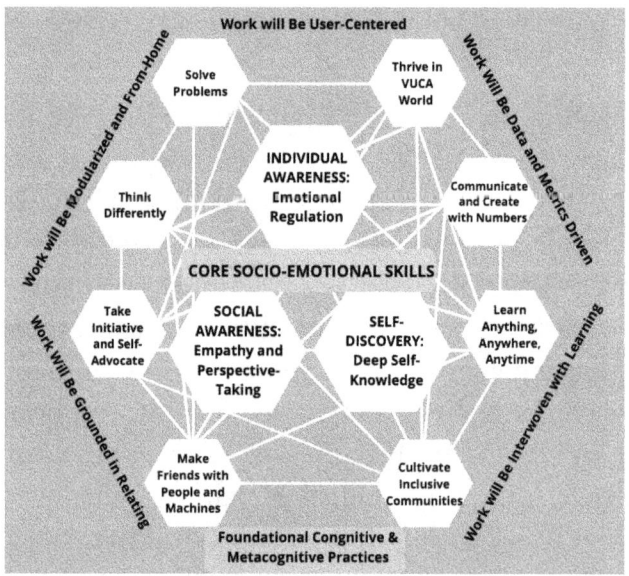

Possible ways of being *competent*

In the future, many employers will look for the *knowmad* (Know-Nomad). That is, nomads of knowledge. These *knowmad* understand that knowledge is part of a life cycle and feel the desire to expand it continuously, without being afraid to quit their current job and undertake new horizons, if necessary. They are creative and innovative people who can work with almost everyone, anytime, anywhere. They are not simply young people who have made the leap to the corporate world. On the contrary, the *knowmad* profile is not determined by age, but rather by mentality. They are
individuals trained in many fields of learning, with a broad perspective that allows them to generate value in different contexts.

They are allowed to fail and retry as many times as necessary. In addition, attitude is more important than knowledge or technical skills. They tend to be constantly updating to adapt to market changes and show a willingness to participate in new projects and ideas that can provide personal value. A *knowmad* prefers to work in open and agile teams without hierarchical structures. They are inclined to collaborate in teams where they can contribute their ideas and opinions.

Millennials

There are a number of studies that have attempted to delineate the positive and negative aspects of the Millennial Generation. They are more similar by the characteristics that identify them (Stein, 2013). According to Caraher (2015) Pew Research in 2010, it was found that there are more than seventy-seven million Millennials, born in the 80s. This generation eclipses Generation X by around forty-six million according to the United States Census Bureau (Population Reference Bureau). There are many myths about Millennials: that they are people who only have rights without any interest in obligations or responsibilities; that they are young people who expect rewards and promotions just for appearing without commitment or teamwork; that they are people who don't work hard but want everything instantly; that Millennials cannot do anything without precise instructions and do not take the initiative in anything that requires extra effort.

That they are they are subordinated with casual language and dress and disrespectful of authority and hierarchy; that Millennials are not willing to pay their debts because they never feel they don´t have to; on the contrary, others seem to be indebted to them; that the young people of this generation want freedom for their projects, flexibility and responsibilities, and a balance between hard work and life of pleasure.

All descriptions before, according to Caraher (2015), are myths that deserve to be considered as a reading from other generations to Millennials but not as determining definitions about this generation.

Today, a Millennial has been part of many labor, relational, emotional banners in a short period of time. For Millennials, this uncertainty is presented in:

1. Fragmented life projects, where long-term plans are far from the real possibilities that children in developing countries face: unemployment rates, violence, informality, etc.
2. Life projects in uncertainty, uncertainty in their possibility of success and without a guarantee that all invidually carried out actions respond to the deepest aspirations of each person against a society regulated by the neoliberal market economy.

For the Millennial generation, the fact of just thinking about staying in a job for long periods is perceived as a failure because the time that could be used in new contexts, different experiences, various stimuli to experience is wasted. This generation is shown in work environments as looking for a quick promotion, because the merits are measured in the intensity and speed of the experiences and not by the team results or by the conflict results or the goals achieved together. It is true that the new challenges keep them interested...as long as new challenges do not appear to the new challenges, and then the focus is on the new of the

new, without major problem of leaving something unfinished or without the necessary depth for decision making. According to Stein (2013), Millennials believe that "they should be promoted every two years, regardless of performance" (p. 28).

Family relationships and traditional roles are also increasingly volatile: common life projects are shortened to a minimum and the reasons for breaking any relationship are increasingly futile (Stein, 2013). The institutions of traditional society (family, school, church, army) considered a guarantee of axiological strength and guarantors of the social order, today are shown as volatile, with incomprehensible, ethereal and/or inconsistent postulates in practice for members of the same institution (Johansen, 2012).

The ethic of the ephemeral and of the moment seems to prevail and permeate all the vital spaces of today's society and of reality of youth in particular. Currently, says Bauman (2006b):

> The idea of self-sacrifice has been delegitimized; people no longer feel persecuted or willing to make an effort to achieve moral ideals or defend moral values;

politicians have put an end to utopias and yesterday's idealists have become pragmatic. We live in the era of the purest individualism and the search for the good life, limited only by the requirement of tolerance and such tolerance is expressed as indifference, said indifference is closely related to indolence (p. 8-9).

Uncertainty in the family and social institutions is reflected in the likeness of the movement in the stock market: yesterday's options were valuable because they reflected personal convictions, but for the next day they
could become a dilemma due to unsustainable social acceptance or a rejection that is considered politically incorrect, or as a socially intolerant posture (Johansen, 2012).
It all depends on the valence that the specific context requires. Uncertainty about the future means that personal and organizational identity, or relationships, and also decisions are made as "liquid" and provisional, as established by Bauman (2008), for whom the shape of the continent shapes the content, the identity under construction is molded according to the moment and individual situation that is transited, taking aside positions or decisions that are seen as rigid and without constant malleability.
In a VUCA world, anyone who has a different life project proposal, a set of values that give an even counter-current mood or a proposal of ethical commitment must prepare to face opposing or diametrically opposed opinions, perhaps fight alone, or live in exile of the visionaries. What is decided today as the best for a specific group may not be the best for the whole as a whole. The global context of a world categorized as VUCA and as UTRU should be delineated if it is intended, as educators-companions, to better understand the proposal of Preventive Leadership within this context and be relevant and significant for less favored students.

Self-reflection of Chapter I

Check List: Contextualizing reality

In your context...	Y	N
1. You feel comfortable with the changes that economic globalization has brought to your life.		
2. You consider yourself capable of educating citizenship in an economically globalized world.		
3. You consider yourself a technologically up-to-date person.		
4. Consider that the society in which you develop is VUCA (Volatile, Uncertain, Complex and Ambiguous).		
5. You consider that you are capable of transmitting hope in the face of the radical uncertainties of the context.		
6. You consider that you are sufficiently updated in the various topics to be able to use the unprecedented transformations of our days as a resource for analysis and learning.		
7. You are able to make intelligent use of technology.		
8. You manage to identify the generation of people you are in charge of. –Millenials, TS, Centennials–		
9. You consider yourself capable of using their generational traits well and getting the best out of each one of them.		
10. You use technological resources to attract the attention of your students and promote their learning.		

2. Self-Appropriation

Preambles

The Jesuit philosopher and theologian Bernard Lonergan (1973) proposed a guide for the construction of a method that could be applied by educators and students alike to facilitate the formation of educators as experts in processes of significant learning and as learners, both educator and student, within learning communities.

The method is a:

> Normative pattern of recurring and related operations that produce cumulative and progressive results. This is a method where, of course, there are different operations and each operation is related to the others, where the relationship set forms a pattern, where the pattern is described as the correct way to do the job, where the operations accord with the pattern may be repeated indefinitely, and where the fruits of such repetition are, not repetitious, but cumulative and progressive (p. 4).

This method is fertile ground for the foundation of the operational dynamism common to all human beings: knowledge. All human beings are empowered to carry out the human process of acquiring knowledge. Furthermore, each person lives according to the stage of development in which they are, the implications of which come with the internalized appropriation of reality (Finamore, 2014). Any decision, inconsequential as it may seem, is binding on what is outside the subject itself, reality, the environment, etc.

Indeed, Lonergan (1992) understands human knowledge as an interior activity produced through a dynamic cognitive structure that is natural and inherent in every person.

The consciousness of the knowing subject

The leader is, obviously, an entity in relation, which is why the community or the collective process in which, and from which, he knows himself as a leader, makes decisions, and takes responsibility. The invariably dynamic structure of conscious intentionality is a four-level structure of successive sets of operations. Lonergan designates each according to the degree of their most important operation: the level of experience, the level of understanding, the level of judgment, and the level of decision. Therefore, in the process of deciding, the subject produces the first experiences, understands and judges their veracity or the existence of alternative courses of action (Fig. 6).

Figure 6 Dynamic structure of the conscious intentionality

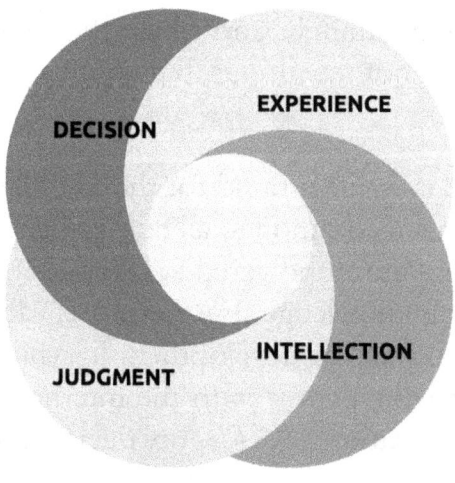

It is not the logic of cause and effect that positivism has defended so much, rather, it is the human process on the basis of the intrinsic faculties of each human being that is capable of carrying out the process of self-knowledge, self-appropriation, and self-determination. Since intelligence "assimilates" the information and knowledge obtained by the senses, reasonableness "assimilates" what intelligence contributes, and the decision or deliberation "assimilates" and "unifies" knowledge and feelings (Doran, 2008).

The method proposed by Lonergan (1992) is "a set of guidelines that serve to guide a process towards a result" (p. 471). So "the result can only exist in the empirical, intellectual, rational consciousness of the subject that affirms itself" (p. 473). The empirical moment can be understood when in the process of internalization not only do I make the process my own (because at this level, there may still be room to think only about oneself and being the sole criterion in decision-making), but it goes from lived experience (which does not imply a reflection of what has been lived and can only remain in emotion) to the understanding of it (using reflection is an entry point into oneself and trying to appropriate one's self without losing the referent of being and of being in relation to others) through questions in order to understand this experience in the whole of the subject's life. Questions such as "What is this that I am living? What does what I have lived mean? Why is this so, how often does it occur or exist?" in a spiral and seeking to exhaust all possible information, such that it significantly reduces blind spots in decision making (p. 413).

The intellectual moment can be understood when moving from the understanding of experiences to the affirmation or denial of judgment (If I affirm that A is B, I am "uniting" A with B; if, on the contrary, I affirm that A is not B, I am "separating" A from B) by asking critical questions and in order to reflect on the largest amount of data collected, I do a reading that "extracts" valuable information from non-relevant information. Questions like, what is the most important of all the data collected? What is the valuable information? Why is this and not something else the relevant information? These are questions that ask if the answers to the questions of the previous type are correct.

According to Lonergan (1999), the human being must judge carefully, and in detail, the substantive value of the alternatives to be considered as more viable and convenient. Thus, the human subject who makes decisions in a position of leadership must verify the results of the total process, passing from and returning to empirical, intellectual, and rational consciousness, always linked to experience, understanding, and judgment based on a value, the responsibility for the chosen alternative of the highest perceived value. This is because "the subject is effectively rational only if his demand for consistency between knowledge and action is followed by his decision and his action in a way that is consistent with his knowledge" (p. 707). Giving value is then a basic element in decision making. The decision, according to Flanagan (1997), is added to the evaluation of a commitment in order to "take a course of action to materialize, if it does not, there will be no such action" (p. 201).

Thus, the method is cumulative when the knowing subject moves from experience to understanding by asking questions; when the knowing subject moves from understanding to judgment, asking critical questions; and when the knowing subject moves from judgment to decision and action, asking questions supported by a value. In order to choose among the existing alternatives, according to Lonergan (1992), the knowing subject must further judge the value of the alternatives. So, the decision-maker must promote the accumulation of experiences, understand and judge the value of the alternatives in the face of the constant question about the completeness or not of the necessary information before choosing the one with the highest value because the subject is effectively rational only if its demand for coherence between knowing and doing is followed by a decision made in a manner consistent with its knowledge.

Outlining the above, Table 1 shows that the last three rows of functions that will be familiar to anyone involved in virtually any job at any level of any company or organization. The following two rows of functions represent the clarification that Lonergan makes regarding the evaluative and projective moments that occur in any type of collaboration that seeks to improve human life (Table 2).

Table 2 Lonerganian Fundamental Precepts and Functions

Level of Transcendence		Retrieving the Past		Moving into the Future
Being Loving	↑	Fusion	↓	Roots
Being Responsible	↑	Dialectic	↓	Foundations
Being Reasonable	↑	History	↓	Doctrines/Policies
Being Intelligent	↑	Interpretation	↓	Systematics/Plans
Being Attentive	↑	Research	↓	Communications/Implementations

Transcendental precepts and decision making

Lonergan (1992) uses the term transcendental precepts to describe the imperatives that drive the human subject at different levels of transcendence towards an ever deeper authenticity of a more genuine human subject with himself and with others; to an increasingly authentic and preventive leadership. These briefly expressed imperatives are shown in Table 3.

Table 3 Lonergan Imperatives

Be attentive	to your experience.
Be intelligent	in your inquiry into the meaning of that experience.
Be reasonable	in your judgments of the accuracy of your understanding of your experience.
Be responsible	in your decisions and subsequent actions based on the conclusions of the accuracy of your understanding of your experience, and base also on the value/givenness of that reality: what can be and what is truly worthwhile.
Be in love	with the mystery that grounds all your human operations, and with the human and the world with which that human is primordially interrelated.

What is preponderant in this method is the process of the subject, hence it has been preferable to call it a process of internalization rather than just the internalization. What is outside the subject can be considered as a set of deductive propositions, recipes, or manuals where the starting point is not the subject who knows but rather what is given by experience, by accumulated personal or community history, by the success achieved, or by the effectiveness of the results achieved. Lonergan (1992) understands human knowledge as an activity that intimately involves the subject he knows, which occurs through a dynamic cognitive structure that is natural and inherent in every human being capable of a cognitive process with conscious intentionality. In other words, there is no neutral cognitive process in itself, each step that makes up the knowledge process is moved by a minimum intention of attention, comprehension, appropriation, decision-making, and responsibility.

Intentionality is the precise objective that the educator has in front of every situation that he lives or faces. Intentionality aims at focused and reasoned ends, it tries to encompass their own experiences and those of the other, seeking to guide them to achievable goals. Intentionality is more than a competence or ability, in Lonergan it is shown as a natural movement of the human being at the moment of trying to understand and understand himself.

Lonergan formulated the operational levels in the first four transcendental precepts; attentive, intelligent, rational, responsible. The four-level structure with its immanent criteria is the fundamental heuristic structure (strategies, rules, syllogisms and conclusions that guide the discovery of new meanings) that is specified in the exercise of all the special methods of the sciences in general (being inherent to the structure of every human being, it is prior to any method be it (scientific, quantitative, qualitative, or mixed, etc.) and is used spontaneously in the practice of daily and social life by all human subjects. The starting point is the experience within the subject, both personal and community, where the level and capacity for self-knowledge of the subject himself in all dimensions, internal dynamics, feelings, sensations, affects that he perceives is an important factor.

A holistic educational intervention involves promoting the correct exercise of all conscious moments of self-appropriation. Consequently, the knowledge acquired by the subject may be at different levels of depth, partly due to the level of expertise that the constant exercise of self-awareness and self-appropriation allows.

This exercise does not exclude the presence of someone who accompanies to facilitate and/or provoke the expected moments and fruits of this personal exercise. At all times, the internal process of the subject who has managed to acquire the necessary knowledge to experience each level of awareness, self-knowledge, and self-appropriation of new and pertinent information allows a greater degree of responsibility against the judgment issued about himself and about the context, since this judgment is bound to the subject and the community of reference, where both can be enriched or both can suffer the inconsistency of the person in their ethical work since value is the pivotal point of the humanization process.

The decision made by the educator based on the suggested methodological process requires a high level of loyalty to the decision made, since the value (respect, order, love, truth, etc.) that has supported such a decision, and not another of the many possible, calls for an existential and ethical commitment of the subject to the consequences of such a decision.

When someone demands punctuality from the teacher, a possible value gained would be respect for the students and for himself, rather than just complying with the Institution's regulations. The consequences of a decision and the concomitant action that follows from it, are assumed responsibly because they respond with what someone is and the roles that are sustained at that time; that is to say: one is responsible as an educator in front of a group, as a citizen in
front of a civil society, as a colleague in front of the academy, etc.
The internal and external knowledge procedure, as well as the experience accumulation process, together with the knowledge process obtained from the exercise of the generalized empirical method, are a whole interacting, overlapping,

and remaining as a unit in the whole process. The brief analysis of the above shows the complexity of the process and the basics common to all knowing subjects (Fig. 7).

Figure 7 Deliberation process

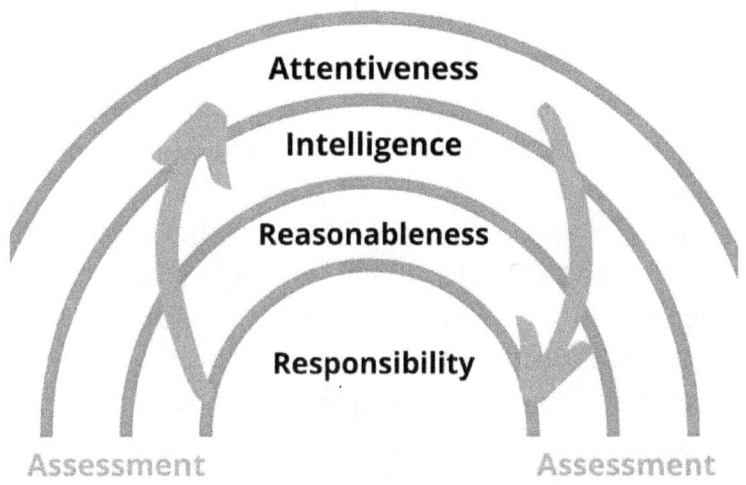

Taking into account the intentionality in the process and its end, the evaluation is then a basic element in decision-making. The decision, according to Flanagan (1997), is added to the evaluation of a commitment in order to "take some course of action to materialize, if it does not, it will not exist" (p. 201). Based on this, it is outlined that an integral human being is capable of transcending the self in order to achieve self-knowledge, self-control and is able to transcend reality to discover and explore it honestly.

The human being who knows how he or she knows and understands how to act responsibly also knows how to transcend towards the other to discover him in the dynamics of love, not only to know him or her, but also to act in favor of him or her.

The concrete person within a determined context is the one who, in his internal structure of knowledge and in his permanent learning process, becomes the center of reflection on leadership with preventive features. Along with the person, also of vital importance for the strengthening of preventive leadership is the community of reference or collective process within which, and from which, the subject that is considered or perceived as the leader becomes a leader, when a leader makes decisions and bears the consequences. Converting the above into an interrogation formula, the answer is presented to questions of a philosophical nature such as: What do I know? How do I know? Why is it that I do not know? What am I responsible for as a human being, as a professional, as a member of a family, as an employee, as a citizen?

For some educators, all of the above may be translated as an exercise in mindfulness by paying attention "intentionally to the present moment, without judging" (Kabat-Zinn, 1994, p. 4). For others, it is the Christian tradition of examination of conscience. It seems to me that the Lonerganian process includes and enriches them both (Andere, 2017; Schoeberlein, 2015; Martí, García-Campayo and DeMarzo, 2014). Over time, this improves responsible and intelligent decision-making based on internal, external, and interdependent progressive steps leading to personal decision. It is therefore perceived that this process is cumulative and gradual (Eurich, 2017).

The cognitive structure of the human subject

Lonergan's (1992) proposal with his Generalized Empirical Method tries to define whether human knowledge is possible, how is it possible, the limits of understanding, and the challenges for the human mind when facing reality. Furthermore, this method provides a broad approach to better understand the person who is undergoing a process of grasping the inner reality and the reality in which that person is immersed.

Knowledge is somewhat structured and is arranged by different operations that function as an optional unit of the subject that knows. According to Lonergan (1992), the realization of each of the knowledge structures implies the updating of four levels at each stage of knowledge. These levels of knowledge are summarized in four operations: experience, understanding, judgment, and decision.

Understanding knowledge "as non-intuitive, but discursive, with judgment as its decisive component" (p. 178) is key in the Canadian philosopher's proposal.

In this sense, the person can assert for himself: "I am a knowing subject, if I am a concrete and intelligible unity-identity-totality, characterized by acts of feeling, perceiving, imagining, inquiring, understanding, formulating, reflecting, apprehending, and judging." Therefore, any isolated element or partial activity, due to its incomplete participation in the cognitive structure, is reductive, partial, or incomplete.

The structure that, as a whole, the human being possesses of his self-knowledge is assembled by intentionality. According to Lonergan (1967): "Human knowledge involves many different and irreducible activities: sight, hearing, smell, touch, taste, asking, imagining, understanding, conceiving, reflecting, evaluating evidence, judging" (p. 222).

In this sense, any isolated element or partial activity, due to its incomplete participation of the elements of the structure, does not define the entire structure. That is, in knowledge, it is not valid only to see or hear and consider that single information as complete or finished, and it is not only the moment to understand or to judge if the most extensive understanding has not been exhausted. Knowledge, in its strictest and most specific sense, is defined not by the performance of an isolated activity or the incomplete convergence of different activities, but by the dynamism of each and every one of the elements that make up the human cognitive structure in the constant recovery of the previously known, investigating the necessary so that a weighing of facts, happenings, experiences, emotions, feelings, and thoughts is achieved as completely as possible.

The question "Would a little more information be missing than what was already collected?" becomes key in the process of appropriation of knowledge, understanding, and evaluation of evidence at the time of making a decision.

The realization of the cognitive structure implies the unity of the empirical moment (feeling, perceiving, imagining, touching, smelling, listening), of the intellectual moment (inquiring, understanding, formulating), of the rational moment (judgment) and of the existential moment of the person (responsibility, respect, love).

A conscious process is what Lonergan (1992) sees as the essence of this internalization; to become more aware (self-awareness) of the mental operations and activities of oneself (Meynell, 2009). The Generalized Empirical Method, if appropriate through the continuous practice of its elements, becomes a personal method that helps improve learning processes, cognitive and metacognitive, and favors decisions that touch the existence of any person, in any situation, and at any time.

Self-appropriation

Lonergan (1967) makes an objectification on self-knowledge: the application of knowledge on self-knowledge such that the moment of the experimenting process with accumulated experience, with intellection, and with judgment comes together. At the same time, the understanding of the self-experience of experience, with intellection and with judgment should come together; and likewise, the moment of the cognitive process of judging whether the intellection of experiences is adequate or not to that of the intellect and judgment. In this conjugation, the individual develops his self-knowledge, an objective knowledge of his own understanding as an internalized activity. In this internalization, the human being discovers the processes by which he obtained this knowledge and, therefore, he or she is able to affirm how he knows his own knowledge. Self-appropriation refers to what a person is already aware of in order to achieve a more complete knowledge and to remove possible omissions at any level of activity within himself. In the words of Lonergan (1973) … "the reader will do it [introspection], not looking inward, but recognizing in their own expressions the objectification of their subjective experience" (p. 9).

In this sense, Lonergan (1967) distinguishes self-knowledge from consciousness itself, arguing that the latter is only relevant to the experience of each of the knowledge activities, but consciousness is unable to achieve knowledge on its own. In other words, putting experience, intelligence, and judgment into action is also a way to experience them. The acquisition of consciousness, according to Lonergan (1967), becomes the application of the first level of knowledge to knowing oneself, without implying that the subject knows how he or she came to know, because for the
subject it only implied having had an experience of their own-ness, of what he or she is to themselves and in their very being, a kind of radical experience of their individuality.

Intentionality in knowledge

Going further without leaving anything behind in human cognitive activity is intentionality. Well according to Lonergan (1967), intentionality is when:

> Conscious, intelligent, rationally it [rationality] goes further: beyond data to intelligibility; beyond the intelligibility of truth and the truth of being; and beyond the known truth, the truth that is known and the truth that remains to be known. However, even though it goes further, it leaves nothing behind. It goes beyond what is added and, when it has been added, it is unified.... It is all inclusive, but the knowledge that we achieve is always limited (p. 228).

Therefore, the relationship between my knowledge and reality is evident by the intentionality, by that movement of going beyond, of the knowledge that tends to all the reality that surrounds it but that does not exhaust it; in addition, there is the "need" to completely satisfy the knowledge of the totality of reality, but that "need" is not satisfied with the content of the knowledge achieved, since it is always a greater but not total, deeper but not full knowledge.

Even when some cognitive problem has already been solved, intentionality, according to Lonergan (1967), "is potential objectivity" (p. 229). That is, the objective knowledge of what the person is, and of what surrounds him or her always remains in the potentiality of being full. One advances in knowledge but does not exhaust it, the person is known yet remains a mystery, the relationship deepens but the fullness of full apprehension is never completed. Intentionality stimulates the cognitive structure since intentionality guides the knowledge process from the data of intellection; it also provokes the passage from intellection to reflection on the experiential elements.

The desire to know-intentionality may, however, be distorted by biases of selfishness or fear. These biases should be more easily overcome through introspection and comparison with the best version of the person that can be imagined for him or herself (Figure 8). Coherence and honesty in the intended process are key elements because, in the words of Lonergan (1992): "if a development is conscious, then its success requires correct apprehensions at its starting point, during its process and in achieving its objective." (Figure 9) (p. 500).

Figure 8 Intentionality

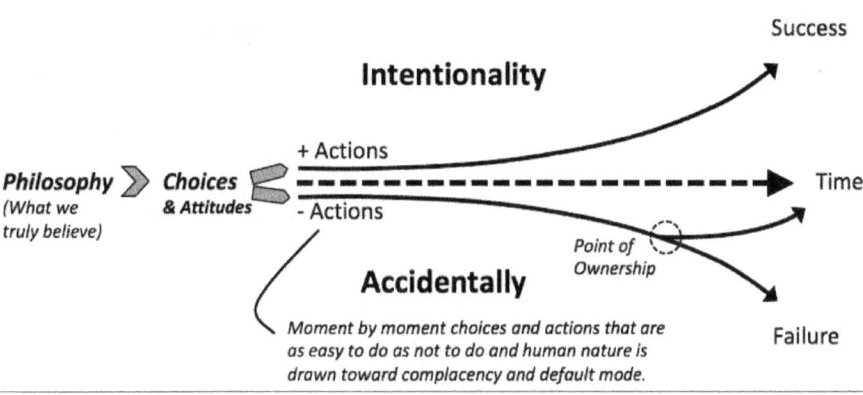

Figure 9 Intentionality in a wide sense

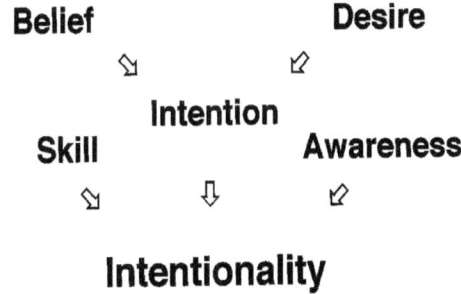

Intentionality is the power that moves one to want to leave nothing behind and to instead know totally and fully. Lonergan (1992) states, "More questions lead to new ideas only to further increase the number of questions. This is how knowledge is accumulated "(p. 494). Because the desire to know is never satisfied, judgments are usually provisional and, as such, should be re-examined from time to time to avoid as much prejudice and/or deviations in the process as possible, cross-checked with new judgments and may eventually be incorporated from a higher point of view, or perhaps the provisional judgments may be re-evaluated to be replaced by better elaborated ones that make up a broader network of related knowledge or that satisfy a greater number of compression criteria (Fig. 10). Something similar happens with feelings: if they are intentional, they will or won't respond to values and the concomitant satisfaction in the Ignatian process of discernment.

Figure 10 Self-appropriation Loop

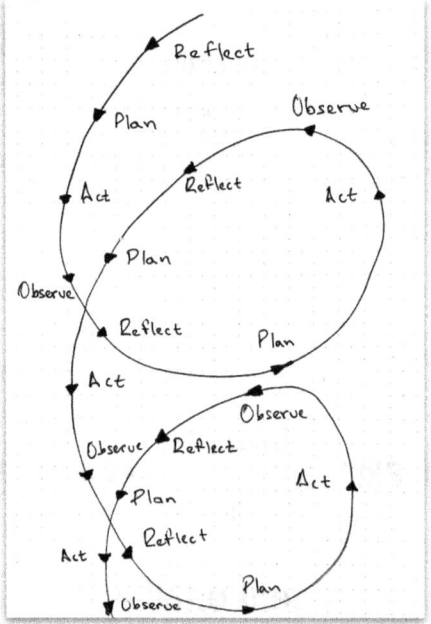

The decision is the last step of practical judgment and corresponds to the transition from your intellectual conception to a possible order for its concrete realization. A greater number of compression criteria or knowledge related to what is known is achieved moral self-transcendence with reference to really good values that return human beings their own value. Making decisions based on values allows a process of humanization that favors those who make the decision and who are affected by it. Value is the dynamic demand of rational consciousness for self-consistency between knowing and doing (Lonergan, 1992, chap. 18).

A teacher in a group makes decisions and, if their internal process and their intentional movement has a value as their support and goal, this preserves the human nature of decision-making it easier for them to take on the consequences and side effects, since the value is a possible object of rational choice. On the contrary, freedom can also lead to human inauthenticity, because if freedom has been exercised with reference to the calculation of complacency or pain inflicted on others or power over others ...both the common good and the values that authenticate a personalized existence will be lost sight of. You will act without assuming the question of what or whom are you responsible for?

Because modern society is massive, a critical and intentionally meaningful action requires many people involved both to act well and to act badly. Today, any field of humanistic action requires experts in all possible branches of knowledge in transdisciplinary dialogue, seeking to achieve the ultimate goal of every human being: a fulfilling and holistic life project. Then, the valuable thing will be then the consistency between knowing and doing, knowing and doing not what you like or please but rather the good, the just, the true. For Lonergan (1974) only "benevolence and beneficence are the principles of collaboration and true love" (Doran, 2008, p. 797).

Method and community

An organization can be a community if it manages to understand itself as the set of subjects who are capable of deciding for themselves and who share ideals, goals, expectations, and life projects in a convergent dynamic. Assets are not measured by their productivity (Rodríguez, 2007; 2015).

The person who acts intentionally goes beyond what is received. But is also the one who uses in all his decisions the values that have been personalized since they are a guarantee of humanization, and intends to permeate them at the institutional level. Lonergan's (1973) words come to reinforce the community aspect:

> A community is not just a number of men with a geographic border. [A community] is an endeavor of common meanings [...] Common meanings are possible when there is a common field of experience, to withdraw [oneself] from that shared field is to be out of touch [with the community]. Common meaning is formal when there is common understanding, withdrawing from that common understanding [may be due to] a lack of understanding, misunderstanding, or mutual misunderstanding. Common meaning exists as long as there are shared judgments, areas in which everyone affirms or denies in the same way, and anyone can withdraw from that common judgment when they disagree, when someone considers true what others consider false or false when others think of it
> as true. Common meaning is realized by decisions and choices, especially through permanent dedication. (p. 79)

In essence, and continuing Lonergan's (1973) reflection, the community unites or divides, ends or begins, just as "the common field of experience, of common understanding, of common judgments, of common commitments begins and ends" (p. 76).

Considering the above, the relevance or failure of any educator lies in whether he accepts and approves or rejects and belittles the convergence of minds, hearts, stories, points of view, emotions and actions, judgments, or intuitions that each student, each person, each partner. Each of them externalizes, the internal process which involves all its faculties and closes a cycle in responsible decision making.

The avoidance of a community of reference distorts the realization of the human being in its empirical, intelligent, rational, and volitional component. Therefore it impoverishes it in its historical construction. The social aspect that is inscribed in every human being is rescued because knowledge requires others so that such knowledge is built and enriched, modified, or discarded. The community of reference links what is beyond personal space but also builds social reality that is essential for a complete human being.

Lonergan gives sustenance to his reflections, to an authentic transcendence that goes beyond the selfish self-reference of the psychologizing consciousness of the self-centered individual, to rediscover the centrality of the human subject in his internal process of self-knowledge and self-possession as necessary conditions for decision making. The community that learns and builds itself enables the proposal of a humanism that involves an intentional educational community practice. The community environment facilitates the educational leadership development of the educator because it allows him to be someone attentive, intelligent, thoughtful, and responsible for a community of reference and learning.

This community of reference, united socially and organizationally, is understood as a vital space for the evaluation of personal and community leadership. According to Johansen

(2012), one of the most important skills of leaders today is the ability to sow, cultivate, and grow shared assets so that they can benefit more people. The social skill of bonding between people, in an intentional educational way, is a competence that points to a leadership process centered on a network built on the accumulation of knowledge from the community, of attitudes or actions of the leader. A leader in educational settings should act based on an intention favored by the axiological in the entire process and focused on achievements from a comprehensive perspective.

By involving the community of reference in the process and its results, within a context, the achievement of the goal is being preserved as an organizational purpose, even if an individual or a small group of the organization makes the final decision.

It is pertinent that the community of reference jointly carry out an attentive, intelligent, reflective, responsible, and affective process, with the aim that at the end of said process the community accepts what is proposed, what is presented, what is judged, what should be approached, and what is decided. For Lonergan (1992), people are united by common experience, by common or complementary ideas, by similar judgments of fact and value and by decisions taken communally. But it is also true that a reference community can lose its educational essence if the members of the reference community are kept out of contact:

  a) By not sharing the same experiences;
  b) By not understanding each other;
  c) By affirming or denying without points of agreement;
  d) By opting for opposite goals.

Proposing the community of reference as a key element in the proposal of an educational leadership with preventive fea-

tures is to seek a paradigm. A paradigm shift in educational leadership is seen more as a process –personal and/or collective– of community learning. That is, a change in the way of perceiving and understanding the human subject, in
this case, the educational leader in their self-possession by self-knowledge, in the construction of their own knowledge, and in decision-making with the support of and coming from a community as a reference.

Faced with a current leadership that seems to look at the subject in their individual possibilities and their ability to modify the organizational culture, to favor the increase of profits, to promote new markets, to create new products, to innovate without ethical guidelines, etc. The paradigm of educational leadership with preventive features is the internal experience of the human subject, both personal and community, and its point of arrival is loyalty to the decision made personally with the community of reference. Over time, this leads to responsible, thoughtful, intelligent, and concrete decisions based on the internal and external series of progressive, interdependent, and cumulative steps that lead to personal and collective decision.

Lonergan's Generalized Empirical Method has shed light on anthropological reflection of "common ground" to all leaders: knowledge, the process of becoming an agent of knowledge, and the implications of appropriating the reality in which he/she is immersed and overwhelms them in richness and diversity. Furthermore, the intentionality of the subject and the practical implications for the connoisseur of self-awareness, self-possession, and self-determination are essential elements for the development of any educational leader and the purposes of the development of his leadership with preventive features. Such a process guarantees sufficient and necessary tranquility for attention, intelligence, reasonableness, and responsibility in a consistent way.

Self-Reflection of Chapter II

Check List: Awareness of my knowing action

In your current life...	Y	N
1. You are attentive to details and data of your own experience.		
2. You investigate the meaning of your experiences.		
3. You manage to make value judgments about the exact understanding of the experience.		
4. You are responsible for the decisions you make.		
5. The people around you (friends and non-friends) consider you a loving person.		
6. You are a respectful person of all humanity and of everything that exists.		
7. You become aware of yourself, your experience and the knowledge you have. (self-knowledge)		
8. You apply knowledge about self-knowledge to achieve more complex knowledge. (self-appropriation).		
9. You make decisions based on self-knowledge and self-appropriation.		
10. You manage to go beyond knowledge without leaving anything behind, that is, you achieve cognitive intentionality.		

3. Scaffolding for an Educational Model

An educator as a preventive leader requires an educational model to converge and support the common process of self-awareness, self-possession, and self-determination with the individual learning process. Learning facilitates increase our sources of knowledge, increases our repertoire of skills, extends the cognitive structures already established, and deepens and expands the frames of reference that each individual possesses.

School displays undergone changes on all fronts and will continue to change as society determines other ways of organizing knowledge, transmitting it, and training its citizens competently to face the demands of life as we saw in previous chapters. The traditional functions of teaching based on orality, repetition, and the direction of being a sage on stage have been replaced, according to Klein (2005), by the models that are still in force as a mentor, mediator, facilitator, coach, guide, and companion. Information, methods, concepts, and theories are used in order to achieve a more complete understanding of the learning experience.

The proposed educational model is constructivist at heart, since it favors the search for increased value, and new content within the already existing forms of our learning schemes. The intended changes in current education should be made not only in what is known but also in how it is known and why it is known (Kegan & Lahey, 2010).

The human mind actively interacts with experience data,

filtering, and selective data processing. People order the world, but they do it in different ways, depending on their learning experiences. And this process of arrangement and organization is always incomplete, as is any human process of knowledge (Werhane et al., 2011). The human mind builds the models of its experiences, on constructions that are socially learned, and contents to alteration and change (Figure 11).

Figure 11 The Inquiry Learning Community

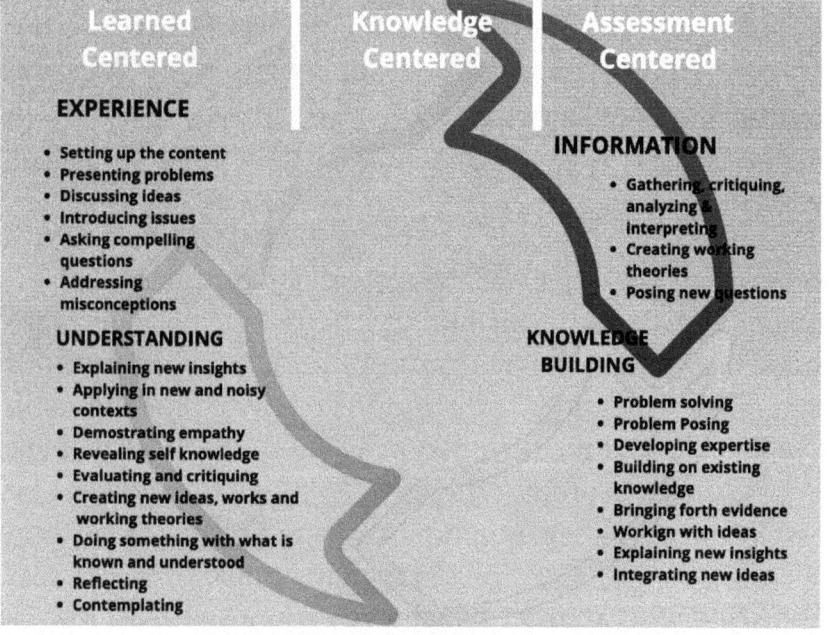

Mental models can be schematics that frame experience, through which individuals process information, conduct experiments, and formulate theories. Such mental models can also be understood as references to human knowledge about a particular set of events or a system. Individuals select and focus on what strikes them or on what they imagine to be the most important phenomena for the ends they pursue.

The connection between social constructions and individual appropriation of knowledge rests on community accompaniment strategies, reasoned and reasonable efforts among members of learning communities, a defined educational intention of the subjects involved in the act of appropriating meaningful learning, and holistic evaluations of the learning experience. That is, a learning community in which the individual can immerse himself in a context of meaning and where meaningful and relevant knowledge is shared, built, and rebuilt. (Bazerman & Chugh, 2006; Chugh & Bazerman, 2007)

Socio-constructivism

Constructivism is a learning theory (Bächtold, 2013; Hartle, Baviskar and Smith, 2012). It assumes that learning can only take place when learners are actively participating in the learning experience itself and in building new knowledge about prior knowledge (Al Huneidi and Schreurs, 2012; Jenkins, 2000). Instead of emphasizing how a learner can memorize and recite a quantity of information, or letting learners do what they want. The constructivist proposal, the learning subject and the internalization process are the focal point where the role of the educator is essential and important, because the educator not only facilitates or mediates, he or she embodies and proposes everything that is intended to be taught.

Learners engage in the "construction of meaning" as the application of knowledge takes precedence over the acquisition and teaching of facts on their own. This construction of meanings requires circular and cumulative internal movements, where the factors in exercise, according to Andere (2017), are:

a) the activation of a dynamic process of propositional affective bonding and personal improvement;
b) the maieutic exercise of questions;
c) the problem statement and its solution process;
d) personal decision-making and the reference group;
e) higher order critical thinking, and
f) reflexivity.

This same approach emphasizes the importance that he who knows a little more facilitates the transfer of culture as education for the enrichment of the subject who finds himself with less knowledge and/or experience. Socio-constructivism highlights the "community" as a key element to transfer, rework, and create knowledge through language (Table 4).

Table 4 Dimensions/Approaches to Constructivist Pedagogies

Dimensions	Narrative
Nature of learner	Constructivism sees learners as unique individuals.
	The unique nature of learner is an integral part of the learning process.
Responsibility for learning	According to constructivism it resides with the learner.
	Constructivism emphasizes the active role of learners in the learning process in looking for meaning.
Learning motivation	According to constructivism, learning motivation develops learners´ motivation:
	Through authentic experiences in handling problems;

	By gaining success, learners gain confidence and motivation to embark on more complex challenges.
Role of Teacher	In the constructivism, the teacher usually asks, supports, provides guidelines, and creates environment for learners to arrive at their own conclusions. The teacher endures continuous dialogue with learners, and the teacher should challenge learners.
Interaction	Teachers and learners learn from each other; learners compare their version of truth with that of teachers and peers to arrive a socially tested/socially negotiate share a version of truth. The learning task is the interface between teachers and learners, both should develop awareness of each other´s viewpoints and should look at their own standards and values.
Collaboration	Learners collaborate to arrive at shared understanding of truth in a specific field; through "scaffolding," learners can extend beyond the limitation of physical maturation to the extent that the development process lags behind the learning process.
Context	Sees the context in which learning occurs as central to learning; learning is directly relevant to application; it acculturates students into authentic and complex practices through activities and social interaction.
Assessment	A two-way process involving interaction between teachers and learners; inextricably linked with the learning process to find out learning achievements and quality of learning experiences; courseware; share possible ways in which learner´s performance may be improved.

Constructivism, according to Bächtold (2013), has one field of reference in the psychology of cognitive development and another in epistemology. Both fields lead to two different points of view about the learning process. One point of view sees the construction process carried out by students as a process of enrichment and/or reorganization of cognitive structures at the mental level.

The other sees the construction process carried out by the students as a process of construction or development of models or theories at the symbolic level. These two types of construction processes are closely related and, therefore, should not be considered independent of each other.

There are two trends in social constructivism. A trend, in Piaget's line, looks at the spontaneous and unconscious enrichment of the individual in the group and/or at the reorganization of the cognitive structures of each individual on the mental plane. The other trend is in line with Vygotsky and looks at the process of understanding and mastering with a certain level of specialization of new models or theories at the symbolic level. These two trends agree that the interaction between the learners favors the enrichment and/or the reorganization of the learning process of each learner, while the interaction between the learners and the expert favors the introduction of the former in the culture and makes possible learning (Bächtold, 2013; Piaget, 1954, 1971; Vygotsky, 1986).

Making the first point of view his own, the educator pays attention to the process that enriches and/or reorganizes the cognitive structures of himself and the learner. Taking the symbolic level as its own, the educator pays attention to the process in which new models or theories are constructed or developed (Bächtold, 2013).

The constructivism that highlights the social environment of the learner and his apprehension of knowledge, presents a series of elements that intervene in the process of construction of knowledge that are outlined in Table 5.

Table 5 Elements that intervene in the knowledge construction process

The learner	Builds knowledge.
The educator	Understands how learners interpret knowledge. Guides during the learning acquisition and modification process.
The instruments	Are used in the learning activity.
The knowledge	Integrates a previous knowledge that has to be reviewed, perhaps needs to find new meanings and be reconstructed, and; the "new" knowledge to be built.
"Learning community"	It is the cooperation between learners. It is the acculturation of the learner in the scientific culture.
Competences	They generate movement, apply, and integrate the declarative, procedural, attitudinal, and causal knowledge acquired.
Emotional intelligence	Means self-awareness, self-control, empathy, and social ability.

The learner who builds knowledge

Socio-constructivism, according to Hartle et al. (2012), proposes a person who constructs meaning by acting in an intentionally structured environment and in interaction with others (Jenkins, 2000; Duit, 2003), intentionally causing the reactivation of knowledge, generating cognitive dissonance, applying new knowledge with its corresponding feedback, and reflecting on learning or metacognition (Fig. 12) (Duit, 1995; Tyson, Venville, Harrison, and Treagust, 1997).

Figure 12 Double loop learning matrix

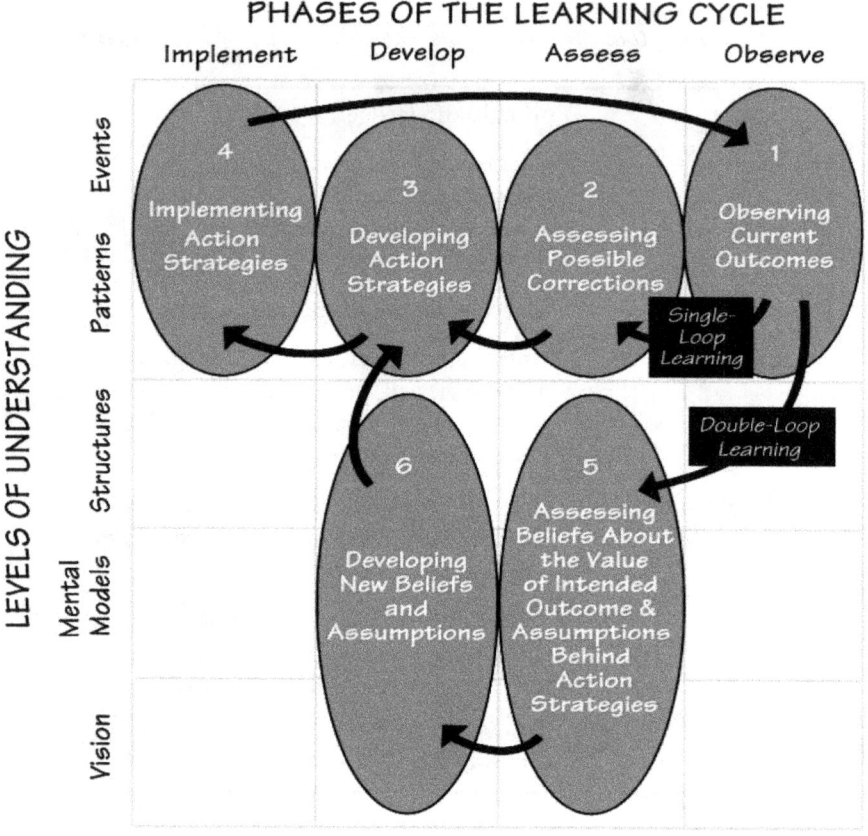

According to Bächtold (2013), to acquire new knowledge, learners must mentally carry out a series of intellectual steps (internalization process) that lead to that knowledge. To carry out these intellectual steps, learners must integrate, modify, or improve new modes of reasoning. This process of construction of knowledge has three defining characteristics: the unity of subjectivity-intersubjectivity linked in this book with the Lonerganian proposal, the semiotic mediation supported by instruments, and the joint construction within asymmetric relationships that every learning community has in its very structure (Posner, Strike, Hewson and Gertzog, 1982).

The subject that constructs knowledge is an active subject that interacts with the environment. Although he or she is not completely limited by the characteristics of the environment itself or by the determinants that his own biology marks, he or she is changing by increase and accumulation in their knowledge according to a set of internal and external restrictions typical of its being labile and finite. Both objects and contexts emerge and converge as part of a single bio-socio-cultural development process (Fig. 13).

Figure 13 Learning Environment Design

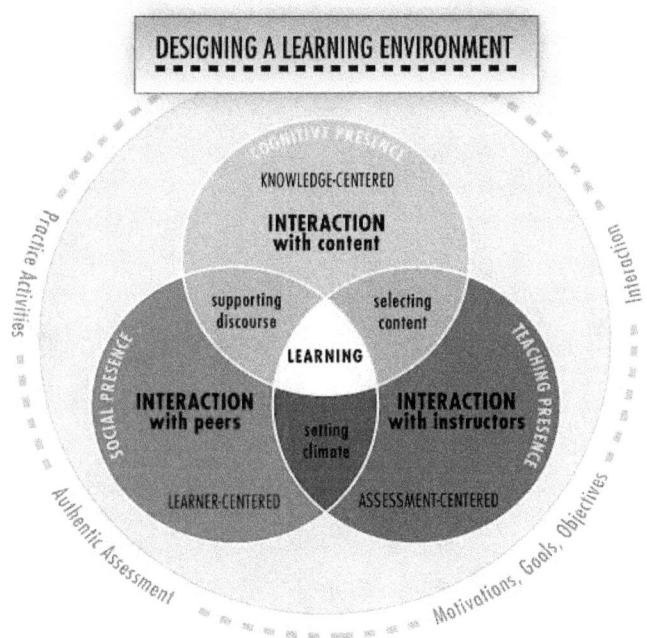

According to Chu Chin and Ju (Crissa) Chen (2010) "the meaning of an action and a context are not specifically independent of each other" (p. 65). The process of construction of meanings that the learner carries out is seen as:

1. An extension of the cognitive process that takes place before and outside the intentional educational process through which learners adapt their cognitive structures to their material and social environments (Posner et al., 1982);
2. It is observed that in this process of construction of meaning and appropriation of knowledge, the continuous construction of new models or theories is verified (Fig. 14) (Von Glasersfeld, 1998; 2013).

Figure 14 Learning Theories

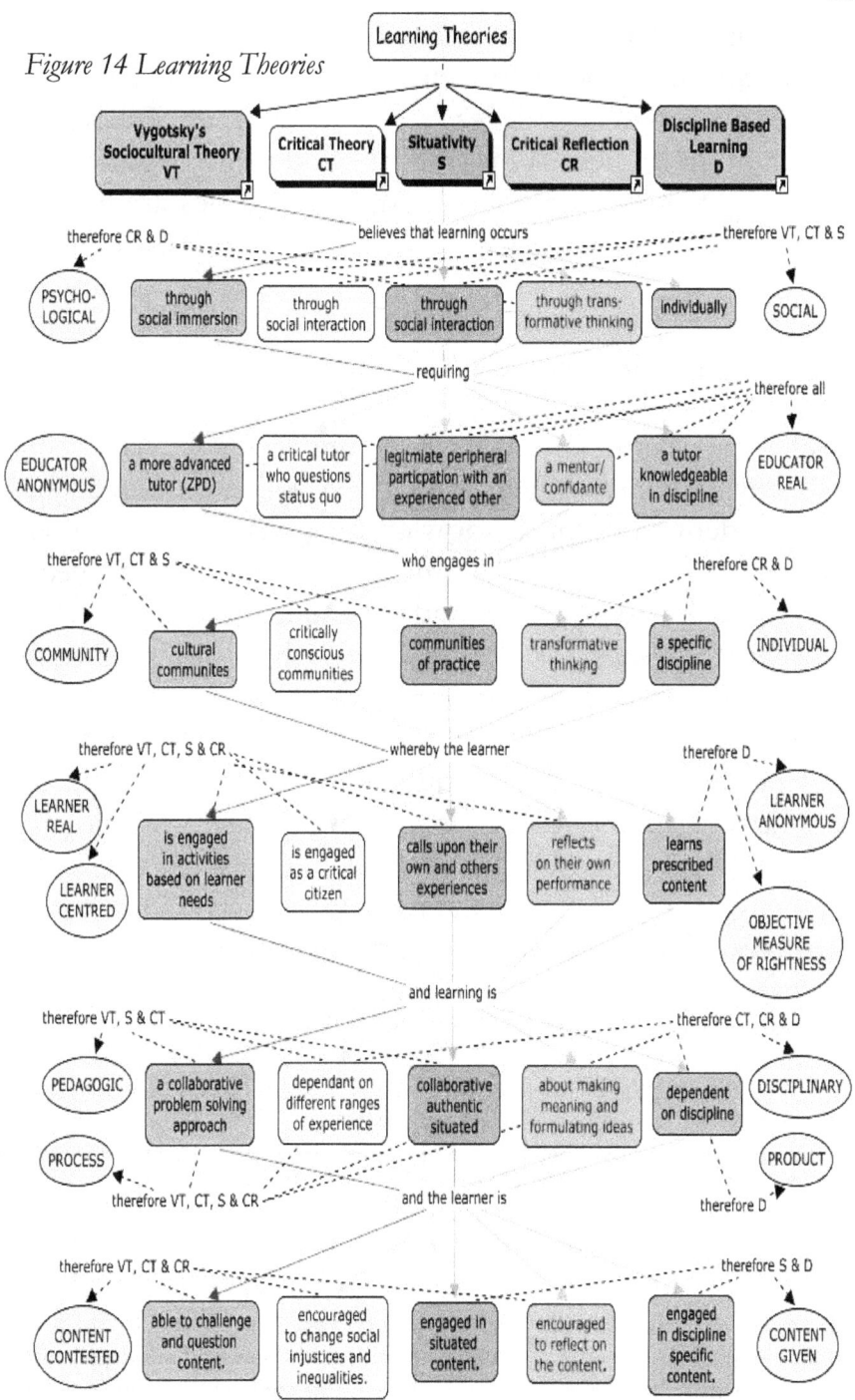

Making the first point of view his own, the educator pays attention to the process that enriches and/or reorganizes the cognitive structures of himself and the learner. Taking the second point of view as his own, the educator pays attention to the process in which new models or theories are built or developed (Bächtold, 2013).

The educator

The role of the educator, for some constructivist theory theorists (Jenkins, 2000; Matthews, 2000), is to understand how students interpret knowledge so as to guide them through the process of acquiring and modifying it. The educator should help refine his understanding and interpretation in new mental schemas. The teacher's job would be to try to correct the misconceptions that may arise in students in previous stages. The aim of the teacher would be focused on improving the quality of the acquired knowledge and lived experiences. To apply the constructivist theory, according to Alonso, López, Manrique, and Vines (2005), a learning environment must be designed and implemented to guide through a process of collaboration and interaction between the learners (experts and novices), to learning that is built by the group instead of a single individual (Table 6).

Table 6 Key elements for a positive school climate

- The development of children and youth is promoted.
- The necessary learning is sought for a productive, contributory, and satisfactory life in a democratic society.
- The presence of norms, values, and expectations that support people, feel socially, emotionally and physically safe and are respected.

- All members of the educational community feel respected and involved.

- Students, families, and educators work together to develop, live, and contribute to a shared school vision.

- Educators model and nurture an attitude that emphasizes the benefits and satisfaction derived from learning.

- Each person contributes to the operation of the school and to the care of the environment.

The work of the adult or the expert is not ruled out (Table 7), or that of the most advanced in knowledge, although it is also not emphasized according to the Salesian educational proposal where the educator is the model of values and educational proposals embodied and suggested by conviction and experience.

Table 7 Key elements for a highly effective learning environment

Components	Features
Individual characteristics of learners	Students ask more questions than teachers themselves.
Teaching and learning goals	Questions are rated better than answers.
Activities that best support learning	Ideas come from various sources.
The evaluative evaluations that best measure and guide learning	Very different learning models are used.
The culture that infuses the learning environment	The classroom as a learning space becomes a hyper-connected community.
	Learning is personalized through a variety of criteria and stimuli.

> Assessment is persistent, authentic, transparent, and never punitive.
>
> Achievement criteria are diverse, transparent, and co-developed with students and families.
>
> Learning habits are constantly modeled.
>
> There are opportunities for constant and creative practice and growth.

The tools used in cognitive activity

Hutchins (1995) considers that external tools and resources modify the nature and functional system where cognitive activities occur, thereby affecting the conception of what, how, and why it is necessary to know (Fig. 15).

Figure 15 Socio-constructivist learning tools

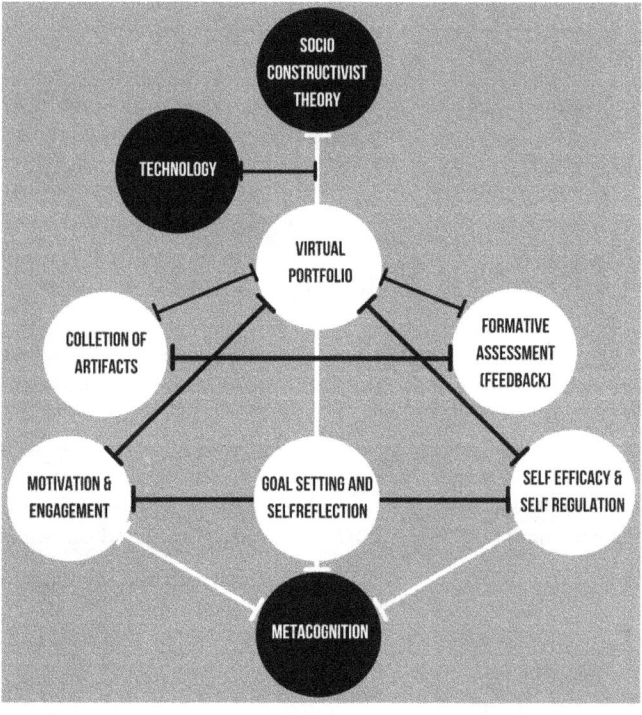

Furthermore, according to Brown and Cole (2001), knowledge is found as part and product of cognitive activity, the context and culture in which this activity was developed and the way it is used.

Wartofsky (1979) defines tools (equipment and language) as objectivizations of human needs and intentions clothed with cognitive and affective content. He distinguishes between three hierarchical levels the notion of tools:

1) Primary tools are those such as needles, buckets, bowls, which are used directly for the performance of things or activities;
2) Secondary tools are representations of primary tools and modes of action using primary tools. These are, therefore, traditions or beliefs, habits or customs;
3) Tertiary tools are imaginary worlds built individually but shared, nurtured, and modified in a given social context.

The idea of a social origin of psychological functions is not the antithesis of the notion of personal construction of it, especially if it starts from a two-way model of cultural transmission in which all participants actively transform knowledge. New technologies and the world of apps, smartphones, Artificial Intelligence, non-contact modes of communication, languages used in social networks that do not respect grammatical, phonetic, or style rules are some examples of artifacts (Fig. 16).

Figure 16 Tools for the learning process

Some concepts are, according to Bächtold (2013), semiotic mediations constructed spontaneously by a subject and then connected or replaced by the corresponding socio-cultural concepts learned by the subject through social interaction (signs used in language, words expressed in signs shared by a group, and especially on social networks). Socio-cultural concepts are mental representations that are always made explicit and communicated by the subject when using them.

Therefore, it is assumed that the construction of knowledge is an experience of internalization that it is guided by other social subjects, like a learning community, in a structured environment. A community of learning takes into account that the learners are responsible for their own learning accompanied by those who can provide a little more knowledge, experience, and who model what they propose (Fig. 17).

Figure 17 New symbols and languages

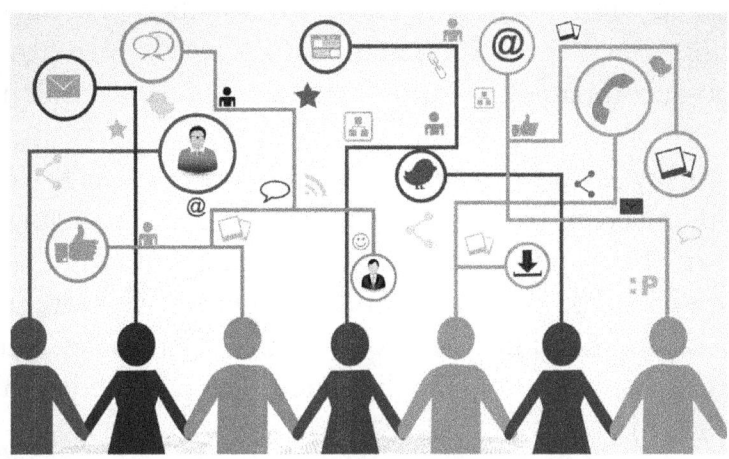

According to Nuthall (2000), the incorporation of socio-cultural and linguistic perspectives in the socio-cognitive model of mental processes offers a vision of how language and social processes constitute the forms through which knowledge is acquired, it is also rebuilt and modified.

In a group or community, one learns and unlearns, interacts and modifies mental models, behaviors, evaluations, decisions, since in a community or group one's own skills and ways of exercising acquired learning and/or active citizenship are appreciated. The learner's previous cognitive structures, according to Bächtold (2013), may or may not be adequate for the construction or understanding of new knowledge. There may be limitations that place conditions on the individual learning process: level of personal development, physiological issues, limiting contexts, reduced experiences, etc. If this is the case, the learner must "build" new cognitive structures to enrich or reorganize the previous ones, since personal achievements should be measured, not standardized goals. Thus, there is talk of a kind of *constructivist synapse* that involves the person, the learning community, language games, and the culture and context in which the person is immersed.

Cognitive processes are presented as a quality of people who act in culturally organized environments where the construction and deconstruction of processes is shared, provoked, accompanied, verified (Lonergan, 1973; Salomon, 2001).

Vygotsky (1987) affirms that human beings manage to separate themselves from the "exterior" through meaning encoded in the symbolic, that is, the cultural systems that are important for the development of thought. This "cultural exterior" and "individual interior" of the cognitive relational process is considered as the dialectic of deep reflective thinking (Fig. 18).

Figure 18 Deep Reflective Thinking

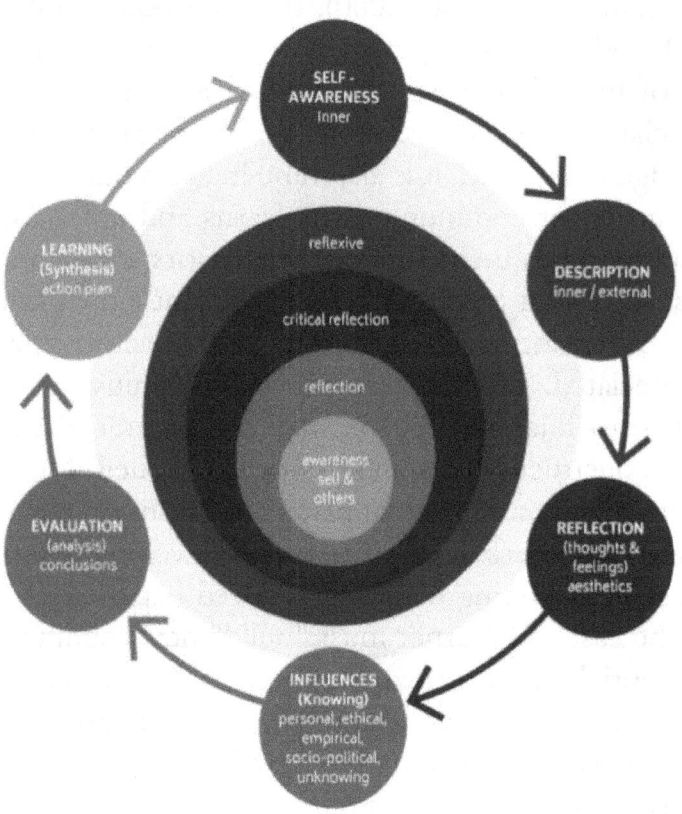

Such reflective thinking can support the reorganization and stabilization of the underlying cognitive structures in the process of reconstruction and/or new acquisition of cognitive processes (Fig. 19) (Bächtold, 2013; Hartle et al., 2012).

Figure 19 Reflective Cycle according to Gibbs

Deep reflective thinking comprises the set of biological, social, motivational, and environmental characteristics that an individual develops from new or difficult information; to perceive and process it, retain it, and accumulate it, build concepts and categories, and solve problems, which together establish their learning preferences and define their cognitive potential.

Deep reflective thinking is characterized by being concentrated on the subject of the discourse, associated with an active approach to learning and the desire to understand the main point of the content, establish connections, and draw conclusions, or according to Pinchao (2016):

> The student personalizes the task, extracting its meaning for his personal life project and for daily life; relates the contents of the task with other knowledge and with everyday situations; tries to make learning have personal meaning (p. 63).

Knowledge

Knowledge is a dynamic and interactive process of the knowing subject through which his cognitive structures interpret and reinterpret information external to himself. According to Bächtold (2013), there are different types of cognitive structures which can be a unique concept, a set of interrelated concepts, a reasoning structure, a symbolic structure, etc. A cognitive structure is considered as such because it allows the cognition of the knowing subject (perception, reasoning, judgment, decision) (Fig. 20). In this process, cognitive structures are progressively building explanatory models, usually of greater complexity, so that reality is interpreted through models that are built ad hoc to explain this interpretation.

Figure 20 Kolbe's model of the Process of learning

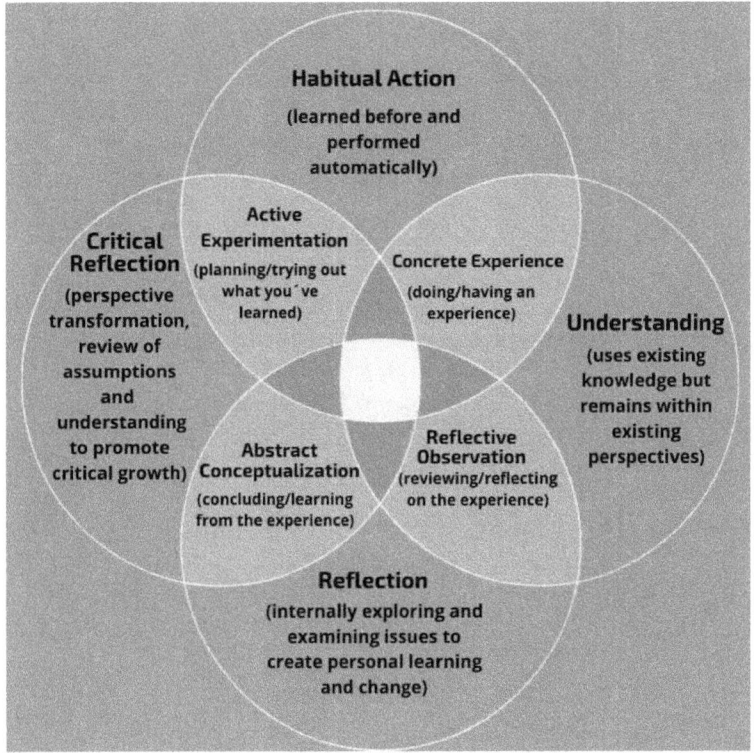

Reflective thinking about new concepts, models, or theories and self-awareness of the operational functions of those who know allow for the conscious activation of the connections between the concepts at stake and also between these and the objects, properties, events, or processes to which they refer (Fig. 21).

Figure 21 The Student learning spiral

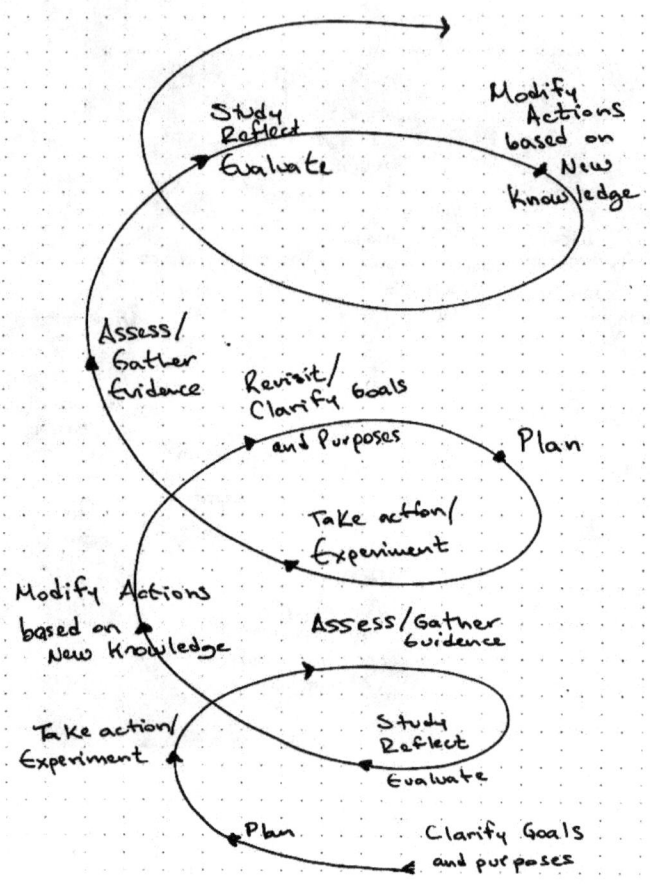

Piaget's (1954) work is primarily concerned with the development of spontaneous concepts, while Vygotsky's (1986) work is primarily concerned with the development of scientific concepts. According to Vygotsky (1986), spontaneous concepts are constructed by the child itself, spontaneously and unconsciously, based on their own experience. Scientific concepts, by contrast, are first constructed by society and then shared with children by adults. Since society took a great deal of time to develop current scientific concepts, it is highly unlikely that children can build them on their own (alone or in groups) in a short period of time. Think about the conceptual scaffolding of any discipline, area of knowledge or academic document; its level of complexity requires experts to unravel the lesser experts in the series of knowledge that requires the understanding of the academic object in question (concept, topic, theory, system, etc.).

The development of scientific concepts assumes that they are explicitly introduced by the educator through language mainly and require that they be integrated by the learners into their old conceptual system. As Vygotsky (1986) emphasizes, both types of concepts interact: scientific concepts are acquired through spontaneous or initial concepts, while the latter are reconfigured due to integration with the former (Fig. 22).

Figure 22 ZPD

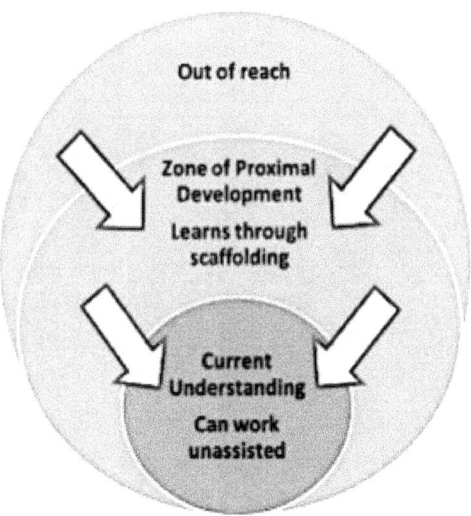

In the case of the Vygotskian tradition, what is constructed is a semiotically mediated activity that includes the variety of ways in which the knowing subject reconstructs cultural mea nings (Fig. 23). Vygotsky (1978) postulates:

> Each function in the child's cultural development appears twice: first at the social level and, later, at the individual level; first between people (interpsychological) and then within the child (intrapsychological). This also applies to voluntary attention, logical memory, and concept formation. All higher functions originate as real relationships between human individuals (p. 57).

Figure 23 Meaning and knowledge

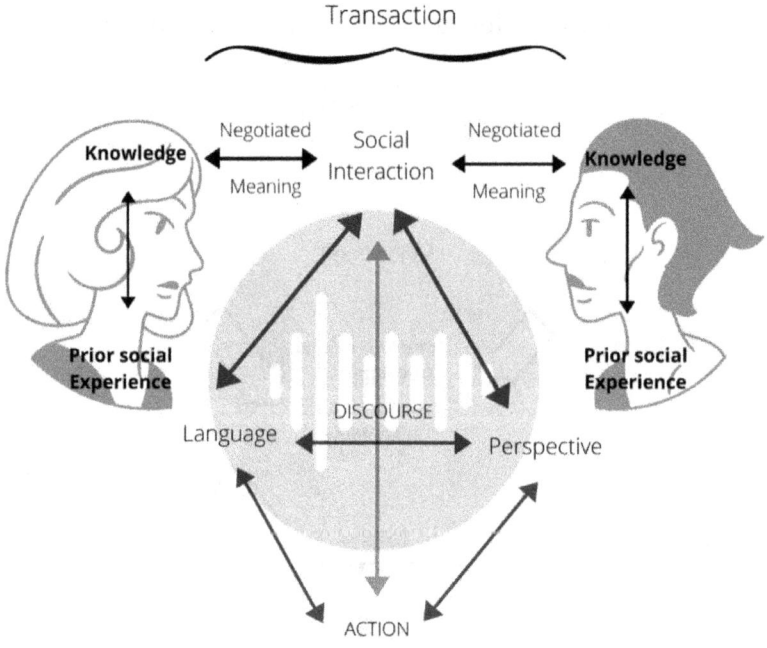

When a new scientific concept is added to the existing conceptual system, a bidirectional effect occurs. In a sense, the new concept is not only assimilated but is registered with the specificities of the previous conceptual system. In another sense the existing conceptual system is reorganized in order to integrate the new concept in the interaction of the learner with the social environment (community). On the one hand, the community of learning introduces and shares these concepts with the learner and, on the other, language is a vehicle that allows this exchange (Table 8).

Table 8 Constructivist theoretical foundation with examples

Theoretical Principles	Theoretical Application
Knowledge is the result of active cognizing by the individual in a social environment (Cobb & Yackel, 1996; Prawat, 1996).	Students should be motivated to reflect on their experiences, to create understanding (and thus knowledge), to evaluate their understanding, and to explain their understanding to others.
Knowledge acquisition is an adaptive function designed to organize one's experiences (Fleury, 1998; Prawat & Floden, 1994).	Students should be confronted with problems or discrepant events that motivate the students to seek, test, and assess answers within socially collaborative environments.
Knowledge is the result of language-based social interaction (Gergen, 1995; Vygotsky, 1978).	Teachers should create activities that necessitate students interacting verbally and students should communicate often with both novices and experts in their field of study.

Vygotsky (1978) considers that knowledge is acquired in accordance with a double training law, with special emphasis on the role of the interaction of the learner with their social environment through language. According to Cole (1996):

> The twofold process of shaping and being shaped by culture implies that human beings inhabit "intentional" (constituted) worlds within which the traditional dichotomies of subject and object, person and enviroment, and so on cannot be analytically separated and temporarily sorted into independent and dependent variables (p. 103).

The social factor of language plays an essential role in the construction of knowledge, both at the inter-psychological level and at the intra-psychological level (Fig. 24).

Figure 24 Socio Emotional Learning

Learners can hope to rebuild only part of the new knowledge to be learned, the other part will be shared by the educator (Driver, Asoko, Leach, Mortimer and Scott, 1994).

A community is where learning is a two-way flow of language, experiments, experiences, knowledge, and where a community is required as part of a learning community.

The individual representations and the mental processes involved in the construction of the universe of meaning are under the direct influence of culturally organized communities or the environments in which people participate, actually the technological environment (Fig. 25).

According to Coll (2001) "the relationship between the individual mind and cultural environments has a transactional nature" (p. 163).

Figure 25 Pedagogical and technological contexts

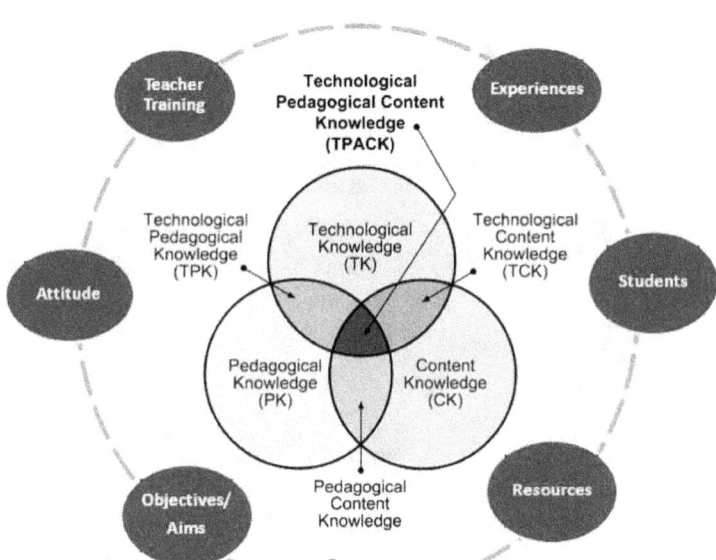

Socio-constructivism, in fact, refers to two different trends: one that revolves around cooperation between learners; and another that revolves around the acculturation of the learner in the scientific culture, a process that is supposed to be managed by the educator-expert.

Drive et al. (1994) do not support the thesis that expert educators and learners work together to build scientific models or theories in the classroom.

Rather, this group of researchers hold the idea that any learning experience involves both a process of personal construction on the part of the learners, as well as the orientation of the educator as an expert to accompany the learners to carry out the process of building the knowledge in its initial stages as well as in its moments of reconstruction of individual cognitive structures (Fig. 26).

Figure 26 Cognitive Structures

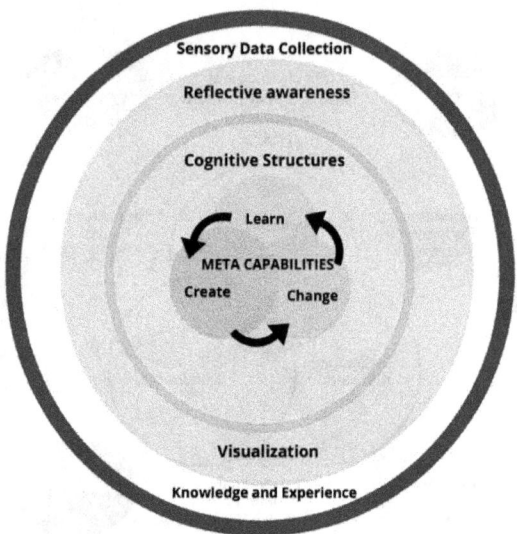

When the centrality of the human subject is in its internal process of self-knowledge, self-possession, and decision-making is rediscovered, then it is possible to propose a humanism that involves the best practices of educator leadership in all social spheres. These practices are based on attention to the other, intelligence in the face of reality, awareness of one's existence, responsibility towards others and the other, and respect for the transcendent.

Additionally, from the discovery of the human subject emerges the importance of a community of inquiry that favors collective work in the process of self-knowledge and decision-making. This community of learning is understood as a vital space for the cultivation and appreciation of personal and community leadership in educational environments.

One of the most necessary skills for leading educators of the new millennium is the ability to plant, care for, cultivate, and expand the assets that are owned individually or organizationally to benefit the most people possible and go beyond the circles of immediate influence. It is the ability to think of and empower the leader who cares for and nurtures the community because he lives in it and enriches or impoverishes it with his sensitivity for the construction of the common good.

It is a good prognosis of an educational leader if the training process of said leader is centered on an accumulation of knowledge built in community, where the attitudes and/or actions of the educational leader are intentionally in interpersonal relationship with others, giving less importance to a self-referenced subject. The community of inquiry, participating both in the process and in the results, in their own context and in their contextualization, preserves the achievement of the goal as a purpose of the organization as a whole, even if only one person or one small group of the organization makes or should make the final decision.

The community of inquiry must jointly conduct a careful, intelligent, reflective, responsible, and affective process with the objective that at the end of it the community accepts or not, what is proposed, what is presented, what is judged, what is evaluated, what must be specified, and what must be decided (Rodríguez & Sánchez, 2017).

For Lonergan (1992), people are united by common experience, by common or complementary ideas, by similar processes to make judgments, and by decisions made in common. Members of the community of inquiry are kept out of contact when they do not share the same experiences, when they do not understand each other, when they do not reach an agreement, and when they choose not to share objectives.

Therefore, from the community of inquiry as a key element in training and accompaniment, a paradigm shift is sought in the structure of thought regarding the leader. That is, a change in the way in which the leader in educational areas is perceived and understood as a human subject; in this case, the preventive leader educator gives relevance and care in his process of self-possession to facilitate self-knowledge and making decisions with and from a community of inquiry. Over time, this leads to responsible, thoughtful, intelligent, and concrete decisions based on interdependent internal and external progressive steps that lead to personal and joint decision-making (Fig. 27).

Figure 27 Responsible Decision-Making

Community of inquiry

The concept "community of inquiry" can be defined as a group of people who are learning together using common tools in a shared environment. Communities of inquiry speak of groups of people with different levels of skill, experience, and knowledge. They learn through their involvement and participation in culturally relevant activities that are possible thanks to the cooperation established between them. Through the construction of collective knowledge and the various types of assistance that they provide to each other. Therefore, the objective is the construction of a "socially competent" subject, a citizen committed to civil values, human rights and caring for others in solidarity, and a citizen who cares about their interiority, their connection with transcendence and that which gives meaning to life as a whole as a strongly unitary project (Fig. 28).

Figure 28 Community of Inquiry in the classroom

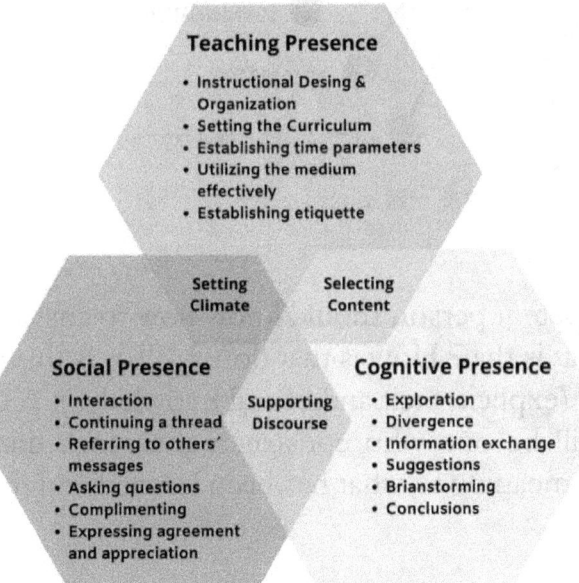

Today's society seems to require educated individuals with skills that allow them to function effectively in a given context. They do this in such a way that a competent person is the one who, in diverse, complex, and unpredictable situations, sets in motion, applies and integrates the declarative, procedural, attitudinal, and causal knowledge that has been acquired. Therefore, competence is based on, but not limited to, knowledge (Fig. 29).

Figure 29 Competencies on education

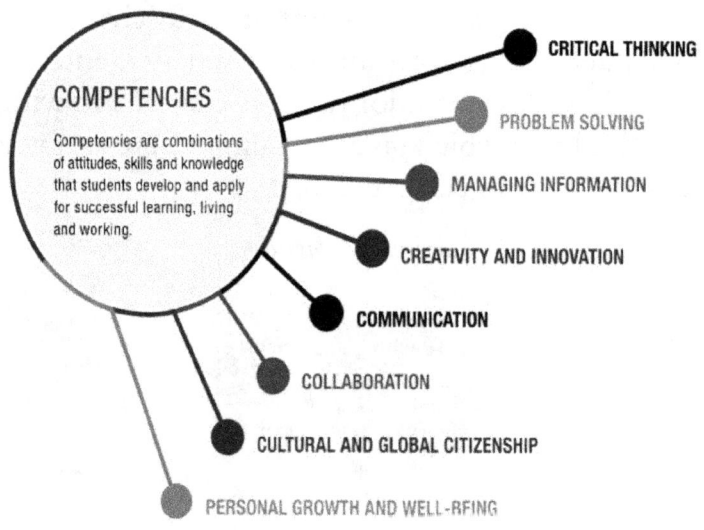

A competent person should know how to answer the questions: What is that? How is that done? What is this for? When is it used? (explicit, tacit and causal knowledge). A competent learner will be one who constructs meanings that attribute sense and meaning to what has been learned and to their own learning.

In this process, the educator becomes a mediator between the cognitive structure of the student, the logocentric structure of the contents, and the objective and subjective aims of learning and its practicality in the application of the same framed in a life project. As a mediator between the constructive activity of the learner and the learning, he or she allows the construction of the cognitive representations of meanings adapted to the training objectives for life, work, society. As a mediator between the affective-emotional characteristics and the instructional goals of the learners, he or she facilitates the attribution of the meaning to the content. As an intentionally projected educator, he or she articulates content and goals in the form of competencies that can potentially be assimilated by the student's cognitive structure and, over time, lead to changes in their deeper motivation and thus, be of greater duration and personal impact for life.

From this point of view, it is possible to find in the educational model proposed by constructivism the link between the teaching and learning processes in a coherent explanatory framework individually and collectively. As seen in previous paragraphs, this educational model postulates the need for contextualization and knowledge construction for adequate individual and collective learning, whether intentional (formal and informal) or incidental (informal). Therefore, to explain these processes, it is convenient to consider four key elements of the process: the subject who learns, the educators who teach, the content that is learned, and the purpose of learning. Educator-expert, educator-learner, content, and goals become an inseparable whole when it comes to explaining and analyzing the teaching and learning processes.

Engeström (2009) proposes five principles for a theory of learning considering activity as a key factor. These principles are explained in Table 9.

Table 9 Principles for a theory of learning whose key factor is activity

Principle	Implication
A system of collective activity, artifact–mediated and object–oriented	Individual and group actions directed at a goal, as well as automatic operations, are relatively independent but subordinate units of analysis, which are ultimately understood only when interpreted in the context of the entire activity system.
	Activity systems become aware of and reproduce themselves by generating actions and operations.
The multiple voice	Multiple voice multiplies in networks of interactive activity systems.
	It is a source of problems and a source of innovation, which requires translation and negotiation actions.
Historicity	Activity systems that take shape and transform over long periods of time.
	Problems and potentialities can only be understood when analyzed against their own history.
	History itself must be studied as the local history of activities and their objects, and as a history of the theoretical ideas and tools that have shaped the activity.
The central role of contradictions as sources of change and development	Contradictions are not the same as problems or conflicts. Contradictions historically are the accumulation of structural tensions within a system and between activity systems.
The possibility of qualitative expansive transformations through long cycles	Transformation is achieved when the object and motive of the activity are re-conceptualized to encompass a radically broader horizon of possibilities than the previous mode of activity.

The link that I perceive between preventive leadership and constructivism lies in the fact that educational reflection prepares leaders for the resolution of problems in complex environments but always referring to a community that accompanies, discerns, evaluates, and rewrites. Starting with constructivism, educational leaders are more active in building communities of inquiry and in creating knowledge in a shared environment, individually and socially, based on their experiences and interpretations, and following a method of discerning reality.

The most experienced leading educators can play an essential and important role in the learning processes of the educators in training because one of the key moments of the experienced educational leader is trying to understand how new leaders interpret knowledge, guiding them in the testing-error process and helping them refine their understanding and interpretation to correct any risk that occurs in an early stage of training and improve the quality of the results expected of those who will accompany others in a community always in formation (Chang & Brickman, 2018).

Any educational leader could change the way teamwork is understood and practiced if he uses the four most important words of leadership when relating to others: What do you think? These words share and empower the other, regardless of the context. If you have had decision-making positions, it is well known that the question is not as easy as it seems. The educational leader must realize that he or she needs to see their role in a different way. The leader must be an educational presence, a kind listener, a builder of an organized preventive environment in communities of inquiry with a clear criterion of identity.

Basic emotional and social skills

Goleman (1998) considers that to achieve better decision-making it is essential that the leader has an acceptable level of self-awareness. But what does self-awareness mean? It means having a deep understanding of oneself and understanding of your own emotions, strengths, weaknesses, needs, and motivations.

People with a strong sense of self-awareness are balanced in their judgment of themselves, avoiding excessive self-criticism or the unrealistic hope of naivety. Honesty with themselves and with others is a clear result of an acceptable level of self-awareness. In this sense, self-awareness extends to the understanding that every human being has his own values that guide or regulate him, his own goals and failures, his own efforts and mistakes, and his own areas of growth.

According to Goleman (2015), self-control is necessary in the management of one's emotions in a fast changing context like the COVID pandemic. Such self-control allows us to better face the context of volatility, uncertainty, confusion, and ambiguity. Goleman (2015) considers self-control to be a continuous conversation with himself. According to Goleman, this exercise of continuous internal dialogue is a key part in the development of emotional intelligence and at the same time it frees you from being trapped in your own feelings when decisions are made that affect others. In teamwork, it often happens that the processes are not simple and that emotions and prejudices cause moments of friction and tension. If a leader has walked in the exercise of self-control, he will be more sensitive to what happens within himself and he or she will have a greater chance of obtaining positive results in their work teams when those types of common situations arise in their environments.

Empathy is another factor that, according to Goleman (2016), is key in emotional intelligence since it plays an important role in decision-making in an organizational context where work teams are modified by the generations to which their members belong. Said factors are intermingled with the globalization of knowledge, cultural diversity, and the members' own contexts in the work teams, where sensitivities and perspectives provoke a transdisciplinary work as the edges of the disciplines seem to dilute and open the necessary possibility of a fusion of horizons. Empathy, for a leader:

> Does not mean adopting other people's emotions as if they were their own and trying to make good with everyone. This strategy would sooner or later become a nightmare and decision making would be practically impossible. Rather, empathy means considering carefully, thoughtfully, with foresight, employees' feelings —along with many other factors— in the process of making smart decisions and acting accordingly (para. 39).

Social ability consists of sympathy with a purpose: "to mobilize people in the direction you want" (Goleman, 2015: 29). Who is socially skilled tends to consolidate a wide circle of relationships and has the ability to create a point of union with people of all kind. "Social ability" is the competence that brings together all the skills to work according to the idea that nothing important can be done alone. Wide bonds in interpersonal relationships are important today in coping with and responding to a world that is volatile, uncertain, ambiguous, and complex. The task of a leader educator is when the work is done linking other people. Social ability allows this to be possible, the future of learning can be conditioned by this communicative factor to a large extent.

Self-reflection of Chapter III

Check List: Praxis for an Educational Model

In your practice as a teacher...	Y	N
1. You promote active participation, where the students are the main builder of their knowledge.		
2. You establish spaces that favor interaction between your students to enrich their knowledge.		
3. You take the role of guide and mediator during the moments of interaction.		
4. You know the particular way in which your students acquire knowledge.		
5. You correct as much as possible the erroneous conceptions that the student may have, either prior or in the moment.		
6. You give your students a meaning that they will have to assume for their life.		
7. You create learning communities where each student cooperates from his/her vision to rebuild or reorganize his/her knowledge.		
8. You have a deep understanding of yourself and understanding of your own emotions, strengths, weaknesses, motivations, and needs.		
9. You have self-control in managing your own emotions in such a changing environment.		
10. You consider that in your decisions you are empathetic with your students.		

4. Leaders and Leadership Development

Leadership

Pfeffer (2015) takes into account the importance of the theories on leadership and the proposals for leadership development that emanate from them. Pfeffer is critical of "the leadership industry," describing the industry as idealizing a practical concept of versatile conformation and adaptability in the most varied contexts. Furthermore, according to Pfeffer, most of the current proposals for leadership, and its ways of developing, have a character of confessional preaching or a narrative of inspiring stories and aspirations common to human beings, due either to their plethora of virtues or their animosity more like recipes for achievers.

This devalues and makes the reflection on leadership so superficial that it makes things worse in many ways. On repeated occasions, "the leadership industry" presents leadership itself as something almost unattainable or as something so trivial that a motivational talk, a series of steps to follow, or recipes to mix carefully is enough that it empties what is in itself an intellectual task that hardly breaks new ground in the new educational, social, economic, or political contexts.

The search for the one true definition of leadership seems to be unsuccessful. Rather, the choice of an appropriate definition should depend on the methodological and substantive aspects of leadership in which one is interested. For example, if one makes extensive use of observation, then it seems important to define leadership in terms of activities, behaviors, or roles performed where the importance lies in group processes and their compliance based on observed performance, rather than on traits of personality, power relations, or influence outside the person's own resources. However, if a lengthy examination of the impact of leadership authority were the focus, then it would be more important to define leadership in terms of perceived influence, control, and power relations.

Many of the theories of leadership seem to emphasize aspects that are external to the leader.

Stogdill (1950) defines leadership as "the process (action) of influencing the activities of an organized group in its efforts toward goal setting and goal achievement" (p. 3). In a similar vein, Northouse (2019) defines leadership as "a process by which an individual influences a group of individuals to achieve a common goal" (p. 3). Recent conceptualizations of leadership suggest that leadership is a more holistic, collective, distributed, political, relational, and contextual phenomenon (Avolio, Walumbwa, and Weber, 2009; Bolden, Petrov, and Gosling, 2008; Day, Fleenor, Atwater, Sturm, and Mckee, 2014). Fischer and Sievewright (2014) argue similarly, as they believe that advances in leadership research should move to stronger levels of contextual and organizational analysis.

Bolden et al. (2008), observe the continuous dominance of the individual perspective on leadership issues, and suggest that leadership be seen as a procedural, relational, social, political, and temporal phenomenon. It can be thought that leadership in educational fields involves five dimensions:
1. The first dimension is the personal one where factors considered include: academic credibility and demonstrated knowledge, personal vision, values and ethics, the level of development of emotional intelligence, openness to criticism, authenticity of life

sustained by what has been said with what has been lived, and interpersonal and persuasive skills (Bryman, 2007; Day et al., 2014);
2. The second dimension is where social and relational processes are highlighted, such as: the figures of mentors, people capable of modeling what they propose because they have assimilated it as part of their personality, the creating multivariate and plural work teams, the creation of networks of both social capital and relevant presence in the mediated reality, the development of trust both in the person himself and in the ethical relevance of doing and deciding, the sensitivity and real delegation and planning of the succession of the managerial position that is sustained (Spendlove, 2007; Hargreaves and Fink, 2006; Hoppe and Reinelt, 2010; Jarvis, Gulati, McCririck and Simpson, 2013);
3. The third dimension is structural, because leadership is situated in and by the organizational and social structures where organization chart, chain of command, levels in decision making, teamwork, problem solving, internationalization, local impact, and types of evaluation are factors to consider. (Bolden et al., 2008);
4. The fourth dimension is contextual due to the organizational, political, social, economic contexts internal to the organization itself where the culture and organizational climate have a real impact on leadership development. Values, beliefs, definitions, roles, non-verbal languages, interpersonal dynamics constitute the environments in which leaders operate, relate, impact, and decide. (Bolden et al., 2009);
5. The fifth dimension is that of leadership development

which alerts about the procedural nature of leadership that has an impact over time where factors of personality, education, context, experience, level of development in skills and competences, and expertise are pieces of a set that at the end of the training process are possibilities of achievement (Bolden et al., 2008).

It is through these five dimensions that leadership theories and leadership development could prepare leaders for a new economic, social, political, educational, and organizational context (VUCA world or UTRU reality).

Leadership Development

Leadership development, according to Avolio and Gardner (2005), can be seen as a complex human process that involves leaders, followers, dynamic contexts, time resources, technology, history, and luck, among many other things. Hannum and Craig (2010) describe the significant conceptual and measurement challenges associated with evaluating leadership development activity, reflecting the concept of highly nuanced and necessarily contextualized leadership as well as the many different forms that leadership can take.

Morrison, Rha, and Helfman (2003) argue that the traditional essence of leadership development has been the ability to first understand leadership theories and concepts and then apply them to real-life settings.

Leadership theories are continually evolving, and an adhering adjectives to the concept of leadership generates more reflection on its conceptualization and praxis —servant, charismatic, transformational, authentic, etc.–

Empirical research suggests that self-awareness has been recognized as a critical component of leadership in the past two decades due to changes in the nature of organizational life (Ashley and Reiter-Palmon, 2012; Axelrod, 2012; Goleman, 2016). Knowledge has become the basic economic resource, which translates into the life of the organization as the capacity for the quickest reaction, extreme flexibility, and innovation. Distributed leadership is an emerging leadership development model. According to Axelrod (2012), this model refers to "leadership exercised at many levels and in many different contexts." (p. 344)

Considering the possibility of a different reflection of leadership, it seems desirable to recover the structure of the subject, rediscover the internal process that precedes and supports the decision-making of those in leadership roles and/or those who are in the continuous process of being and acting as leaders. Self-awareness is a concept with many meanings that can be "broadly described [as] an inwardly focused assessment process in which individuals make a standard self-comparison with the goal of improving self-knowledge and self-improvement" (Ashley and Reiter-Palmon, 2012, p. 2).

Avolio and Hanna (2008) have related that the improvement of organizations with the importance that the leader gives to the formation of conscience is essential because it underlines the processes of self-integration and self-alignment, which contributes to leadership development. The outcome is that there are fewer individual and internal conflicts thus allowing for more ability to articulate, socialize, and follow a direction with commitment, energy, purpose, and integrity. Ashley and Reiter-Palmon (2102: 2) consider that "leaders with greater self-awareness tend to perform better than those with lower levels of self-awareness."

According to Rodríguez and Rodríguez (2015), in research on current leadership theories, the central factor to address is the human subject, which means the personality and character of someone who continually exercises an intentional influence on others. A second factor, common to all leadership exercises, is the group that is immersed in the radius of influence of the leader. A third factor in reflecting on leadership is the context (physical, cultural, historical, organizational, etc.) in which the leader operates or will function, and the group in which the leader has influence. A fourth common factor refers to the task that links both the leader and the group that is influenced as well as the context.

Leadership can also be understood as an influencing process related to "meaning management" (Smircich & Morgan, 1982), a "social construction" (Grint, 2005) or a "framework" of organizational context (Fairhurst, 2009; 2011), or contextually situated "practice" (Denis, Langley & Sergi, 2012). The literature has emphasized the traits, skills, behaviors, styles, and adaptations of individual-centered leadership, but this approach may overlook how leadership influences and instills purpose, values, and meaning in organizations themselves.

In today's education, it is very important to have a more relational dynamic and instill values. the influence of the leader attempts to make sense of what is done, going from research driven by the single theory that currently characterizes the field to research, reflection, and praxis more focused on the problem. (Fig. 30)

Figure 30 Common elements for a Leadership Theory

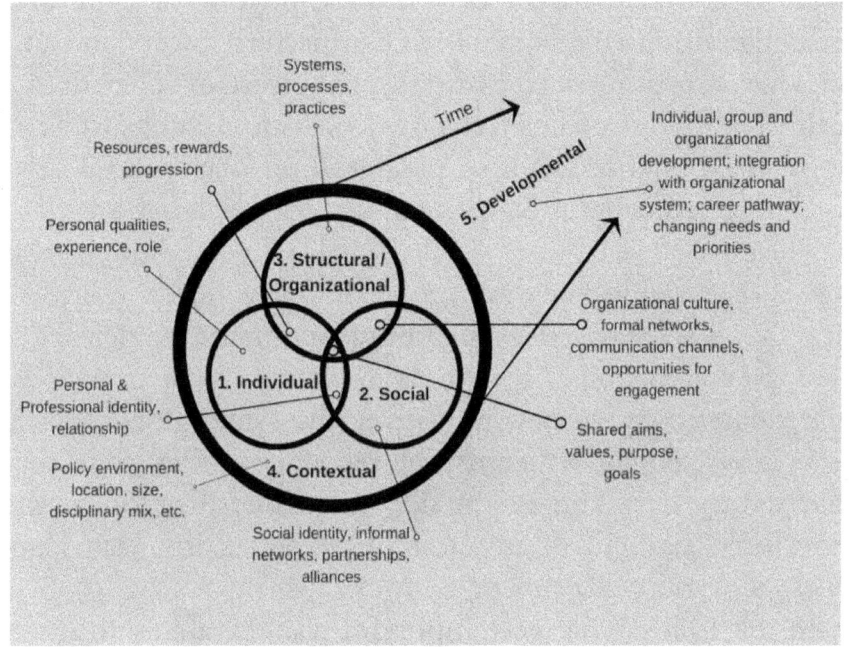

Parry and Bryman (2006) say that these "stages of leadership theory and research" are generally associated with specific time periods. According to Bass and Bass (2008), representative definitions of leadership in the 1920s focused on the leader's will, traits, and behaviors that would lead him to induce obedience, respect, loyalty, and cooperation in his followers. Personality, as part of the traits of good leadership, caught the attention of different early theorists on the subject, who tried to explain why some people are more capable than others of exercising leadership.

In the 1930s, leadership was considered a process through which a group of employees was organized to move in a specific direction set by the leader, as the leader was considered the nucleus of a trend.

In the 1940s, leadership was understood as the ability to

persuade and lead a group regardless of the effects of power, position, or circumstances. Leaders provide insight and meaning into situations that their confused followers find ambiguous, confusing, vague, diffuse, or uncertain. They define reality for followers. Leaders always provide credible explanations, interpretations, stories, parables, and stories about what has happened, what is happening, and what will happen.

The next 70 years after World War II witnessed three great waves of sustained research, reflecting an interest in leadership that was catalysed by theoretical and methodological developments, as well as by contextual factors such as war, exponential growth of new industries, recession, globalization, technology, ethical concerns, the recognition that leadership may have a dark and bright side, and diversification of the workforce, particularly in terms of gender (Lord, Day, Zaccaro, & Avolio, 2017).

In the 1950s, what was important was the ability to influence, motivate, and empower others to contribute to the effectiveness and success of the organizations of which they were members.

In the 1960s, leadership was the influence to move others in a shared direction. Larson (1968: 21) considers that "leadership is the ability to decide what to do, and then make others want to do it."

In the 1970s, the influence of the leader was viewed with discretion and varied from member to member. While in the 1980s, leadership was seen as the action of inspiring others to take on a task with a purpose. This implied a reciprocal relationship between the leader and his followers, but it was not necessarily characterized by domination, control, or induction of compliance by the leader.

For the 1990s, the commonalities within the leadership literature focused on the influence of the leader on his followers, who sought to make real changes in organizations. In the first decade of the 21st century, the leader was seen as the person with the greatest ethical responsibility who provided explanations about actions within an organization supported by organizational values, mission, and vision. The reasons, arguments, and motives provided by the person who served as leader were a point of agglutination or separation. Leadership theories were concerned with the knowledge, interpersonal behaviors, and attributions of both leaders and their followers and also with how they influenced each other in seeking to realize their common goals.

Parry and Bryman (2006) state that each time period is associated with a change of pre-eminence whereby each of these stages signals a change in cultural sensitivity rather than a demolition of previous theoretical constructs regarding leadership. Northouse (2019) developed 15 categories of leadership research that have evolved over time. Athanasopoulou and Dopson (2015) further expanded Northouse's categorization by including three more leadership approaches. There are also many leadership theories whereby anyone who wants to improve their leadership can draw from a set of essential skills, knowledge, and experiences as essential tools. Today, the field of leadership focuses not only on the leader, but also on the followers, peers, or supervisors, or perhaps in the workplace or workplace context, or organizational culture, including a much broader range of people representing a wide spectrum of diversity: public sector, private non-profit organizations, companies, churches, governments, and increasingly evident in all organizations, together with the leader, a team is considered: multiracial, multiethnic, diverse, multidisciplinary (Avolio, 2007; Yukl, 2006).

The last twenty years of research on the topic are presented on Tables 10 to 37.

Table 10 Trait Focus Leadership Theory

Theory	Trait Focus Determine the personal qualities and characteristics of leaders.
Implications	Successful leaders differ from other people and possess certain core personality traits that significantly contribute to their success. Core personality traits that predict leader effectiveness can help organizations with their leader selection, training, and development practices.

Author's proposals	Author's Inferences
Northouse (2019) Athanasopoulou & Dopson (2015)	Leadership is a phenomenon of organizations, not groups as such, and the organization defines and delimits the scope of the leadership. Leadership must be viewed from the standpoint of influence on organizational activity, rather than on group members.
Stogdill (1950)	Traits such as intelligence, level of alertness or perception, responsibility, initiative, persistence, self-confidence and sociability are strongly present in all leaders.
Zaccaro, Kemp, & Bader (2004) Zaccaro (2007) The two most recent categorizations have organized traits into: (1) demographic vs. task competence vs. interpersonal; (2) distal (trait-like) vs. proximal (state-like).	*Extraversion*: represents the tendency to be sociable, assertive, active, and to experience positive effects, such as energy and zeal. *Agreeableness*: refers to the tendency to be trusting, compliant, caring, and gentle. *Conscientiousness*: it comprises two related facets, namely achievement and dependability. *Openness*: the disposition to be imaginative, non-conforming, unconventional, and autonomous. *Neuroticism*: represents the tendency to exhibit poor emotional adjustment and experience negative effects (anxiety, insecurity, and hostility). *Honesty/Integrity*: The correspondence between work and deed, and as being truthful and non-deceitful. *Charisma*: is the influence by articulating a compelling vision for the future, arousing commitment to organizational objectives and

inspiring commitment and a sense of self-efficacy among followers.

Intelligence: has been identified as one of the most critical traits that must be possessed by all leaders.

Creativity, and Achievement motivation: They have been proposed as an important component of effective leadership.

Need of power: Characterized by the satisfaction leaders derive from exerting influence over the attitudes and behaviors of others.

Oral/written communication, General problem solving, and decision making: They are correlated with leader effectiveness

Interpersonal skills: associated with an understanding of human behavior and the dynamics of groups.

Technical Knowledge: It includes methods, processes, and equipment for conducting the specialized activities of the managers' organizational unit.

Hoffman, Woehr, Maldagen-Youngjohn, & Lyons (2011) Focus on distal (dispositional/trait-like) characteristics of leaders and proximal (malleable/state-like) individual differences.	Distal characteristics correlated with leader effectiveness: achievement-motivation, energy, flexibility, dominance, honesty/integrity, self-confidence, creativity, and charisma. Proximal characteristics correlated with leader effectiveness: interpersonal skills, oral communication, written communication, management skills, problem solving skills, and decision making.
Derue, Nahrgang, Wellman, & Humphrey (2011)	Most leader traits can be organized into three categories: *Demographic* (male and female leaders are both equally effective). *Task competence* (how individuals approach the execution and performance of tasks). *Interpersonal attributes* (Intelligence, Conscientiousness, Openness to Experience, and Emotional Stability).

Table 11 Skill Approach Leadership Theory

Theory	Skill approach Leadership focuses on capabilities. Three skill approach: Conceptual, Human and Technical.
Implications	People have leadership potential, and if they can learn from their experiences, they can become more effective leaders.

Author´s proposals	Author´s Inferences
Katz (1974) Mumford, Zaccaro, Connelly, & Marks (2000)	*Conceptual.* Analyze and diagnose complex situations to discover the way things fit, as well as facilitate assertive decision making. *Human.* Work well with others both individually and as a team through communication, motivation, guidance, and delegation. *Technical.* Knowledge, experience, specific job techniques for good performance at each level in the organization.

Mumford, Zaccaro, Connelly, & Marks (2000)
Zaccaro, Mumford, Connelly, Marks, & Gilbert (2000)
Mumford, Campion, & Morgeson (2007)
 	
Leadership outcomes:
  Effective Problem Solving
  Performance
  Career experience
  Environmental influence
	Individual attributes:
	General Cognitive Ability means perceptual processing, information processing, general reasoning skills, creative and divergent thinking capacities, and memory skills.
	Crystallized Cognitive Ability means a type of intelligence that remains relatively consistent and generally does not diminish with age. It positively affects our leadership potential by increasing our social judgment skills, conceptual ability, and problem-solving skills.
	Competencies
	Motivation.
	First, a person must want to lead.
	Second, leaders must be willing to exert influence.
	Third, the leader must be willing to advance the "social good" of the organization.
	Personality.
	Leaders possess tolerance for ambiguity, openness, and curiosity. Leaders with confidence and adaptability may be helpful in situations of conflict.

Table 12 Style Approach Leadership Theory

Theory	Style Approach
	A model for training leaders that describes leadership behaviors as plots on a grid with two axes: concern for results (task behaviors) and concern for people (relationship behavior).
Implications	Instead of focusing on who leaders are, style theories consider what leaders do.
	Leaders engage in two types of behavior: task behaviors and relationship behaviors.
Author´s proposals	Author´s Inferences
Parry & Bryman (2006)	Style theory refers to three main lines of research: the Ohio State University studies, the Michigan University studies, and the Blake and Mouton Managerial Grid.

Blake & Mouton (1964)	The model outlines five main plots on the managerial grid:
	 Authority-compliance (9,1)
	    Also called dictatorial style. Here leaders are more concerned about production and have less concern for people.
	 Country club management (1,9)
	    This is a collegial style characterized by low task and high people orientation where the leader gives thoughtful attention to the needs of people thus providing them with a friendly and comfortable environment.
	 Impoverished management (1,1)
	    The leader has low concern for employee satisfaction and work deadlines and as a result disharmony and disorganization prevail within the organization.
	 Middle-of-the-road management (5,5)
	    This is basically a compromising style wherein the leader tries to maintain a balance between goals of company and the needs of people.

	Team management (9,9) The leader feels that empowerment, commitment, trust, and respect are the key elements in creating a team atmosphere which will automatically result in high employee satisfaction and production.
Shartle & Stodgill (1950) Fleishman (1951)	Proposing scales to measure what the leader does, how the leader operates in the leadership role, how the group perceives their leader and their group, group expectations of leaders, and status attitudes, status perceptions, and status position of leaders.

Table 13 Contingency Leadership Theory

Theory	Contingency Leadership Theory
	It argues that effective leadership is contingent upon a match between the leader's style and the work situation.
Implications	Contingency theory examines the leader in conjunction with the situation the leader is in.
Author's proposals	Author's Inferences
Fiedler (1967)	Variables provide a means for situational measurement:
	Leader-Member Relation: how the leader interacts with employees.
	Task Structure how tasks are set up by the leader
	Positional Power: the amount of power a leader has over followers.
	There is no one best style of leadership. A leader is effective when his or her style of leadership fits with the situation.

Table 14 Situational Leadership Theory

Theory	Situational Leadership Theory
	Situational leadership defines four leadership styles: S1 (high-directive but low-supportive), S2 (high-directive and high-supportive), S3 (low-directive but high-supportive), S4 (low-directive and low-supportive).
Implications	Situational leadership theory argues that any leader can work best in any environment by changing their style accordingly.

Author´s proposals	Author´s Inferences
Hersey & Blanchard, 1969, 1982, 1988	The Situational Leadership theory promotes a particular leadership style depending upon the development level of the follower: D1: low–competence but high commitment, D2: moderate-competence but low-commitment, D3: moderate–competence but no commitment, D4: high-competence and high-commitment. Effective leadership is a matter of assessing the development level of a follower and acting in the correlating leadership style to elicit the best response from followers (D1s respond to S1, D2s respond to S1, and so on).

Table 15 Path-Goal Leadership Theory

Theory	Path-Goal Theory
	It was developed to explain how leaders motivate their followers toward a determined end.
Implications	The theory suggests that a leader's behavior is motivating or satisfying to the degree that the behavior increases subordinate goal attainment and clarifies the paths to these goals.

Author´s proposals	Author´s Inferences
House & Mitchell (1975) People will be motivated if they believe that: a) putting in more effort will yield better job performance, b) better job performance will lead to rewards, such as an increase in salary or benefits, c) these rewards are valued by the person in question.	The four kinds of leader behavior included in the theory are: *Directive leadership* is a leader who lets subordinates know what is expected of them, gives specific guidance as to what and how it should be done, makes them part of the group, maintains standards of performance, and tasks oriented leadership to follow standard rules and regulations. *Supportive leadership* is a friendly and approachable leader who shows concern for the status, well-being, and needs of subordinates as equals. *Participative leadership* is a leader who consults with subordinates, solicits their suggestions and takes these suggestions seriously into consideration before making a decision. *Achievement-oriented* expects subordinates to perform at their highest level, continuously seeks improvement in performance, and shows a high degree of confidence that the subordinates will assume responsibility, put forth effort, and accomplish challenging goals.

Table 16 Leader–Member Exchange (LMX) Theory

Theory	Leader- Member Exchange (LMX) Theory
	LMX focuses on the interactions between leaders and an individual follower: strangers, acquaintances, and partners.
Implications	The central concept of the theory is that effective leadership processes occur when leaders and followers are able to develop mature leadership relationships (partnerships) and thus gain access to the many benefits these relationships bring.
Author´s proposals	Author´s Inferences
Graen (1969)	Three phases that each leader–follower dyad goes through as one moves from out–group to in–group: stranger, acquaintance, and partner.
Graen & Uhl-Bien (1995)	As the relationship moves from stranger to partner, mutual trust, respect, and obligation toward each other develops.
The leader's relationship to the follower unit as a whole is viewed as a series of these individual relationships. These relationships are referred to as vertical dyads. Leadership's focus, then, should be on developing these dyads.	

Table 17 Charismatic Leadership Theory

Theory	Charismatic leadership
	Charismatic leaders have potent effects on followers because of their transcendental ideals and authority that facilitate the followers' identification with the leader.
	In those conditions, trust is solidified as psychological exchanges occur.
Implications	Charisma in leaders referred to specific gifts of the body and spirit not accessible to everybody.

Author´s proposals	Author´s Inferences
Weber (1947, 1968) Weber was the first to use the term and describe the charismatic leader as one who could bring about social change.	He identified these types of leaders who arise in times of psychic, physical, economic, ethical, religious, or political distress. These leaders were attributed with supernatural, superhuman, or at least specifically exceptional powers or qualities and could undertake great feats. Weber believed that followers of a charismatic leader willingly place their destiny in their leader's hands and support the leader's mission which may have arisen out of enthusiasm, or of despair and hope.
Downton (1973)	A system of personal rule may derive its legitimacy from the manipulation of rewards as well as punishments, from the manipulation of myths and symbols that give meaning to action and suffering, and from the presence of leaders who are able to provide security, a new identity, or cultural reinforcement for those whose psychological dispositions or socialization require that they obey orders.

House (1977) The basis for the charismatic appeal is the emotional interaction that occurs between followers and their leader. Charismatic leadership is basically the method of encouraging particular behaviors in others by way of eloquent communication, persuasion, and force of personality.	Charismatic leaders display a high degree of self-confidence, pro-social assertiveness (dominance), and moral conviction. These leaders models what they expect their followers to do, exemplify the struggle by self-sacrifice, and engage in image-building and self-promotion actions to come across as powerful and competent. House argued that these leaders become role models and objects of identification of followers, who in turn emulate their leader's ideals and values and are enthusiastically inspired and motivated to reach outstanding accomplishments. These types of leaders are seen as courageous, because they challenge a status quo that is seen as undesirable. Charismatic leaders are very skilled communicators – individuals who are verbally eloquent, but also able to communicate to followers on a deep, emotional level. They are able to articulate a compelling or captivating vision, and to arouse strong emotions in followers.
Etzioni (1961, 1964) Symbolic power is what Etzioni referred to as "charisma."	Three types of power bases that leaders may use: (a) physical power, entailing the use of threats or coercion; (b) material power, entailing the use of rewards; (c) symbolic power, entailing the use of normative or social power. Greater commitment and less alienation will be displayed in followers when their leaders are using symbolic over material or physical power, and material over physical power.

Table 18 Servant Leadership Theory

Theory	Servant Leader
	Servant leaders get results for their organization through whole-hearted attention to their followers and followers' needs.
Implications	This theory argues that the most effective leaders are servants of their people.

Author´s proposals	Author´s Inferences
Greenleaf (1970, 1977, 1978, 1987, 1996, 1998, 2003)	The leader has to have a strong ethical basis and a clear and explicit basis for their leadership and what the value is of what they believe.
The leader should be a servant first, leading from a desire to better serve others and not to attain more power. The assumption is that if leaders focus on the needs and desires of followers, followers will reciprocate through increased teamwork, deeper engagement, and better performance.	Integrity, trustworthiness, authenticity. Ambition never must surpass moral compass. Servant leaders are distinguished by both their primary motivation to serve (what they do) and their self-construction (who they are), and from this conscious choice of 'doing' and 'being' they aspire to lead. Servant leadership is an inward lifelong journey. Servant leadership puts its emphasis on collaboration, trust, empathy, and ethics.
Spears (1998)	10 characteristics of a servant leader: *Listening to what is said:* which allows them to identify the will of the group and help clarify that will. *Empathy:* striving to accept and understand others, never rejecting them. *Healing:* they have the opportunity to make themselves and others 'whole.'

	Awareness: which enables them to view situations holistically. *Persuasion*: relying on convincement rather than coercion. *Conceptualization*: seeking to arouse and nurture theirs' and others' abilities to 'dream great dreams'. *Foresight*: Intuitively understanding the lessons from the past, the present realities, and the likely outcome of a decision for the future. *Stewardship*: committing first and foremost to serving others' needs. *Commitment to the growth of people* nurtures the personal, professional, and spiritual growth of each individual. *Building community*: working within their institutions, which can give the healing love essential for health.
Russell and Stone (2002)	*Core attributes* as vision, honesty, integrity, trust, service, modeling, pioneering, appreciation of others, and empowerment. *Accompanying attributes* as communication, credibility, competence, stewardship, visibility, influence, persuasion, listening, encouragement, teaching, and delegation.
Barbuto and Wheeler (2006)	Five factors: altruistic calling, emotional healing, persuasive mapping, wisdom, and organizational stewardship.
Van Dierendonck (2011)	Six key characteristics of a servant leader: empowering and developing people, humility, authenticity, interpersonal acceptance, providing direction, and stewardship

Table 19 Authentic Leadership Theory

Theory	Authentic Leadership Theory
	The essence of authentic leadership is emotional intelligence.
Implications	Authentic leaders monitor their words and behaviors carefully to be attuned to their audiences and to incorporate their colleagues and teammates.

Author´s proposals	Author´s Inferences
George (2003, 2016) Character is the ingredient that matters most. They are constantly developing themselves to increase self-awareness and improve relationships with others. The core of authentic leadership are: • Self-awareness, • openness, • transparency, and • consistency. Being motivated by positive end values and concern for others is essential to authentic leadership. Authentic leader model positive attributes such as hope, optimism, and resiliency.	Being authentic as a leader is hard work and takes years of experience in leadership roles. Everyone behaves inauthentically at times, saying and doing things they will come to regret. The key is to have the self-awareness to recognize these times and listen to fellow colleagues who point them out. To become an Authentic Leader: *Explore* your life stories and your crucibles. As leader, discover your truth, your True North, gain confidence and resilience to face difficult situations. *Engage* in reflection and introspective practices such as meditation, mindfulness, prayer, long walks, etc. *Obtain* real-time feedback by listening to their "truth tellers." *Understand* your leadership purpose so you can align people around a common purpose. This is more important than metrics like money, fame, and power. *Adapt* your style, without compromising your character. Authentic leaders are capable of judging ambiguous ethical issues aligning decisions with their own moral values.
Harter (2002)	Authenticity is conceived as both owning one's personal experiences (thoughts, emotions, or beliefs, "the real me inside") and acting in accord with the true self (behaving and expressing what you really think and believe).

Luthans & Avolio (2003) Stajkovic & Luthans (1998) Bandura (1986, 1988) Snyder, Irving, & Anderson (1991) Snyder, Rand, & Sigmon (2002) Authentic leadership is a process that draws from both positive psychological capacities: self-awareness and self-regulated positive behaviors and fostering positive self-development. The authentic leader does not try to coerce or even rationally persuade associates, but rather the leader's authentic values, beliefs, and behaviors serve to model the development of associates.	An authentic leader must be: *Confident* as the ability to mobilize the motivation, cognitive resources, and courses of action necessary to execute a specific task within a given context. *Self-efficacy* is derived and supported by self-regulation. The more efficacious the individual, (a) the more likely the choice will be made to really get into the task and welcome the challenge; (b) the more effort and motivation will be given to successfully accomplish the task; (c) the more persistence there will be when obstacles are encountered. *Hopeful* as a positive motivational state that is based on an interactively derived sense of a successful. *An optimist* is motivated to work harder; optimists are more satisfied and have high morale and tend to feel upbeat and invigorated both physically and mentally. *Resiliency* is the ability to rebound from adversity, uncertainty, conflict, failure and increased responsibility. *Self-awareness/Self-regulation* is a sense one can be ethical relying upon different core values, may regulate the target leader's attention.
Masten & Reed (2002)	Authentic leaders provide three resiliency development strategies: (1) risk-focused (prevent/reduce risk); (2) asset-focused (improve the quantity and quality of support resources or social capital); (3) process-focused (mobilizing the power of psychological adaptation systems such as coping and efficacy).
Coutu (2002)	Three common themes are: (1) a staunch acceptance of reality (2) a deep belief that life is meaningful; (3) an uncanny ability to improvise and adapt to significant change

Table 20 Adaptative Leadership Theory

Theory	Adaptative Leadership Theory Adaptive leadership would build a culture that values diverse views and relies less on central planning and the genius of the few at the top.
Implications	Adaptive leadership is the practice of mobilizing people to tackle tough challenges and thrive. Adaptive leadership is specifically about change that enables the capacity to thrive.
Author´s proposals	Author´s Inferences
Heifezt, Grashow, & Linsky (2009)	The concept of thriving is drawn from evolutionary biology, in which a successful adaptation has three characteristics:
A challenge for adaptive leadership is to engage people in distinguishing what is essential to preserve from their organization's heritage from what is expendable.	(1) it preserves the DNA essential for the species' continued survival; (2) it discards (re-regulates or rearranges) the DNA that no longer serves the species' current needs; 3) it creates DNA arrangements that give the species' the ability to flourish in new ways and in more challenging environments.
Successful adaptations are thus both conservative and progressive. Successful adaptations enable a living system to take the best from its history into the future.	Organizational adaptation occurs through experimentation. Those seeking to lead adaptive change need an experimental mindset. They must learn to improvise as they go, buying time and resources along the way for the next set of experiments.
Leaders make the best possible use of previous wisdom and know-how.	Adaptation relies on diversity. Evolution is variation, which in organizational terms could be called distributed or collective intelligence.
Useem (2007)	Adaptation takes time. Progress is radical over time yet incremental in time.

Uhl-Bien, Marion & McKelvey (2007) Linsky & Heifetz (2002) Bryman (1996)	This leadership focuses on change but distinguishes between leadership (as a product of interactive dynamics) and leaders (people who influence this process). As such, adaptive leadership occurs when interacting agents generate adaptive outcomes.
Adaptive Leadership is an interactive event in which knowledge, action, and behaviors change, thereby provoking an organization to become more adaptive.	Individuals act as leaders in this dynamic when they mobilize people to seize new opportunities and tackle tough problems. As the situation changes, different people may act as leaders by leveraging their differing skills and experience.

Table 21 Ethical Leadership Theory

Theory	Ethical Leadership Theory
Implications	Ethical leaders attempt to influence followers' ethical conduct by explicitly setting ethical standards and holding followers' accountable to those standards by the use of rewards and discipline.

Author´s proposals	Author´s Inferences

Brown, Treviño, & Harrison, (2005)
Factors to consider:
  Role modeling.
  Ethical contexts.
  Agreeableness.
  Conscientiousness.
  Moral reasoning.
  Locus of control.
  Self-monitoring.
  Moral intensity.
  Inhibition.
	Outcomes:
	  The well-being of the individual.
	  A positive working atmosphere.
	  The energy of the team.
	  High Morality in the workplace.
	  The health of the organization.
	
	The 4-V´s model: Values, Vision, Voice, Virtues.
	
	The main goal is to create a world in which the future is positive, inclusive, and allows the potential for all individuals to pursue and fulfill their needs and meet their highest potential.

Table 22 Psychodynamic Organizational and Leadership Perspective

Theory	Psychodynamic Organizational and Leadership Perspective
	It is defined as the study of unconscious patterns of work relations and their influence on leadership and authority and how role formation, conflict, identity, and boundaries influence relationships and relatedness in the leadership system.
Implications	The approach is theoretically informed by five basic behavioral assumptions, namely dependency, fight or flight, pairing, me-ness and one-ness or we-ness.

Author's proposals	Author's Inferences
Brunner, Nutkevitch, & Sher (2006) Miller (1993) Freud (1921) Klein (1988) Bertalanff (1968) Jaques (1970) Menzies (1993) Bion (2003) Adams & Diamond (1999) Cytrynbaum & Noumair (2004) Armstrong (2005) Neumann, Kellner & Dawson-Shepherd (1997) Turquet (1974) Koortzen (2005) Czander (1993) Gould *et al.*, (2001) Klein (2005) Hirchhorn (1997) Lawrence, Bain & Gould (1996)	Psychodynamic approach believes that the macro, meso, and micro systems mirror one another and that the system as a whole strives towards equilibrium between consciousness or unconsciousness, rational or irrational behavior, inclusion or exclusion, and attachment or detachment. *Anxiety* as the fear of the future, acting as the driving force of the relationship and relatedness between leadership and followership. *Task* refers to the leader's adherence to a behavior where confusion and free-floating anxiety are manifested. *Role* encompasses the boundary around the leadership position that differentiates it from the followership role. *Authority* is the formal and official right to take up the leadership role, bestowed from above (organization, manager or leader), the side (colleagues), below (subordinates) and from within (self-authorization). *Boundaries* (such as tasks, time, or territory) act as the space around and between parts of the system, keeping it safe and contained. *Identity* describes the nature of the leader's role behavior and the branding, climate and culture of the organizational system.

Table 23 Spirituality and Leadership

Theory	Spirituality and Leadership
	This leadership is role modeling comprised of the values, attitudes, and behaviors that are necessary to intrinsically motivate one's self and others.
Implications	A person in a leadership position embodies spiritual values such as integrity, honesty, and humility, creating the self as an example of someone who can be trusted, relied upon, and admired.

Author's proposals	Author's Inferences
Fry (2003) A sense of call from leaders and followers. Organizational cultures characterized by altruistic love, hope, and faith. Leaders and followers express genuine care, concern, and appreciation for self and others.	The main elements are integrity, the search for meaning, deep reflection, inner connection, creativity, Personal transformation, sacredness, energy. The end effect of spiritual leadership is to create a sense of fusion between the four fundamental forces of human existence (body, mind, heart, and spirit) so that people are motivated for high performance, have greater organizational and personal commitment, work as vocation, experience joy, peace, and serenity.
Reave (2005)	Spiritual leadership is also demonstrated through behavior, whether in individual reflective practice or in the ethical, compassionate, and respectful treatment of others.
Fry, Vitucci & Cedillo (2005)	An instrument designed to measure spiritual leadership: a) vision, which describes an organization's vision and identity, b) hope/faith, which reflects confidence that the vision will be realized, c) altruistic love which results from the caring work environment.

Table 24 Transformational Leadership Theory

Theory	Transformational Leadership Theory
	Leaders go beyond the use of external rewards, inspiring followers to identify with a vision that is beyond their own immediate interest.
Implications	This leadership focuses on how leaders can create valuable and positive change in their followers.

Author´s proposals	Author´s Inferences
Burns (1978, 2010) Antonakis & Sivasubramaniam (2003) Leaders and followers help each other to advance to a higher level of morale and motivation. Yukl (1999)	Transformational leaders inspire and motivate their workforce without micromanaging, they trust trained employees to take authority over decisions in their assigned jobs. It's a management style that's designed to give employees more room to be creative, look to the future and find new solutions to old problems. Employees on the leadership track will also be prepared to become transformational leaders themselves through mentorship and training.
People transform through a process that includes four factors:	a) Idealized influence. b) Inspiring motivation. c) Intellectual motivation. d) Individualized consideration.
Bass (1985; 1991) Employees will be inspired to follow suit. Transformational leadership was the first developed and validated theory to emphasize morals and values in leadership.	A leader is someone who: *Encourages* the motivation and positive development of followers. *Exemplifies* moral standards within the organization and encourages the same to others. *Fosters* an ethical work environment with clear values, priorities, and standards. *Builds* company culture by encouraging employees to move from an attitude of self-interest to a mindset where they are working for the common good. *Holds* an emphasis on authenticity, cooperation, and open communication. *Provides* coaching and mentoring but allowing employees to make decisions and take ownership of tasks.

Table 25 Transactional Leadership Theory

Theory	Transactional Leadership Theory
This theory can be defined as leaders or managers motivating the group to perform, based on punishment and incentives that will persuade the group to perform at an exceptional level.
Implications	Leaders allow followers to fulfill their own self-interest, minimize workplace anxiety, and concentrate on clear organizational objectives.
Author's proposals	Author's Inferences
Burns (1978)
Bass (1991)
Avolio, Bass, & Jung (1995)
McCleskey (2014)
Spahr (2018)	The Transactional Leadership includes three basic concepts:
• Organizing
• Controlling
• Short-term planning

Table 26 Pragmatic Leadership Theory

Theory	Pragmatic Leadership Theory
Pragmatists usually have a straightforward, matter-of-fact approach and don't let emotions distract them.
Implications	A pragmatist is someone who is practical and focused on reaching a goal.
Author's proposals	Author's Inferences
Mumford & Van Doom (2001)
A pragmatist can also ignore his/her own ideals to get the job done.	1. Create the conditions to enable performance: Rather than asking yourself 'how do I get the maximum out of these people?', ask yourself 'how do I set the conditions for optimum performance?'
2. Ask yourself, what demotivates my people? Reframe the challenge, accept that each individual has their own intrinsic motivations. Spend the time examining and analyzing certain practices and processes which are cumbersome, ineffectual, and antiquated that impedes performance.

Pragmatic leaders communicate to others exactly what, when and how they want it. The strategic goals they send tend to be SMART –specific, measurable, achievable, realistic, and time-bound– focusing on the period for which they can plan.	3. Train as you mean to fight: this military axiom refers to the importance of preparing yourself and your people in a way that fits the challenges they will face in their line of work.

Table 27 Symbolic Leadership Theory

Theory	Symbolic Leadership Theory
	The approach emphasizes that the meaningful world of organizations is the outcome of numerous interaction processes creating the organizational reality.
Implications	Symbolic leadership is defined as leadership which refers to, and is based on, the category of meaning. Meaning becomes tangible and can be experienced in the form of symbols.

Author´s proposals	Author´s Inferences
Neuberger (1990, 1995, 2002) Bartölke (1987) Kezar, Carducci, & Contreras-McGavin (2006)	*Enhancing self-awareness.* What do I stand for? What are my values? How can I bring life to what matters most? Is my ego or conviction driving me? Is what I'm doing about substance or show? These are the questions symbolic leaders must ask (and answer) before taking any action. *Demanding* an entirely new vocabulary. Communication extends far beyond the written or verbal realm. *Standing* in the employee's shoes. Symbols are all about meaning. And meaning is defined by the receiver. As a result, leaders must always consider their followers.

This frame is based on anthropology (Geertz 1973), research on corporate culture (Hofstede 1980; Schein 1985; Sackmann 1991; Martin 1992), and organizational symbolism (Pondy et al. 1983; Turner 1990; Alvesson & Berg, 1992).	*Reality*, created and lived by people, is a social construction, with leadership being a part of this reality. Symbolic leadership concentrates on studying values, meaning, interpretation, history, context, as well as other symbolic elements in the leadership process.
Sociological concepts of symbolic interactionism (Mead 1934; Blumer 1969) and the constructivist approach (Hosking et al., 1995).	

Table 28 Complex Leadership Theory

Theory	Complex Leadership Theory (Shared, collective, distributed, relational, adaptive leadership; organizational meta-capability) Leadership as a perceived segment of action whose meaning is created by the interactions of agents involved in producing it rather than being "caused" by the specific acts of individuals described as leaders.
Implications	Leadership is a dynamic that transcends the capabilities of individuals alone, it's a system phenomenon; it is the product of interaction, tension, and exchange rules governing changes in perceptions and understanding.
Author´s proposals	Author´s Inferences
Lichtenstein, Uhl-Bien, Marion, Seers, Orton & Schreiber (2006) Marion & Uhl-Bien (2001, 2003) Uhl-Bien, Marion & McKelvey (2007)	This theory considers leadership within the framework of a Complex Adaptive System (CAS). In such systems, relationships are not primarily defined hierarchically but rather by *interactions* among heterogeneous agents and across agent networks.

Hazy (2006) Marion (1999) "Leaders" in the formal sense can enable the conditions within which the process occurs, but they are not the direct source of change.	CAS is composed of agents and individuals as well as groups of individuals, who "resonate" through sharing common interests, knowledge and/or goals due to their history of interaction and sharing of worldviews. Focusing on events as the prime unit of analysis: *Identifying* and bracketing the events, episodes, and interactions of interest; *Capturing* these events or interactions as data in a systematic way; *Gathering* individual/agent level data that describe interaction over time; *Modeling* these data in ways that highlight their longitudinal and relational qualities; *Analyzing* these data in terms of their relational net.

Table 29 Shared Leadership Theory

Theory	Shared Leadership Theory
	Leadership is therefore not determined by positions of authority but rather by an individual's capacity to influence peers and by the needs of the team in any given moment.
Implications	The absence of hierarchical authority is what distinguishes these groups from traditional organizational forms.
Author´s proposals	Author´s Inferences
Pearce & Conger (2012)	The fastest growing organizational unit is the cross-functional teams.
	Each member of the team brings unique perspectives, knowledge, and capabilities to the team.

Table 30 Distributed Leadership Theory

Theory	Distributed Leadership Theory It is about leadership practice.
Implications	This practice is framed in a very particular way, as a product of the joint interactions of leaders, followers, and aspects of their situation such as tools and routines.

Author´s proposals	Author´s Inferences
Gronn (2002)	This distributed view of leadership shifts focus, from formal and informal leaders to the web of leaders, followers, and their situations that gives form to leadership practice.
Spillane (2006) The key for the distributed leadership is the collective interactions among leaders, followers, and their situation.	Three elements are essential: Leadership *practice* is the central and anchoring concern; Leadership practice is generated in the *interactions* of leaders, followers, and their situation where each element is essential for leadership practice. The *situation* both defines leadership practice and is defined through leadership practice.

Table 31 Relational Leadership Theory

Theory	Relational leadership Theory Meaning emerges in the "spaces between" people rather than in the acts of individuals *per se*.
Implications	All of the agents need not play equivalent roles in the action, but all of the roles are interrelated.

Author´s proposals	Author´s Inferences
Bradbury & Lichtenstein (2000) Buber (1970) Cilliers (1998) Drath (2001)	People construct reality through their interactions within worldviews. They do it when they explain things to one another, tell each other stories, create models and theories and in general when they interact through thought, word, and action

Table 32 Collective leadership Theory

Theory	Collective Leadership Theory It occurs over time, as participants together define "who we are" and what we are doing through our interactions.
Implications	The emergence of a social object occurs through the "informing" of a joint social identity.
Author´s proposals	**Author´s Inferences**
Gioia, Schultz, & Corley (2000) Weick & Roberts (1993)	Social objects arise jointly, through the mutual interactions of its participant creators. This driver of collective identity formation can be forgotten as soon as the participants create a common-sense conception of a formal leader "out there," with themselves holding complementary follower roles.

Table 33 Cross-cultural Leadership Theory

Theory	Cross-cultural leadership Theory Leaders must spend time living in different cultures to be prepared to lead.
Implications	The competencies a leader needs to have to lead effectively and successfully in a variety of cultures.
Author´s proposals	**Author´s Inferences**
Hofstede (2001) House, Hanges, Javidan, Dorfman & Gupta (2004)	There are substantial differences and approaches in how global leadership is conceptualized and defined.
Mobley, Gessner & Arnold (1999) Goldsmith (2003) Green, Hassan, Immelt, Marks & Meland (2003) Lane (2004)	GLOBE project: The study involved more than 160 researchers working in 62 societies. Objectives: To develop cultural dimensions both at the organizational level and at the societal level; to examine the beliefs that different cultures had about effective leaders.

Table 34 E-leadership

Theory	E-leadership Leading virtually involves leading people from different departments, organizations, countries.
Implications	Much of the work on E-Leadership focuses on leadership in virtual work teams which are called "group decision support systems."

Author's proposals	Author's Inferences
Zigurs (2003) Zaccaro & Bader (2003)	Feedback, encouragement, rewards, and motivation must be re-examined when leadership is mediated by technology.
Xiao, Seagull, Mackenzie, Klein & Ziegert (2008) Malhotra, Majchrzak & Rosen (2007)	E-Leadership practices included the ability to: (a) establish and maintain trust through the use of communication technology, (b) ensure that distributed diversity is understood and appreciated, (c) effectively manage virtual work life cycles, (d) monitor the progress of the technology team, (e) improve the visibility of virtual members within the team and outside the organization, and, (f) allow individual team members to benefit from the team.

Table 35 Implicit Leadership Theories

Theory	Implicit Leadership Theories
	They imply that they are cognitive structures containing the traits and behaviors of leaders.
Implications	Implicit theories represent a special form of cognitive schemata which are seen as a cognitive network of everyday concepts.

Author´s proposals	Author´s Inferences
Offermann, Kennedy, & Wirtz (1994)	People try to explain and predict their own and the behavior of others as well as derive their action strategies.
Epitropaki & Martin (2004)	
Lord, Foti, & De Vader (1984)	The same behavior may be interpreted in a different way by different people based on their implicit leadership theories.
Eagly & Karau (2002)	The basic idea of leadership categorization theory is that perceivers (followers) classify stimuli persons (their supervisors), by comparing them to prototypes of a category (effective leader).
Judge, Bono, Ilies, & Gerhardt (2002)	
Antonakis, Day, & Schyns (2012)	

Table 36 Multi-level Theory and Methods in Organizations

Theory	Multi-level Theory and Methods in Organizations
Implications	Multi-level Theory discuss at various levels of analysis (entities) that are relevant to leadership theory: persons, dyads, groups, and collectives.

Author´s proposals	Author´s Inferences
Dansereau, Alutto, & Yammarino (1984) Markham (1998) Waldman, Yammarino, & Avolio (1990) Yammarino & Dubinsky (1990) Anderson (1999) Gupta, Tesluk, & Taylor (2007) Meyer, Gaba, & Colwell (2005)	Individuals in organizational settings acting independently of one another represented the person level. Dyads encompassed two individuals that were interdependent on a one-to-one basis. Groups reflected two or more interdependent individuals interacting with each other. Collectives were composed of a clustering of individuals, groups, departments, organizations, and/or societies where interdependency rests on shared expectations.
Markham (1985) Markham & McKee (1995)	The multi-level framework promotes branch out to other areas of organizational research: Group absence behavior.
Berson & Avolio (2004) Chun, Yammarino, Dionne, Sosik, & Moon (2009) Markham S. E. (2012)	The incorporation of a multi-level framework into leadership and organizational research introduced explicit levels of clarification regarding individuals, dyads, groups, and collectives, where implicit clarification had been the norm.

Table 37 Leadership Affect and Emotions

Theory	Leadership Affect and Emotions
	Leadership will benefit by incorporating the research on emotional labor, emotional regulation, and happiness.
Implications	A better understanding how the workplace context, and leadership demands influence affective events.

Author´s proposals	Author´s Inferences
Gooty, Connelly, Griffith, & Gupta (2010) Sy, Côté, & Saavedra (2005) Bono & Ilies (2006) The term 'affect' is often used as the umbrella term that embraces both emotions and moods as well as other constructs with relevance to emotions.	Integrating these concepts: (1) emotions are present in the workplace, (2) employees may experience emotional events outside of work and bring their emotions to the workplace, (3) other employees can trigger emotional events during the day, (4) emotional events that occur during the workday or are relived through memories while at work will create emotions, (5) these emotions must be dealt with, either through self-regulation or emotional labor, (6) emotions may be transferred to other employees, (7) leaders are susceptible to these same emotional events, and (8) leaders are capable of influencing the emotions and moods of their followers (both positively and negatively).
Ashkanasy & Humphrey (2011a, b) Humphrey (2013)	This model examines emotions in organizations at five levels: (1) within person, (2) between persons, (3) interpersonal relationships, (4) groups and teams, and (5) organizational.

Menges & Kilduff (2015)	Individuals, groups, and therefore, organizations, are pervaded by feelings, or emotions, which affect individuals and their organizations. These effects can have far-reaching impacts since emotions are transferable between followers, from leader to follower, or from follower to leader. Emotions are usually discussed at the individual level where an event, object, or affiliation elicit a short-lived feeling of joy, happiness, fear, anxiety, sadness, pride, anger, guilt, or shame. Once these emotions are evident, they must be dealt with in social settings.
Izard (1991)	Cognitive Appraisal Theory defines emotions as organized mental responses to an event or entity.
Fisher (2000)	Moods are less intense than emotions and range from positive to negative, with no focal stimuli, and are often not consciously recognized by the individual.
Hatfield, Cacioppo, & Rapson (1994) Tee (2015)	Emotional contagion is defined as the tendency to automatically mimic and synchronize facial expressions, vocalizations, postures, and movements with those of another person and, consequently, to converge emotionally.
Conger (2011) Inspirational, charismatic leadership may be especially critical during times of crisis or during times of great opportunities when emotions are likely to be highly engaged.	The leadership literature on charisma, transformational leadership, LMX, and other theories have the potential to shed light on how rhetorical techniques and other leadership techniques influence emotional labor, emotional contagion, moods, and overall morale. Charismatic leadership attributes an important role to the leader's ability to inspire followers and create a sense of a common identity.

Bass & Riggio, (2006)	Transformational leadership researchers acknowledge that leaders need to be charismatic and inspirational if they want followers to buy into their visions.
Schriesheim, Castro, & Cogliser (1999) Liden & Maslyn (1998)	Leader-member exchange theorists state that affect is important to leader-follower relationships, and scholars developed leader-member exchange subscales to measure affect in terms of the amount of liking and friendship between leaders and followers.

Burns (2010) highlights something that every leader must consider: the desire for power and the risks that it entails. Power itself must be considered made up of motives and resources, symbolic and real, concomitant or subsequent, etc. Power relations are fundamental factors to understand the "true nature of leadership." (p. 11)

Several authors (French & Raven, 1959; Lunenburg, 2012; Raven, 1992; Tracy, 1990) categorized and defined the types/bases of power that exist in human domination which are more explained in Table 38.

Table 38 Bases of Power

Bases	Descriptors
Informational Power	Use of information by a supervisor to convince the subordinate to acquiesce
Empowerment	Power flows from the bottom up. If you are successful in giving your people power, they will surely lift you on their shoulders to heights of power and success.
Reward Power	The power whose basis is the ability to reward. Can lead to better performance as long as the employee sees a clear link between performance and rewards. Associated with short-term results.

Coercive Power	The power whose basis is the ability to punish. Often associated with negative side effects and short-term results.
Legitimate Power	A person's ability to influence another's behavior because of the position that the powerful person holds. Sometimes referred to as *position power*. Can be depended on initially, but can create dissatisfaction, resistance, and frustration among employees.
Referent Power	Defined as a feeling of "oneness" between the powerful and the subject or a desire for such an identity. Based, in part, upon the subject's attraction (not just in the physical sense) to the powerful person. The subject has a desire to be closely associated with the powerful person. The greater the attraction, the greater the identification, and consequently the greater the referent power. Develops out of admiration for another. Can lead to enthusiastic and unquestioning trust, compliance, loyalty, and commitment from subordinates.
Expert Power	Based on the powerful person's knowledge, skills, or ability and depends on the subject's perception that the powerful person has these qualities.

Educative Leadership

Aware of the high demands of educational environments and their demanding training and accompaniment dynamics, coupled with daily stressful situations and the demand for quick responses from well-formed criteria.

Roberts (2018) defines leadership as "the process of influencing people by providing a purpose, direction, and motivation to fulfill the mission and improve the organization." Table 39 shows the twelve approaches it proposes for leaders in highly demanding environments and with a solid degree of mutual collaborative work involving high-impact existential situations.

Table 39 Key elements for a leadership in high demanding environments

Be technically competent	As a leader, you must know the work and the tasks of your different employees.
Develop a sense of responsibility in your collaborators	Helps to develop the character that will help your collaborators to meet their professional managers.
Make sure tasks are understood, supervised, and accomplished: communication is key	A leader must be able to communicate effectively. Leaders must spend most of the day engaged in communication.
Keep your collaborators informed	Learn how to communicate not only with junior staff, but also with senior staff and other key people.
Know your people and take care of their well-being	Be well versed in the basic elements of human nature and recognize the importance of taking care of others with sincerity.
Know yourself and seek self-improvement	To know yourself, you must understand what you are, what you know and what you can do. Continually seeking self-improvement. This can be achieved through self-knowledge, education, continuous training, personal reflection, and interaction with others.
Make wise and timely decisions	Use good problem-solving, decision-making and planning tools
Seek responsibility and take responsibility for your actions	Find ways to guide your organization to new goals. When things go wrong, don't blame others. Analyze the situation, take corrective action and continue with the next challenge
Be an example	Be a good example for your collaborators. Your team should not only be told what is expected of them, but they should also see leaders embody the qualities and ethics of the organization. Leaders must embody what they want to see in their collaborators.
Work as a global team	It does not focus only on your department, section or close collaborators, but it visualizes the entire organization as an entity that must learn and succeed together.
Use the full capabilities of your organization	By developing team spirit, you can use the skills of your entire organization to achieve common goals.

Miller (2006) proposes that being a leader requires a strong ethical conviction of the person to commit to doing what is best for the world where the characteristics of collaborative work are present.

Derridá (2004) wrote about leadership in educational institutions in his essays published as *Eyes of the University*. The Algerian philosopher begins his reflection by returning to the questions raised by Immanuel Kant (1997) two centuries earlier, regarding the foundation of the modern public university. He focuses on questions that have to do with the responsibility of the faculty to assume leadership within formal education. Teachers are the eyes of the school, who are dedicated to thinking and teaching young generations, and who take primary responsibility for their leadership.

Derridá raised a series of questions that teachers and administrators might face when leaders begin to think of education collectively and individually. The strong questions pointed out by Derridá (2004) are: "What do we represent? Who do we represent? Are we responsible? For what and for whom?" (p. 83).

It is possible to infer that the type of idea that one has about others, about the school environment, about the values that sustain relationships, about the modes of action and the objectives that will be pursued organizationally. These together directly influence the final result that is attempted as identity traits of the educational community. What a person is today affects the future they seek. A similar thing happens with an educational community except for the dimensions and complexity of both.

A life project that involves the student, the educator, and the educational community that, taking advantage of the unique period of valuable experience of formal education, forges the honest citizen who, focusing his life on the passion that springs from the heart for self-knowledge and self-appropriation, is capable of giving himself up. He is capable of being passionate about others in totality, of suffering for love, of accepting with serenity and joy the daily demands and renunciations of the life placed at the service (Ratzinger, 2008).

Educational and pedagogical leadership (efficient, sustainable)

Foster (1986) argues that educational leadership requires contextualization in terms of social and community impact. This author affirms that all leadership in the classroom "must be critically educational; not only can it look at the conditions in which we live, but it must also decide how to change them" (p.185). In addition to this, Freire (1998) asserts that education should not be considered as the lever
with the greatest impact and influence on social transformation, but in the absence of it, such transformation cannot occur.

The confirmation that both participants in leadership training processes, both those who serve as leaders and those who follow (in traditional leadership schemes), are transformed and empowered, is fundamental to the current notion of leadership. Bennis (1986) wrote an article entitled Transforming Power and Leadership in which he identified three factors as components of transforming power: the leader, the intention, and the organization. The educational organization requires educators in front of a group with decision-making power and intelligent conflict resolution, in addition to other soft skills.

Bennis (2012) defines the power of educational leadership from a very humanistic perspective. That is, as "the leader's ability to reach the souls of others in a way that raises human consciousness, builds meaning, and inspires the human intention that is the source of power" (p. 70).

Aronowitz and Giroux (1985) identified the need for the educator in the formal educational setting to be a context-sensitive person "to encourage social justice" and to practice "leadership that can transcend [to] democratic education for the benefit of all students and staff" (p. 5). The educator is a leader in the middle of the community because the classroom is not a space isolated from reality or an alternative experience to the society in which one lives immersed. The classroom is society in a privileged context of intervention. Philip and García (2013) state that what is important is the context and not the tools used when it comes to making decisions in learning environments. It is the power to influence the generation of significant environments, capturing the student's interest, using relevant pedagogical strategies, valuing individuality and inclusion, using creativity to facilitate the relevance and connection of knowledge and learning environments, without confusing in the case of technological tools with contexts.

King and Biro (2000) call for transformative learning to begin with a disorienting dilemma and to "progress through a dynamic path of stages ... [to] a final reintegration of a new frame of reference" (p. 19). Common elements in these approaches include the need for social improvement and a complete remodeling of the element-structures of all knowledge and belief.

The educational leader proposes and facilitates spontaneous interpersonal relationships for improvement and growth because without those relationships, education would act to deform rather than transform. Freire (2012) states: "Every time the *you* is transformed into an object, dialogue is *subverted* by an *it* and education is transformed into deformation" (p. 89).

The educational leadership recognizes the need to start with critical reflection and analysis of all the information available, to pass through understanding illuminated by self-reflection turned into action, not only with regard to access to teaching processes-learning, but also with respect to the academic, social, and civic impact. In other words, it is not simply the task of the educational and pedagogical leader to ensure that all learners succeed in the tasks associated with learning the formal curriculum and demonstrating that learning has been achieved according to standardized test assessments. It is the essential role of the educational leader to

create learning contexts or communities in which social, political, and cultural capital is continually improved in such a way as to provide equal opportunities for all students.

Educating for life is not educating for what happens outside of school and the classroom. Rather, it is educating in the society that is also the school and within the micro-reality that is the classroom where the student interacts, learns, lives, grows, and is affected by all its dimensions. A leader with educational and pedagogical intentions recognizes that the final end of education is not only the private good and individual achievement, but also democratic citizenship and participation in civil society (Shields, 2009).

Astin and Astin (2000), associate educational leadership and social change, saying:

> We believe that the value ends of leadership should be to improve equity, social justice, and quality of life; to expand access and opportunity; encourage respect for difference and diversity; strengthen democracy, civic life and civic responsibility; and promote cultural enrichment, creative expression, intellectual honesty, advancement of knowledge, and personal freedom along with responsibility (p. 11).

The learning that is proposed in the formation of a leader requires some transformative features proposed by Davis (2006). These features involve the acquisition of knowledge that interrupts previous learning and stimulates the reflexive remodeling of deep-rooted structures of knowledge or previous beliefs. Transformative learning involves the critical self-reflection of deeply rooted assumptions and, the validation of one's beliefs by sharing experiences and perceptions of and with others. These features are provided by the Lonerganian proposal of self-appropriation. It also implies the ability to interpret past experiences from a new set of expectations about the future, thus giving new perspectives of meaning to those experiences. In order to make sense, learning requires that new information be incorporated into well-developed symbolic frames of reference.

These are then redesigned through critical reflection and discourse and then used to guide future action and behavior (Fig. 31).

Figure 31 Things that learners pay attention to

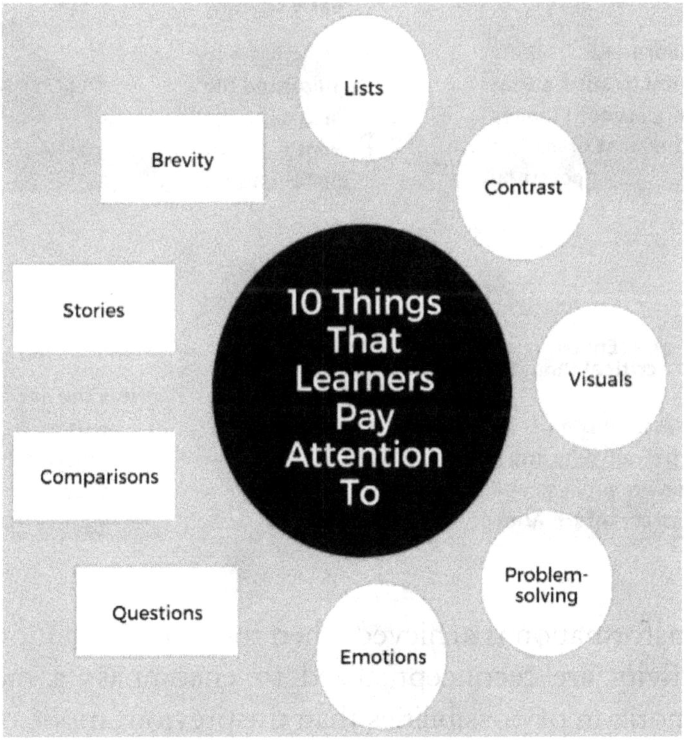

The process can be uncomfortable because it affects the *status quo* of those who do not want to continue transforming. The process affects the *modus vivendi* of those who have accommodated themselves to what they already know, to what they believe is a given in the way that they have always understood it.

Disruptive interventions create a feeling of imbalance that encourages the educator and manager to see the world with new eyes, to get out of what is already established simply because it is tradition even though it lacks any reasons to support what is done, said, believed, or how it is done, lived, and projected (Fig. 32).

Figure 32 Disruptive Education model

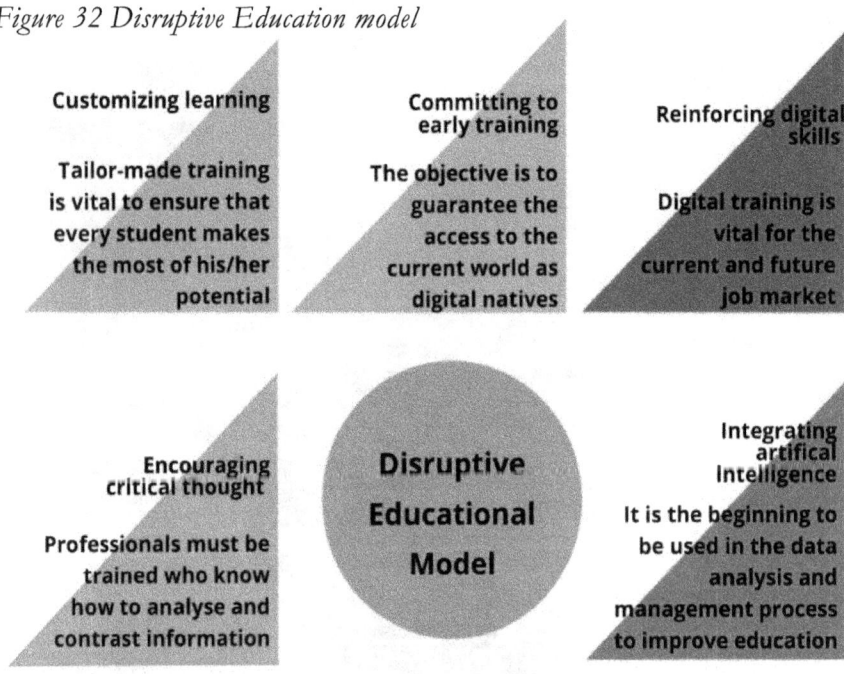

Transformation is achieved when the object and motive of the activity are reconceptualized to encompass a radically wider horizon of possibilities than the previous mode of activity (Engeström, 2009).

Taylor (2006) has highlighted the importance of having the educator be present with all his being, involved intentionally and actively in interpersonal relationships and for educational purposes with the learners, and that such presence requires being firmly grounded in multiple forms of expression. An authentic educational and pedagogical practice appears to be multidimensional, where educator-experts develop a greater awareness of the self (both personal and cultural), an appreciation of the spiritual, and recognition of the ethical dimensions associated with fostering transformative learning. It seems to me that Taylor's proposal requires being present intentionally (Lonerganian-style) in educational settings if students are to be leaders with a high and positive impact in a changing cultural context. We require effectiveness in our leadership as educators. Hence, effective educational leadership is essential for the effectiveness and improvement of the school (Ololube, Egbezor, Kpolovie, & Amaele, 2012).

Effective Educational Leadership

An effective leader, educational leaders must develop a sustainable scholar environment. He/she protects and commits to teach and learn in schools seeking achievement of individuals. Effective leaders support themselves and the followers around them to promote and support learning process.

Leaders should learn how they can avoid burnouts among followers and increase the impact of their leadership on school management.

Most leaders want to do important things, inspire others to do it with them, and leave a legacy once they are gone. To a large extent, the specific school context, the management systems or the bureaucracy in which they have to be leaders, is what hinders or limits the exercise of leadership (Munford, 2003). Therefore, to maintain effective educational leadership, Hargreaves and Fink (2004) presented seven principles of sustainable leadership (Fig. 33).

Figure 33 Effective Educative Leader

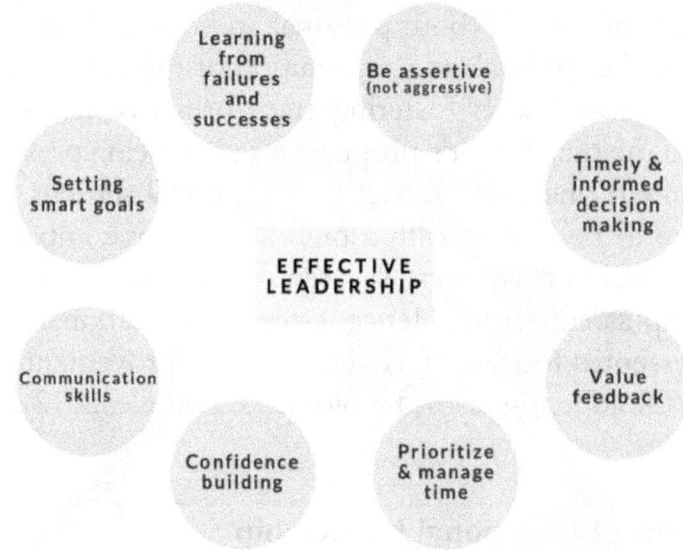

Sustainable Educational Leadership

Sustainable leadership allows for better understanding of the link with school leadership by:
1) Emphasizing learning goals; defining and prioritizing them among all the demands of the educational institution. These goals have to be integrated in all the tasks and procedures of the classroom, hence the need to generate a consensus about them among teachers.
2) Ensuring that staff, materials, and financial

resources are aligned with the pedagogical purposes and goals. This implies having a systemic view of school improvement and resource allocation skills, especially when these are scarce.

3) Involving practices such as: reflecting with the staff on teaching, coordinating and reviewing the curriculum with teachers while seeking a sequence and articulation between all grades, providing feedback to teachers in their classroom practice based on observation of their learning session, and systematically monitoring student progress to improve their results.

4) Encouraging student learning and engages in the process itself. In the same way, it takes part in the learning and professional development of teachers as leaders and apprentices at the same time. These learnings are formal (courses or degrees) or informal through reflections on specific aspects of teaching.

5) Ensuring that teachers can focus on teaching and students on learning thereby establishing an orderly environment both inside and outside the classroom. For this, it is necessary to have clear and relevant rules. Teachers need to feel support and appreciation from the principal, which is reflected by the confidence in their work.

Self reflection of Chapter IV

Let's see how that leadership is going, educator

Characteristic traits of leadership	Y	N
1. You have a professional ethic linked to your values and vision.		
2. You are able to model what you propose as it is a substantial part of your personality.		
3. You have well developed decision making skills.		
4. You have well developed teamwork skills.		
5. You have well developed problems solving skills.		
6. Your values, beliefs, dynamics and even language are related to the contexts that surround you.		
7. You remain in a constant training process for the development of your leadership.		
8. You promote awareness of your own worth.		
9. You act accordingly of who you are as an educator and what you represent.		
10. You have the capacity for interpersonal relationships and a sense of community.		
11. You have a sense of community.		

5. Salesian Preventive Leadership

An attempt at definition

The Preventive System is a synthesis so rich and with so many edges of understanding, experience or interpretation that it becomes method, methodology, spirituality, project, criterion of life, and action. The Preventive System is like a living ecosystem, an essential atmosphere in any educational action, a DNA grafted onto the chromosomes of the person who, after the example of Saint John Bosco[1], is intentionally aware of his being and doing as an educator open to transcendence for all, at all times, on any occasion and at every opportunity. Three statements about Salesian Prevention:

Being Preventive is building up from the positive in each person, always having a look at the best in each person.

---

[1] Saint John Bosco died in Turin, Italy, on January 31, 1888. The almost 73 years of his life were accompanied by profound and complex political, social and cultural changes: revolutionary movements, wars and a migration of people from the countryside to the cities, all factors with an emphatic effect on people's lives, especially the poorest classes. Locked up as they were on the outskirts of cities, the poor in general and the youngest in particular became victims of exploitation or unemployment: in their human, moral, religious and occupational development they were not sufficiently accompanied and were frequently gave no attention at all. Sensitive as they were to each change, young people often became insecure and bewildered. Traditional methods of education became disjointed and ineffective in the face of this uprooted mass of people. Efforts were made for various reasons by philanthropists, educators, and ecclesiastics to meet new needs. One of them, who came to the fore in Turin thanks to his clear Christian inspiration, his courageous initiatives and the rapid and widespread extension of his work, was Don Bosco (John Paul II, Juvenum Patris, para. 2).

Being Preventive means bringing out the best possible version of each person for everyone, every day and in every situation.

To be preventive is to discover the energy of the good, to stimulate and develop it, because this energy is "a small guarantee of the future"
(Vecchi, 1992, p. 3).

The whole Salesian educational Preventive System presents a specific purpose that justifies its practice and is explicitly present when it speaks of the formation of the good Christian and the honest citizen. At the same time, we can say that the ultimate goal of those who live the Preventive System is to support strongly unitary life projects (Rodríguez, 2007).

Each life narrative is an important personal story, and each personal story matters because you cannot understand any human relationship, organization, or social group without understanding the active participation and contribution of the human resources that sustain, nurture, affect, and modify.

The Preventive System, as a way of life and action to study, practice, enrich, innovate, and adapt to current times, is based on the Documents of the General Chapter No. 23 (GC 23) of the Salesians of Don Bosco (1990).

Salesian prevention

Prevention is the founding principle and criterion of life and is an action that acts as a permanent filter of discernment and decision-making that aims to extract the best from each educator and others, even if construction and collaboration efforts are therefore hindered (Vecchi, 1992, p. 8).

The rich and complex meaning of Salesian prevention extends to all the moments that make up the life of the educator who decides to be preventive. Each action, each decision, each intervention is intentionally and consciously an expression of the genuine interest in educating from the positive in the person and always seeking the best version of oneself and of the other.

Salesian prevention needs an atmosphere, an environment, with a personalized and personal accompaniment. Accompaniment that, according to the Fundamental Table of Reference of Salesian Youth Ministry (2016), is clarified with a specific vocabulary:

- Anticipation of any risk situation,
- Intentional development of personal positive energy,
- Construction of an almost natural atmosphere with features of individual and organizational family nucleus,
- Promotion of the constant presence of the educator who proposes everything that his creativity offers him to generate trust, closeness, and balanced mature affection,
- Interest in educational proposals that intentionally seek the integral formation of the student,
- A family environment that allows for benevolent and healthy interpersonal relationships,
- Personalized help to overcome current challenges while projecting the individual´s future.

The ecosystem, generated and sustained by the Preventive System, requires high personal commitment, the harmony of the parties in the educational-pastoral experience, and the balance between self-appropriation with interpersonal relationships for a suitable experience.

The benefit of Salesian Preventivity is the educational relationship that springs from the positive and tends towards the positive relationship that uplifts, rebuilds, and takes advantage of the healthy energy that every person has.

Educational-pastoral assistance as an expression of Salesian Preventivity is a desire to regenerate the sense of dignity where it is required. It is the joy of shared gratifying moments in a family atmosphere. It is the attraction for noble, beautiful, and useful things that the educator intentionally generates and tries to bring together. It is the assistance that lives and shapes the openness to transcendence that Love asks, calls, launches, fulfills.

Masiá (2004) emphasized: "Without hope, there is no future, without future there is no present, without present there is no past" (p. 9). Likewise, every human being who considers himself a leader, regardless of the most appropriate definition of leadership, needs to have a future full of hope. The human being, according to Ricoeur (2004), requires this openness to possibilities, to interconnections with the social environment, a presence of others beyond oneself that cannot be understood without seeing it in relation to one's own and the past of one´s community's.

The differentiated range of offers and demands of specific contexts makes Preventive Leadership in Salesian Schools in the Americas (ESA in Latin America) an educational proposal valid for the global context VUCA and the reading of the historical moment as UTRU, because such leadership is a flexible proposal to be adapted into different contexts and it also provides a theoretical structure rich in intuitions for its implementation.

Salesian Schools in America have a unique approach because they affirm that their preferred recipients are young people in economic and social conditions more disadvantaged by globalized markets affecting formal educational settings.

These institutions have a sense of urgency to accompany students and help them to carry out their life project in a unitary way. The principles coming from the Preventive System are supported by an educational philosophy which permeates any administrative or pedagogical management style. Each Salesian educational work, according to the criteria of prevention and renewal, challenges pedagogical strategies, educator´s practice and assessment instruments.

Table 40 presents a very brief theoretical compendium of the Preventive System, considered Saint John Bosco's intuitions, experiences and reflections, and adaptations in the most varied contexts in the field of formal education.

Table 40 Salesian Preventive System reading on organizational perspective

Philosophy	This philosophy is based on the optimistic conception about the dignity of the person.
	Total respect for personal history and individual processes.
	Honest interest in the integral promotion of both the expert leader and the leader in training.
Principles	Reason, Transcendence, and Benevolence (*Amorevolezza*).
	Intentionally purposeful and positive environment.
	Creative proposal to generate any experience that shows the best of each person.
Strategies	They are used as applications and verifiable hinges of the Preventive Leadership proposal
	Intentional presence.
	Atmosphere where the essential elements of the best version of yourself are lived and potentiated.
	Accompaniment.
Means or instruments	Leader as benevolent and reasoned presence.
	Leader as an embodiment of deep life with a transcendent meaning.
	Leader as embodiment of service according to shared interests.
	Leader as a person always sensitive to the other and in an ethical attitude of humanizing commitment.

School is the period of life where boys and girls discover, organize, choose, and foresee; for many at the high school level, make the first personal decisions, decisions that will later have great personal and social importance.

Salesian Preventive Leadership

A leader, according to Fisher, Turner, and Morling (2009), can achieve the potential to realize a harmonious organizational culture; he or she can create a healthy "ecosystem" environment, he or she can live an environment that promotes and respects life as a balanced interrelation. Today, it is important to train a future educator as a preventive leader whose stamina is to seek the truth about himself, about reality, about the person, about the citizen, and about others supported by ethics. Preventive leadership training is accompanied by a set of person-centered options that allow educators a process of transformation, both personal and of any organization. The fusion of shared goals, assimilated values, common purposes, unified processes, correct procedures, and the care for the environment are sought, above all else, through honest dialogue, harmonious intervention, and
an encounter where each social agent has a voice that can and should be heard.

Wright (1999) emphasizes that leadership seeks "fundamentally to promote a better quality of humanity" (p. 6). Chapman and Aspin (2001) have argued that leadership development can be achieved through explicit programs, since the intent of these programs can be fundamental to promote social responsibility, community leadership, active citizenship, or service to the community.

An educational leader with preventive traits can influence the culture of any school classroom by promoting that students acquire the knowledge, abilities, and skills necessary to generate and sustain more harmonious social ecosystemic environments. It is an arduous task that requires going beyond what is scheduled, beyond the books, beyond the walls of the classroom each educator is looking for a convenient and possible result that he/she should try to achieve during the time he/she has with the students. As a preventive leader, it is worth remembering that the modeling of values, character, and personality is an essential part of the Salesian educational proposal: you are always an educator, for everyone, at all times. There is no break between being an individual and what you do as a professional.

Myers (2005) states that opportunities to exercise educational leadership provide students with additional skills and confidence that will help them later in life. Therefore, the school and the teacher as educational leader cannot be separated from the context of the human being as an individual and a social agent with a worldwide impact.

In the specific case of the Salesians, they decode the youth with the "preventive" approach and use this perspective as a model to make the educational institutions and comprehensive educational activities that are sheltered under the traditional umbrella concept of the Salesian "pastoral work." In the present book, this educational-pastoral-educational perspective it is rethought from a singular paradigm: convergence. Convergence of a method, a model, and a body of founding principles coupled with educational criteria and strategies to guide any proposal for preventive educational leadership (Fig. 34).

Figure 34 Salesian Preventive System new approach model

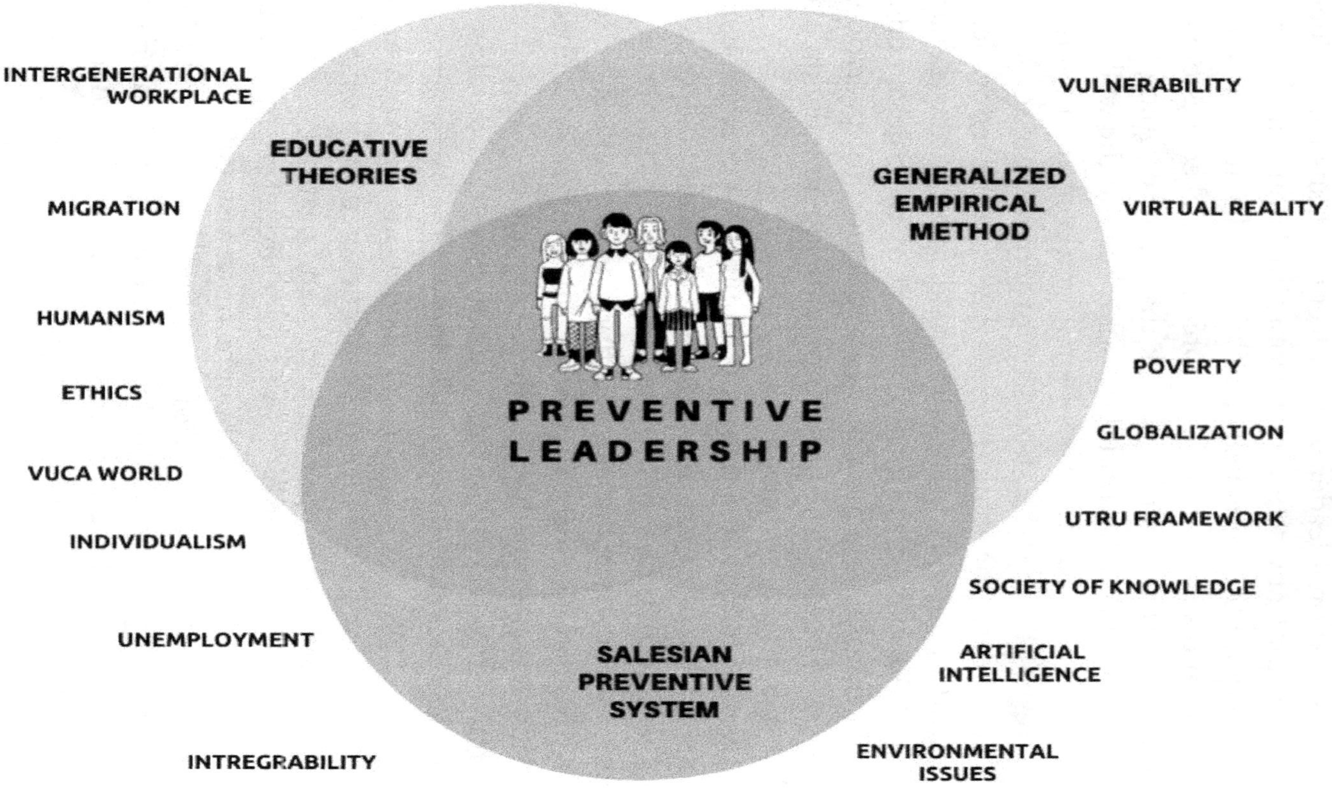

The Preventive Leadership proposal is the narrated story of educators with a vocation to serve, in the broadest sense of the term. Preventive leadership is the reflection on educators passionate about the integral human growth of the new generations. It is the narration of educators for whom the history of young people is a history that becomes their own because it is a dialogue always open to the fullness of life. It is the choice of educators who educate from the positive energy that each person has within themselves, and who educate towards the positivity of history, of humanity, of the person himself. This "convergence of stories" deserves to be studied as a new event, full of hope and causing renewal in the educational fields in the face of a society of despair, of a radical individualization that blocks one from the other, and the consequent dehumanization.

The human being, in his cognitive structure and his permanent self-awareness process, is the center of preventive educational leadership. That is to say, a leadership that demands the action of a human subject who concretizes its leadership from the Lonerganian imperatives or precepts: "be attentive, be intelligent, be reasonable, be responsible, be loving" (Lonergan, 1973, p. 27); who combines them to the daily practice of the principles, criteria, strategies, and actions that from Salesian preventiveness can be linked to the life and action of the leader.

Salesian Preventive Leader

A leading educator with preventive traits tries to "highlight" the positive in each person whom he/she meets along the way in all areas of life.

A Preventive Leader, within his/her immersion in each context, uses the best tools available at the moment, and seeks the best possible interventions according to his/her own capacities and resources. In subsequent sections, the Principle of *amorevolezza* (benevolence, beneficence, *hesed*) is explained as the axis of a polyphony of constructs. Like a light that passes through a prism it allows the human eye to see the polychromatic reality of what seems like a single beam of light. Reason and transcendence together with love act as the polychromatic light of the Preventive System. As the Preventive System passes through each person and context, there will be a "reflection, refraction, diffraction, dispersion of the light beam" which, in the person and praxis of Saint John Bosco, was a means that fulfilled all the conditions for the light beams to be sharp.

After him, members of the Salesian Family are a handful of beams of "preventive light" for the world. How can one be a vivid example of prevention for others? The analysis of each one of the criteria of Preventive Leadership —educate from the positive and towards the best; present the best version of oneself and of others at all times; embody the proposed values; accompany personally and in a personalizing way—, with the parameters necessary —*oratory* criterion, intentionally educational presence— to allow a better understanding of the foundational Salesian educational strategies —family educational relationship, joyful, cordial; educational assistance that inquires, discerns, values and lives the best educational practices— trying an amalgam of tradition and current affairs, is a reflection of years with challenges of the current moment with contextual educational strategies —solidarity, dialogue, discernment—.

Intentionally, these standards began with the statement "Be …," because it implies embodying what is said, makes life what is proposed, experiences what is exercised.

It is a provocation to the educator's ontic structure, his DNA, his best version of himself.

It is not enough to list actions or list things that claim to be proven formulas of Salesian prevention. It is required to be a sign and bearer of each of the challenges listed. This is the only way I could speak of the preventive leader educator who is, knows, knows how to make, and knows how to coexist with the new reality of young generations (Table 41).

Table 41 New conceptualization of Preventive System according to the Preventive Leadership

	Today	Don Bosco	Educational Meaning
Conditions	Be Benevolent Loving-kindness Beneficient	*Amorevolezza*	Benevolence is what makes the leader very willing to be affectionate and to responsibly commit his person to others who are part of the educative process. The Preventive Leader becomes a friendly and spontaneous individual encounter activating humanizing and cordial interpersonal relationships. A leader whose own person is an atmosphere of respect and freedom to seek answers that open to transcendence and give the deepest meaning to life.
	Be reasonable	*Reason*	This criterion is defined as *justice* because the leader, as well as the learner, is subject to the norm. It is also *reasonableness* since everything that is required must be proportionate and possible. It is understood as *rationality* since the ultimate reason and the good for all decisions and demands must be evident.

			Motivation as the importance and validity of the educational process must be evident for the learners, and their active and conscious participation are required for their achievement.
	Be an educator with transcendent intent	Religion	Intentionality is nourished by the desire to go beyond what is required or assigned by a role. It seeks a communion of hearts, minds, goals, projects; it does not deny previous experience, but it does not stop solely on what has been given to it. The leader knows himself and is the embodiment of a deep interior life with a transcendent meaning.
	Be a person of reflection and self-awareness	Heart Citizenship Virtues	By consciously practicing the method of self-awareness, self-knowledge, and self-possession, he or she finds ways of human fulfillment by applying the cognitive and rational capacity in the experience of Love that is educational, fulfilling, and human. This means clarifying the objective of all the values of leadership: making the person someone who can exercise their autonomy ethically, attentive to their own internal movements, interacting with the context in which each individual develops, and being responsible for decisions that have been made showing self-appropriation between knowing and doing.

Criteria	Be the Salesian Oratorio anywhere, anytime	Oratory	The preventive leader becomes him or herself a *center* who is perceived as a person that welcomes because relationships are based on the educational benevolence. The *oratory criterion* is understood as the attitude of each Preventive Leader who is seeking a holistic promotion in being and doing. The educator with preventive features becomes a center and an *atmosphere* of humanity; personal attention, service, kind relationships, intellectual motivation, axiological reference in any activity, place, and event where he or she is present (university, parish, youth center, etc.)
	Be a builder of a family environment, in joy and trust	Assistance Presence Accompaniment	The key "operative" words of the method were familiarity, affection and trust. The deep friendship thrives and is born of the gestures and the desire for familiarity. In turn, familiarity breeds confidence, and confidence is everything in education because the only time it is possible to begin to educate is when the young confides his/her interiority. Spontaneous groups formed by shared interests are an essential and indispensable part of the Preventive Leadership proposal because they represent a valid instrument for sharing and collaboration.

Parameters	Be a promoter of integral and personal development	Community	A leader capable of proposing and accompanying an organic and articulated set of initiatives, interventions, and means aimed at jointly promoting the development of others in the work of their own maturation by activating their potential, their mind, heart, will, and opening them to transcendence with an intentionally educational presence.
	Be a promoter of an accompanying community	Goodwill Honesty	The leader listens, intervenes, arouses interest, welcomes proposals from different members of the community, and proposes activities that aim for an environment rich in humanizing initiatives and educational intent.
Educative Strategies	Be a constant presence with an active and focused accompaniment	Timely advice	Presence and availability for others as to be present and available for everything necessary, intervening in their integral maturation in any educational situation, particularly from the point of view of values, and to help the other to make free decisions.
	Be a generator of a pedagogy of possibility	Friendship Dialogue	The pedagogy of possibility is when one considers the complexity that life has within it and all the wealth of possible responses to diverse existential situations that it is intended to accompany with and in the group.

Social Parameters	Be a promoter of discernment	Family environment	Means to clarify the goal of all values of education: to make the person someone who can exercise their autonomy ethically, being attentive to their own motivations, interactions with the social environment in which each individual evolves, and be responsible for the decisions that have been taken.
	Be a promoter of a culture of encounter and dialogue	Dialogue Community	Dialogue involves balanced confrontation rather than silent acceptance, honest and timely debate rather than conformity. Dialogue demands respect and benevolence, closeness and the ability to listen. The Preventive leader is convinced that the other has something good to say, or has a different perspective to communicate, or a horizon of interpretation to enrich.
	Be supportive in solidarity	Compassion Charity	It is lived when the human being is aware of the mutual responsibility for others, especially those who need it. Solidarity is the ability to see people, very different from us, included in the "us" category.

There are preconditions for the linking, both the functional and voluntary, of anyone who wishes to form part of any educational presence with a preventive identity; I would suggest starting with six. These criteria are spontaneous in the personality of each potential preventive educator.

They are a kind of internal natural inclination of perceptivity and specific receptivity: Be benevolent (loving-kindness), be reasonable, be intentional, be a deep person, be a companion with and through the community, and be reflexive and critical thinker.

It seems to me that these criteria of natural adherence to the preventive proposal must be carefully intuited, read between the lines in the work of the one who intends to educate preventively, "scented" by the person who, at any level of decision-making, will be the one to generate a Salesian preventive atmosphere. The absence of one of these six criteria compromises the Salesian Preventive System.

These six criteria, referred to as the Salesian educational atmosphere of preventivity, are a *sine qua non* condition which is not possible to think of the educational proposal as Preventive. Each of these six criteria has a significant influence on the way of living and proposing the Preventive System. Each of these criteria has a decisive impact on the results of prevention as a criterion of life, criterion of action, and criterion of decision-making.

The aforementioned is affirmed because, in the daily praxis of experiencing the Preventive System, there is something natural in the way of doing things, as an essential element in resolution of any conflict, and as the password to face any circumstance. These conditions –Be benevolent (loving-kindness), be reasonable, be intentional, be a deep person, be a companion with and through the community, and be reflexive and critical thinker– become the DNA of the educational presence intentionally preventive of a Salesian environment.

Conditions

Be Benevolent (*amorevolezza*, *loving kindness*)

The true understanding and experience of Preventive Leadership lies in Love. Loving, like education, is an art. It implies a sense of reciprocity, benevolent empathy, and beneficial actions. The leading educator knows that as soon as he relates to others from his whole being, the capacity to love requires an emotional maturity that can only be achieved through self-appropriation as a result of self-knowledge. The educational leader with preventive traits, thanks to this routine exercise of self-appropriation, can reach the hearts of others with less effort. When the educator-student relationship is built on trust gained and cultivated in mature equilibrium, familiarity springs spontaneously, achieving maximum cooperation based on the conviction that the educational relationship only seeks the best in and for the person (Braido, 2001; Cian, 2001; Viganó, 1991).

This educational leadership combines the humility of those who know themselves as vulnerable, labile and fragile, with the professional will of those who seek to serve others well, serve them with dedication for the greater good, and serve them from and for the most positive version of themselves and the others to whom he or she devotes himself as an educator.

Leadership that seeks to live and act with benevolence (loving-kindness) becomes an art when it intertwines organizational values with the daily life of those who are active members of the institution. Art is achieved when the educational relationship reaches an acceptable level of human maturity in those who form and in those who are formed.

When in a continuous dialogue, the family environment that nurtures people, is built, this environment is then modified because people continually enrich it by seeking the most positive from each member of the educational community. The word *amorevolezza* (loving kindness) is not identical to Platonic or Straussian love, nor does it indicate some features of the *hesed* of the Bible or the theological virtue of charity in its closest expression to the Pauline *agapic* interpretation. The first and essential virtue of the educator is benevolence. It is "his loving educational goodness" (Braido, 2001, p. 320) which is an expression of Don Bosco's *Da mihi animas coetera tolle* (Give me souls, take away the rest). This virtue requires a real concern for the individual, for the "personality" of each of the members of the educational community and the level of development found in each of them.

The educator who "comes out from within the self and goes to meet the other" does so with the clear intention of valuing the life and history of others but respecting their process of personal maturation and leading them to achievable goals and paths of achievement. They should be humanizing. That is why it is necessary to suspend all judgment before knowing and to try to understand the "other" in depth.

The educator, according to Stella (1973), is honest with what he finds in the life and history of the members of the educational community, and also remains open to the novelty that each personal story has in itself. His educational love is human, and he seeks reciprocal humanization. He loves with and from what he is, considering the most complete expression of human fullness as the ultimate reference of his educational exercise of giving life.

The principle of promotion and acceptance of others from their current stage of individual development and humanization process in which they find themselves requires a type of understanding that is expressed in a benevolent empathetic attitude. Empathy, according to Cian (2001), means penetrating the "referenced and axiological framework" of the person to know and appreciate the characteristics of their being and the wealth that each person has from their historical moment and their horizon of interpretation. Empathy goes beyond "putting yourself in the other's shoes." This is existentially impossible and emotionally it has very little benefit. Empathy intentionally goes to the center of the person, to his heart.

Empathy looks at the deep motivations that make the world see from where he or she interprets it and tries to decode the person's mental frameworks to accompany and be accompanied in the process of personal growth. Empathy is an expression of human love that vibrates, understands, welcomes, accepts, values the personal situation of the other and does not stop there. It moves him to seek to achieve the best version of the other and of himself using the resources that the person has at that point (considering the moment of psychological, emotional, spiritual development, etc.).

For Goleman (2016), empathy is not just a feeling for others, it is the confluence between rational decisions and growth processes, trying to ensure that whoever pretends to be empathetic should be aware of other people's emotions and the possible affectations to others for the decisions made by the person who must make those decisions.

Empathy is the foundational ability, according to Goleman (2016), of all social skills that allow teamwork and goal achievement. It is an empathy that proposes specific models of achievement for those who are being educated.

Empathy makes it easier for the teacher to relate to the "deep and positive being" of the student. Empathic understanding fearlessly faces the change, both in educator and in learner, that brings about freedom of proximity with the learner without generic judgments of moral values or degrading statements that minimize the experience of the other.

The empathic relationship favors openness towards the other and tries to obtain, with well-weighed decisions, the best for them in educational resources, leadership skills, and social capital. It is a cognitive empathy that allows you to feel how other people think about the world, which means that you can contribute what you possess in terms that others will understand because it is the ability to understand the perspective of others. It is an emotional empathy whereby you instantly resonate with what the other person is feeling. It is the ability to experience in yourself what others feel. Empathic interest is when you express the ways in which you will take care of the person helping` with what you feel and what he or she needs. It is the ability to feel what the other person needs from you (Fig. 35) (Goleman & Senge, 2016).

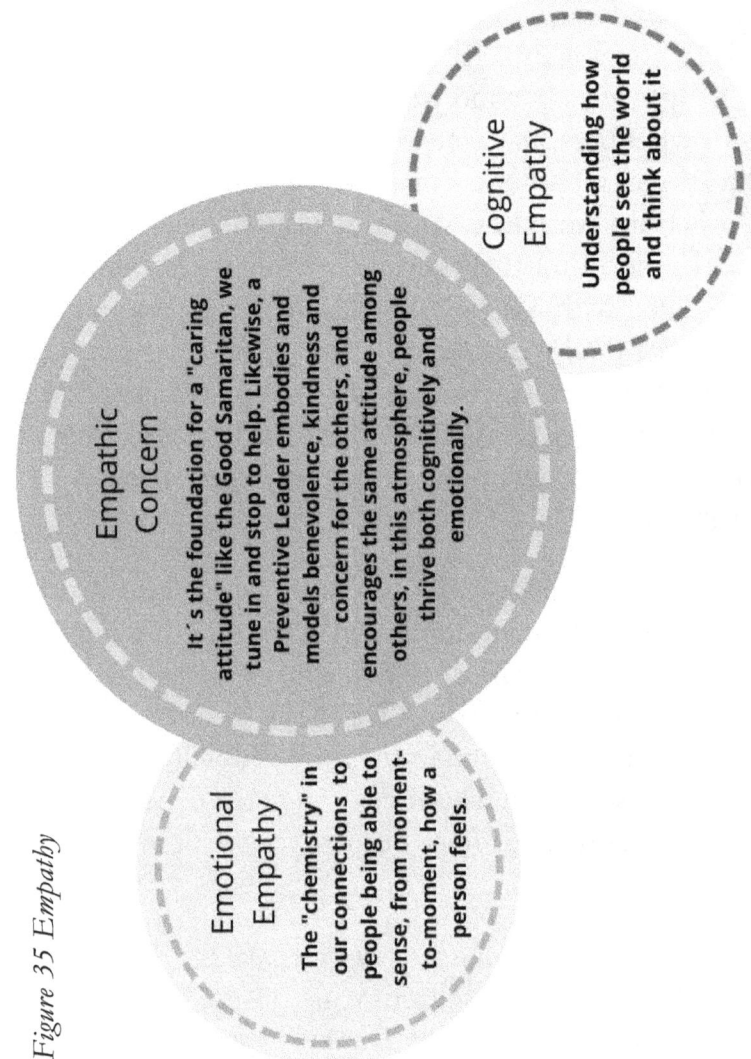

Figure 35 Empathy

Educational benevolence (loving-kindness) is what cultivates in the educator a deep availability to be affected by others and to be affectionate with others and to offer the best that his deep self-possesses to others who are part of the educational process. That same benevolence (*loving-educational-kindness*) is what makes the educator's presence alive, cordial, competent, continuous, and significant (Cian, 2001; Vecchi, 1997a; Viganó, 1993). This means that being among young people goes beyond what the employment contract requires or what personal time allows. Being among them is not an educational technique, it is a movement of the heart that loves, it is born from love with traits of balanced and harmonious fatherhood-motherhood, it is being with them because they are loved with a benevolent educational love, embodied expression of the love received existentially in gratuitousness and prior to any rational option, it is the love received, and for a believer, by a God who is love and mercy. Saint John Bosco expressed this same sentiment in his *Introduzione all Giovane Provveduto*:

> Dear young people, I love you all with all my heart, and it is enough for me that you are young for me to love you extraordinarily. I assure you that you will find books written for you by people who are much more virtuous and wise than me, but you will hardly be able to find someone who loves you more than I do in Jesus Christ and who most desires your true happiness (p. 8).

Educational benevolence (*loving-kindness*), according to Cian (2001), means "transparent trust on the part of the educator with the ability to stand by the young person to make him/her a collaborator, a responsible animator" of his/her life and in solidarity with the dynamics of those who share interests and projects (p. 45).

Whoever acts as the bearer of the values he proposes becomes a role model who arouses admiration when present and close to the learner. Cian (2001) says that "identification encourages assimilation, generally not through rationality, but through the values that the educator lives as a model and that these values become, naturally, part of the way of seeing and evaluating [the learner]" (p. 157).

The educational experience reports that values such as honesty, solidarity, respect, compassion, etc. support clear in cognitive and metacognitive learning processes (value weeks, bulletin board and public announcements, campaigns and awareness-raising exercises), but it is not enough. The emotional part, the aspect of seeing them embodied in others, makes the experience of assimilation of values more effective and holds longer-term effects if it is through a process that touches the experiential and that it be modeled by whoever proposes it. This educational benevolence (*loving-kindness*) itself expresses one's sympathy, one's affection, understanding, wanting to share deep life with the other. An educator-expert who is humanely balanced and integrated is benevolent and capable of a generous disposition for meeting with the other as a spontaneous movement of genuine promotional interest.

He/she is an educator who wisely promote solidarity between peers, coworkers, and stakeholders to better support learners' personal life projects (Table 42).

Table 42 First non-negotiable condition in Preventive Leadership®

Benevolence *Loving-kindness*	It implies a sense of reciprocity, benevolent empathy, and beneficial actions. It is born out of genuine and deep love for people. It is real when the leader adopts organizational values and radiates them in daily actions to those within the organization. It is verifiable when leaders perform benevolent and beneficial activities for the good of people, outside of the schedule and beyond organizational chart positions.

Educational loving kindness is the expression of mutual benevolence (both parties want the mutual good), which is understood as trust, esteem, integrity, appreciation of the other, willingness to want to take the risk in favor of, like a trait embedded in the DNA of a person who seeks the maximum achievement and well-being of the other. They are also advancing on the path of improvement. It is a force that unites despite the differences, that moves to want the good of another despite not presenting traits or aptitudes *a priori* that they do it kindly (Aquino, 1994, II-II, q. 25, a. 3, in c.; Schoorman, Mayer, & Davis, 2007). Benevolence promotes and recognizes the differences of the other and the unique personal reality, the individuality (Cortés Pacheco, 2016). This implication of benevolence manifests itself as reciprocal close friendship and support in the decisive moments of life. It is also an instrument through which educational love is translated into charitable action: timely and sincere appreciation, honest and transparent personal encounter, mutual trust, family spirit that facilitates understanding and coexistence, optimism and joy (PVSDB, p. 232). In his famous Letter of Rome (1884), Saint John Bosco writes:

> What he should do to break this barrier between superiors and students? With familiarity. Familiarity with young people especially on the playground. The teacher who is only seen at the conference is a teacher and nothing else, but if he participates in recess, he becomes a brother (p. 261-269).

According to Rodríguez and Sánchez Tapia (2020), family structure means many things; a single parent home, extended family, a family with no children, stepchildren, etc. Each family has a set of values that constitute its *nucleus* (love, security, a sense of belonging, nutrition, mutual care, growth, respect, joy, trust, patience, freedom, limits and roles, feedback and honest dialogue, etc.). In the Preventive System, a *family nucleus* is what inspires and fosters an educational environment that is transformed intentionally into a "family environment." A family environment places the educator and the students on even ground, which allows a socioemotional experience nurturing both of them with hope, gives them confidence in the good that others possess within them, and mutual trust is established. In a family environment the most genuine desires arise: the hearts are connected, dreams are supported, and educator and student are united in expectations of a better quality of life.

"Family environment" is an educational experience that generates a sense of belonging, a sense of family relationship, a sense of home, a sense of genuine friendships, a sense of gratitude and transcendence, and a feeling of life fulfilled in benevolence and loving kindness.

A Preventive Leader is whom with preventiveness his DNA is capable of create an atmosphere of family that generates ties of belonging where the orphan finds a family, where is possible a sense of home for those who feel homeless, where friendship happens for those who feel lonely, where the heaven could be touched for those who are open to transcendence, and where the heart of the human being is fulfilled benevolence and loving kindness.

Be reasonable

Speaking from the Salesian point of view, the concept of *reason* has several levels of meaning, and they all converge. Reason is understood as justice, as reasonableness or measure, as rationality and as motivation (Table 43).

Table 43 Second non-negotiable condition in Preventive Leadership®

Reason	It is the foundation of every expression of benevolence and beneficence.
	It means trust, understanding, deep motivation, where mutual knowledge is built.
	It makes a person aware of his own identity and responds to the other person's individuality.
	It is a criterion of life that allows us to intuit the best and to decide in search of the common good.
	It is a motivational not just an emotional intervention.
	It is dialogue that allows understanding the perspective of others and facilitates conflict resolution.

Reason is understood as justice when, for both parties, external criteria and goals are used, seeking to facilitate the achievement of objectives, ordered coexistence and preventive training against any situation that could give rise to experiences of injustice. An example in Don Bosco's practice is the generation and continued use of the Regulations. Writing certain regulations and requesting that they be followed by all, generated spaces for coexistence, avoided emotional decisions that could be unfair, and formed habits and virtues in their observance more as norms. These norms appeal to the conscience of the individual rather than punitive norms and constricting character for a group. *The regulations of the Oratory of Saint Francis de Sales* for resident students such as the Regulations for the houses of the Society of San Francis de Sales, according to Lenti (2011, Volume II) "Establish the environment in which the educational work, such as Don Bosco understood and practiced it, was going to be put into practice." (p. 77)

Don Bosco used the *Regulations* in his schools, boarding schools and oratories as necessary elements and as a tool for experiencing justice. These regulations were an expression of this aspect of Salesian reason: the safeguarding of decisions motivated for the greater good of the people. Currently, the codes of conduct, and the protocols of preventive intervention assess the Salesian educational experience. They try to promote the person to their best version of themselves.

Reason is understood as the use of *reasonableness,* or measure when its use seeks to recover the categories of critical judgment, metacognition, conscious-knowledge of personal and community conditioning, areas of growth, spaces of humanization in accordance with the demands at the time, qualities, personality, history of who is involved in the training proposal.

According to Lonergan (1992), in the continued use of self-appropriation, self-awareness, judgment and decision, responsibility, respect, are all present to enable reasonableness in the interpersonal relationships, assimilating knowledge, and feelings in the decision for a greater good.

Lonergan (1992) traced the transformation of experience into understanding through discernment, and the judgment that asks whether perception from experience approaches or distances it from truth. The same author incorporated this knowledge structure into a broader decision structure, which includes determining the value of alternative courses of action and committing to give life to the most valuable alternative with the individual's internal consistency in his being and doing.

It is a *reason understood as rationality* when it facilitates the process of self-awareness in the educator and in the student, and this leads to winning the heart of the learner, because external stimuli, results of personal and community effort, are perceived as reasonable. The demands of all educational actions are translated into expressions of reasonableness because they arise from the educational intentionality that knows the moment in which the other is and proposes everything and only what he is capable of achieving at that moment. Unreachable achievements are not requested. Although apparently optimal, the possible is requested, not more nor less. This requires a deep knowledge of the other and an authentic benevolent educational love.

Reason understood as motivation allows us to perceive the vital experience of mutual trust and deep friendship, and as a result, the level of consciousness that requires the validity of living and working together in shared projects stands out, which is an effective introduction to a humanizing socialization (Vygotsky, 1987; Viganó, 1991; Vecchi, 1997b; Braido, 2001; Cian, 2001).

According to Eccles and Wigfield's (2002) expectation-value theory, a person chooses to take on a challenging task if the person (1) values the task and (2) hopes that they can succeed in the task based on their own beliefs. Beliefs about self and beliefs about the value of the task are important in predicting choice, persistence, and achievement. In addition, task values can play an important role in developing interest. According to the theory of interest, the fact of being interested in an activity motivates us to continue the activity as much as possible (Hidi & Renninger, 2006). Interest can be triggered by interventions that emphasize the value of a task, and then develop as the individual experiences positive feelings and comes to value that activity even more.

Well-developed interests can motivate continued engagement with the activity. Hence, in Don Bosco's praxis and Salesian tradition, reason as motivation looks at investing in an organizational culture that provides purposes and responds to the reasons for actions, plans, decisions. The motivation that springs from the depths of those who educate and know that they are preventive leaders is because they feel satisfied with all the factors that affect the achievement of the ultimate goals of what is done. A motivation to propose to others that the value of the action lies in the continuous construction of the person and his achievements (perhaps small, but proper to oneself in the end), and not in the results only (Harvard Business Review, 2016).

The Preventive System is a pedagogy of possibility and freedom that is based on the strength of interpersonal relationships, and that gives due value to the affective component (Chiosso, 2014). The Preventive System is radically different to a pedagogy of authority, that presupposes a distance between teachers and students, that is based more on impersonal rules than on living relationships.

There is a big difference between the talented educator who is able to translate the great principles of the system in creative ways into everyday life. The one who lowers everything to the minimum standards is constantly tempted to hide his own insecurity by breaching the rules, norms, and standard behavior. To be reasonable is to be deeply human, in all aspects of life.

Be an educator with transcendent intent

Transcendent intentionality as a conscious operation is nourished by the desire to go beyond what is required or assigned by a role, it seeks a communion of hearts and minds, objectives, goals that *verticalize* the educational work that tends to *horizontalize*. Transcendent intentionality does not deny previous experience, but it does not stop at what has been given, it seeks more, deeper, broader, clearer without violating the interiority or consciousness of the other.

Intentionality means leaving the self, because the self is already self-appropriation. Intentionality is an expression of love for the person: the self and the "other."

The educator with traits of preventive leadership knows himself to be an incarnation of a deep and spiritual life with a transcendent meaning because he/she intentionally knows that only in opening to Love does he/she find the path to human fulfillment. Love can do everything, everything good awaits it, endures it, believes it, because he/she educates from the heart (Lonergan, 1992; Rodríguez, 2007).

For Don Bosco, religion is a multipurpose and educational concept: it establishes a context of life and is expressed in practices suitable to support the educational and moral effort.

It is also an educational strategy that directs and shapes the way of thinking and acting: constant reflection on life and death, the futile and the valuable, the essential of the accidental as realities embedded in the evolution of the human being; the exercise for a good death that monthly generated an evaluation of one's existence in its fragility and constant recovery of the sense of the spiritual and transcendent; for Don Bosco the *word in the ear* (timely advice) makes the educator an attentive companion of the student and allows him timely, personal, and positive feedback; spontaneous but intentional personal talks that individualize the educational experience and drive personal growth; the guiding thoughts daily (Don Bosco's "good nights") as a family moment of group attention to issues of educational and pastoral interest, where the closing message of the day has a greater impact on the deep psyche and achieves good results if there is positive reinforcement due to a climate of deep and spiritual life (Lenti, 2011).

Deep life is the hidden sustenance of the entire Preventive System (Rodriguez 2020). Deep life is the center of the person and the sanctuary of maximum transcendence. Don Bosco knew this and appealed to the elements that his being a Catholic priest and educator confirmed to him: frequent confession, constant Communion, spiritual accompaniment, group meetings, and inner life nourished in community life. For Don Bosco as educator, all this meant to educate the mind and heart, to be good Christians and to be upright citizens.

The educational process is intentional when its focus includes details, the bigger picture, and the in-between, but always in continuity with the demands of the person's being and the difficulties inherent in life.

Life is a force of fulfillment even when it is not free of contradictions, even when it is oppressed and seems ruined by the environment or negative experiences. The main task, and the art of the educator, is to think the content of his teaching from the integral point of view. It is to put all the resources at the service of the individual in the processes of formation and personal growth in each educational action, in each pastoral activity, and at each moment of leisure (Table 44).

Table 44 Third non-negotiable condition in the preventive leader educator

Transcendent intentionality	It is described as an aspiration for openness to the Other, which is a mixture of reason, hope, optimism, and interiority. Transcendence for a comprehensive educational intention. A strongly unifying personal life project. A deep interior life which is the fruit and life experience of Don Bosco's motto *Da mihi animas coetera tolle* (Give me souls, take away the rest).

Any educational proposal cannot focus solely on an area of technical or social competence or ability, but on the promotion and development of the whole person, from the discipline that is taught or the daily routine in which it is found.

It is to think of the human being as a whole (Viganó, 1993). The ultimate intention of the educational process is full development: biological, psychological, physical, intellectual, moral, social, spiritual, and emotional. An educational proposal that seeks integrity is present when the methodology used is one that activates a set of organic interventions (family environment) appropriate to involve the learner in his or her most significant potential (mind, heart, will, faith) and when an educator-expert is present seeking the best of and for those involved in the process. Therefore, educating intentionally means participating with paternal/ maternal love in the growth of the human subject, being interested in collaborating with others, and forming an educational relationship. In fact, it involves a collective effort with different organizations that work for the same objective: the full development of youth (Viganó, 1991). Lenti (2011) places similar intuitions from prevention:

> At a basic level [...] it is a strategy designed to provide support to young people in their personal problems, to help them face the difficulties and temptations that come their way as individuals and as Christians in a constructive way. At a second level [...] it aims to define and control the risk faced by young people, so that they can be rescued or can at least avoid being in high-risk situations (p. 91).

The educator knows himself as an incarnation of deep and spiritual life with a transcendent meaning because he/she understands that this level of internalization is an important component for the level of individual preparation that guarantees full personal development. He or she is also a fundamental motivational part in guiding an individual's life project.

One's deep life and transcendent openness are a necessary condition for those who want to get involved in the Salesian educational proposal. Experience suggests that those who show greater sensitivity to learn and live this essential element to every human being are the most likely to seek and generate events that stimulate and nurture their inner life and spirituality as part of their own development from the perspective of a founding element to improve their effectiveness and efficiency in leadership (Avolio, Walumbwa and Weber, 2009; Fry, 2003).

Be a person of reflection and self-awareness

Being a preventive educational leader requires showing that he/she is willing to be accompanied, perhaps re-educated and trained by educator-experts in preventive leadership. An educational leader needs to learn to practice the method of conscious self-knowledge and self-possession. Preventive leaders as educators sooner or later must accompany in a personal process of human fulfillment through the use of rational, affective, cognitive, emotional capacities. The preventive leader must be trained so that, by enriching the expressions of educational love in his being and his daily tasks, he/she can build and help others to elaborate personal meanings with social impact. It is convenient for the educator with preventive leadership traits, to be competent in their area of expertise. It is also necessary for them to be sensitive to accompaniment in Preventive Leadership training. The expectations of a Preventive leader educator, open to the action of founding Love, dispose him/her to the Transcendence and existential commitments that derive from this opening, and are best achieved by taking on a strongly unified personal life project. According to the General Chapter 23 of the Salesians of Don Bosco (GC 23), the reflective and self-conscious leader shows that:

> Loving a life that is not fragmented, but projects itself as a vocation, means accepting the call to work as builders of humanity, justice and peace [...] Loving life in all its depth, [it means being] open to culture and ideals, to sharing and being understanding, being capable of the courage to dream new worlds, new men [and women] (para. 164).

Rodríguez and Rodríguez (2015) presented a model that examines two specific ways in which leaders can influence the way followers decide to behave in terms of the motivations that they use to regulate actions/behaviors. The first way of influencing is related to values. The cited authors emphasize building on specific and intentionally proposed values so that the person being trained is motivated to conscious and deliberate action. The second way of influencing is related to the self-concept of who is forming preventive leaders. Supported by the concept of self, the preventive leaders favor a specific identity by proposing a kind of common criteria. It is preventive criteria, the mental model, the internal structure, the guarantee of an experience of Salesian Prevention in an educational leader. Both values and self-concept are considered mediators of the link between the interchangeable actions of the leader and the behaviors of the followers.

The idea of a self-concept that works as an appropriation of a preventive criteriology refers to the agreement that results from the reflective process and self-appropriation at the moment in which the person asks questions that question their being, their decision, their projects, and their deep motivations. One of the essential components of leadership is the idea of a mental-emotional schema that, acting as a broad framework of organization, more personal than organizational, helps the person understand and make sense of a given context or experience.

Criteria

"Be the Salesian Oratory, Be a builder of family environment" are the criteria and standards by which something done can be judged or decided. Criteria are the mental structures through which Salesian Preventive Leaders understand, analyze, evaluate, and act. The objective of these criteria is the assimilation and the application to each situation faced. These criteria are the new DNA implanted in each cell, each judgment, each breath, each perspiration, and each action taken by the preventive leader educator.

Be the Salesian Oratory anywhere, anytime

The educational environment is born from the oratorian criteria and the family spirit. The oratorian criterion is the basis, the guide, the renewal reference of all the structures, organizations, proposals and personnel identify with the educational model, philosophy, principles, and Salesian strategies. The Special General Chapter of the Salesians of Don Bosco in 1971, clearly indicated the enduring criterion for the renewal of Salesian action:

> Don Bosco in the oratory is the ideal criterion [...] faithful, dynamic, creative and docile, firm and flexible at the same time, he continues to be a role model for all [...] The return to

> Don Bosco's Oratory is, therefore, a postulated not a priori, or a brilliant idea, it is rather an act of dynamic fidelity to the original mission...Guess the formula of homogeneous development, find the operational options that require the loyalty of the Salesian mission, know what Don Bosco would do today[...] we know of no other method than the lay of the land in the Oratory, where his ministry is exemplary, [it] germinates and grows (para. 192-273).

The most important normative document of the Salesians of Don Bosco, their Constitutions, declares in its article 40: "the experience of *Valdocco* [the Oratory]continues to be the enduring criterion for discernment and renewal in all our activities and works" (Salesians of Don Bosco, 2009). Cleary, it is not about looking at the first Oratory (Valdocco) as a single concrete work, but rather about considering it "as the matrix, the synthesis, the sum total of all the great apostolic creations of our Founder, the ripe fruit of all their efforts" (PVSDB, p. 381).

To form the criteria of the mind and heart of the educator-expert in the rich experience of the Don Bosco Oratory is to train those who will know how to decide and act with preventive criteria at the moments when they assume the role of a preventive leader in the midst of others. To form the *oratorian criterion* is to form the feelings of the educator-expert, who looks for the sheep, who cares for the needy, who is empathetic with the historical-personal moment of the other, who is capable of giving his own life for the good of those entrusted to it because it is a greater good. And, furthermore, a life without continuous self-sacrifice is a life without meaning.

The Fundamental Frame of Reference of Salesian Youth Ministry (2016) states that an educator who brings the experience of Valdocco's Oratory closer to the boys and girls today, must engage them with for dimensions:

1. The family climate, establishing the necessary mediations so that every young person grows up in a cozy and familiar environment ("home"),
2. A spontaneous and joyfully encounter with friends ("playground");
3. An educative environment to develop all the students´ potentials, new knowledge, skills and competencies for life ("school") and,
4. An experience of faith as vital adhesion to God ("parish").

If the educator achieves the perfect symbiosis between something external to him —Salesian oratory— with his own person, we then have the Salesian preventive leader. We have the educator who, like Don Bosco, affirms that he or she is the Salesian oratory for today's youth. Since, as Don Bosco understood himself as the oratory, so today the oratory is you, the preventive leader. The most amazing thing is that it is possible to transmit this way of living and understanding each or other to the youngest. The sheep become Shepherds... ***the 9-year-old dream is still valid and compelling***[2].

The *oratorian criterion* is understood as the attitude of each Preventive Leader who is seeking a holistic promotion in being and doing. The leading educator with preventive features becomes a center of humanity; personal attention, service, kind relationships, intellectual motivation, axiological reference in any activity, place, and event where he or she is present (school, university, parish, youth center , etc.) The Preventive Leader is that educator whom young people per-

---

[2] The complete version of Don Bosco´s Dream at Nine Years of Age can be retrieve from http://www.sdb.org.hk/dbway/source/article/article/Teresio%20Bosco-DB-Biography.pdf

ceive as one who values interpersonal relationships and promotes them.

Relationships are based on educational benevolence (*loving kindness*). The Preventive Leader intentionally proposes a pedagogy of possibility that generates and transmits culture, transmits faith, transmits experience, transmits deep life and experiences of spirit (Fig. 36).

Figure 36 Be the Salesian Oratory

The professional formation of the educator requires the vocation to internalize the Salesian oratory until it becomes a criterion for life and action and they themselves become a Salesian Oratory. Essentially, this means a friendly individual who seeks personal encounters and humanized relationships, an educator who turns himself or herself into an atmosphere of respect and of freedom to seek answers that open the transcendence and give a deeper meaning to existence.

A leader, with a strong sense of life and methods, helps achieve the personal goals for which he or she feels responsible. This *Oratorian criterion* imprints an identity in the process of internal knowledge and self-understanding of individuals, while at the same time being an essential reference for any situation involving decisions, policies, or organizational structures in any educational environment.

This environment called Oratory is not a specific educational structure, but an atmosphere and an internalized criterion that must characterize each educational space, each proposal, and each person (Oratorian heart, typically Salesian pedagogical method, fundamental criterion for the discernment and renewal of any activity and work). General Chapter 23 considered that such an atmosphere is based on relationships which in turn are based on trust and family spirit, on joy and celebration that are accompanied by hard work and the fulfillment of duties. The Salesian family atmosphere is imbued with friendship and authentic relationships that seek a friendly educational proximity and is rich in meaningful activities, relationships open to sincere and frank friendship, and interpersonal relationships in search of bringing out the best in oneself and others.

This environment is the external part of the self-awareness process that arises from a deep level of interiority, generating a healthy organizational culture, an environment rich in experiences with a strong existential charge. The Preventive System requires an environment of intense participation and friendly interpersonal relationships, an atmosphere of respect and openness, optimism and joy. A Salesian Oratory was devised by Don Bosco, was lived by him daily and was consciously assumed to the extent that **Don Bosco is the Oratory.**

Adult educators play an important role from the point of view of active and supportive animation. Their wisdom, experience, and intentional presence are fundamental factors in achieving and maintaining this atmosphere and criteriology at the same time. And yet, educators must accommodate the most diverse forms of youth association, so that through small community commitments they prepare for broader forms of civic participation.

In Don Bosco, it was the *Companies* (organized groups) that crystallized his intuition that young people seek the presence of peers to achieve joint goals. Today, those same groups are made up of shared interests: clubs, associations, teams, both physical and virtual (Braido, 2001; Cian, 2001; Viganó, 1991; 1993).

Be a builder of a family environment, in confidence and joy

The basic elements that make up a family nucleus are love, nutrition, care, growth, respect, joy, trust, donation, patience, and freedom. Experience says that one way to achieve a better personalization process is to create an atmosphere of familiarity, a relational environment where the factors that support the *family nucleus* are lived by each of the members that make up the *family nucleus* experience as second nature.

In the letter to the Salesians of Valdocco on May 10, 1884, Don Lemoyne, Don Bosco's first biographer, interpreted Saint John Bosco's idea of familiarity and the atmosphere of trust by affirming that love is the basis of an educational proposal:

> Be a friendly informal relationship with children, especially in recreation. You cannot have love without this familiarity, and where this is not evident there can be no trust. If you want to be loved, you must make it

clear that you love [...] Someone who knows that he is loved, loves in return, and *he/she* who is loved can obtain anything, especially from the young (Braido, Da Silva Ferreira, Motto and Prellezo , 1992: 365-374).

This educational loving-kindness will be persuasive to the extent that those who are loved feel "loved in the things they like, participating with them in their desires" (Braido et al., 1992: 382-385). Benevolent educational love must be reciprocal and share in freedom of expression. It cannot be a love that suffocates or is omnipresent to the degree of destroying what it claims to protect (*helicopter* parents effect, suffocating overprotection, etc.). Respect for the person is essential to allow the achievement of their best possibilities in the rhythm and the way that best suits their individuality. Confidence is expression of the internal resources of the goodness of the human being searching for the best. Confidence is the passion of being a subject of benevolent fulfillment. Confidence is the understanding that benevolent love is a gift received. Confidence and joy are lived in an imperfect world but called to make it better through the force of that same educative love.

A friendly informal relationship that arouses proximity and openness will facilitate the disposition to share with a freedom. According to Lenti (2007-2008), Don Bosco based his educational method on an affectionate relationship between the educator and the student that can be found in a family environment, the *operative* keywords of the Salesian method are familiarity, benevolence, and trust. Familiarity breeds trust, and trust permeates everything in Salesian education. The Salesian preventive leader must live up to those moments with integrity of his person, with a coherent experience of the values that he/she claims to live by, and with procedures that ensure a safe environment of those who are younger than he or she. There are moments when this familiarity achieves its zenith: gatherings, camps, retreats, excursions, etc. The responsibility to take care of those who participate, guaranteeing humanly the absence of risks, is a Salesian preventive requirement.

One of the parameters determining the family environment as preventive is the joy. It is experienced by each person and expressed in personal commitment to strengthen and improve the same atmosphere. When friendship is an experience of sharing time and life in a healthy and harmonious coexistence, the natural feeling that flows through each member is joy. Joy is also an expression benevolence. It is a logical consequence of interpersonal relationships based on reason and openness to transcendence (Salesians, 1996; Bosco, 1988, Vol. II, p. 186).

The joy, displayed spontaneously and in the most varied forms of expression, becomes a diagnosis of the level of Salesian atmosphere for both educators and members of the educational community. The educator has an invaluable source to understand personalities in the spontaneity of the joyous family life of the students. The educator has an opportunity to contact young people individually in confidence as an expression of a personalized and spontaneous dialogue. It challenges to the educator to desire the greater good for the young. Examples of this spontaneous shared joy would be the conversations that happen on the playground, in social settings, in the hallways, at recess, or between activities. These spontaneous, cordial, and direct interactions contribute to the creation of caring and safe protocols that incorporate the presence of the educator in various settings.

In the Letter of Rome (1884), Don Bosco affirms:

The teacher who sees himself alone in the classroom is a teacher and nothing else; but if he joins the recreation of the students, he becomes their brother. If someone is only seen preaching from the pulpit, it will be said that he is doing nothing more or less than his duty, while if he says a good word in the recreation, it is heard as the word of someone who loves.

Parameters

Salesian parameters help define, clarify, prioritize, or evaluate the level of commitment of the work team and mission in the objectives, mission, vision, and, especially, institutional values. For the Salesian Preventive Leadership, the basic parameters are being a promoter of integral and personal development and being a promoter of a community that accompanies people.

These challenges are elements present in every situation where an individual must give an answer based on his own frame of reference (fruit of loving kindness), on the particular axiological system, on individual criteria for decision-making, on his own experience and wisdom fruit of his solid interior life. Both parameters are useful and critical to identify, intervene or evaluate the performance and enrichment of the educational atmosphere in the Salesian environment.

Be a promoter of integral and personal development

An organic and articulated set of initiatives, interventions, and means aimed at jointly promoting the development of young people in their own maturation is foreshadowed by activating appropriate interventions to involve their most significant potential, their minds, hearts, wills, and to open a door to transcendence for them, with a collaborative, connected, creative presence by those who serve as educational leaders.

Education from the heart requires the intentionally active, effective and efficient presence of educators to become mediators of the encounters of the learners with their physical, social, spiritual, and relational worlds. Being a promoter of this education that looks through the decision center (heart) requires that educators be expert facilitators in the interpretations and re-conceptualizations in the process that learners will build in shaping a life project.

Being a promoter of effective and efficient integral development requires social and emotional competences to educate from the full conviction that the learner can, and must, possess the perception of his own personal identity and his own potentials. Any itinerary of human growth requires that self-perception and self-awareness be recognized, supported, and intensified by a person with a certain level of visionariness and expertise who has consciously sought the best possible version of himself, avoiding unrealistic or projective goals based on the aspirations of the other and do not spring up or are not sustained by their own aspirations (Braido, 2001; Cian, 2001; Lonergan, 1992).

The preventive leader, as promoter of effective and efficient integral development, requires a high degree of mature and realistic optimism.

Every person aspires to something better, although sometimes the ongoing formation leads to new horizons of interpretation of what is considered the best. A kindergarten child does not perceive the best in the same way that a university student does. In fact, Don Bosco affirmed:

"In all young people [...] there is an accessible *attribute* for good, and the educator's first duty is to find this *attribute*, [access] this sensitive chord of the heart and bring out the best in them to make the person entrusted to the educator a better person "(MB V, p. 367; Braido, 2001).

Therefore, it is essential that all educational actions intentionally awaken and mobilize young people in the values and the virtues that are reasonably possible to them (second and fourth meaning of the concept of reason).

Any intentional educational action helps the preventive educator leader to look for an integral development of students. The use of deep knowledge of himself offers the appropriate and conscious affective heritage, benevolence, and interior life as a path to any the others to transcendence themselves. The educator promotes a comprehensive and personal development that is a mixture of reason, hope, optimism and interiority (Braido, 2001).

An educational approach with this type of argumentative basis maintains that education cannot be reduced to mere methodology, to only business quality criteria, nor to standardized measurement parameters. Educational action is vitally linked to the evolution of the subject and the community. From the preventive leadership perspective, educators are invited to develop a kind of educational paternity/maternity, is an intentional expression of education.

As an educator he/she seeks for a human co-generation of values such as: truth, freedom, love, work, justice, solidarity, participation, dignity of the life, common good, and rights. (Viganó, 1991)

Be a promoter of an accompanying community

An educational community is one that is lived as a daily lifestyle and not only as an organizational model of coexistence. According to Braido (2001), a community as a lifestyle leads each and every one of its members to commit themselves, to listen to each other, to intervene for the common good, to show interest for the common good, and to welcome new proposals for intervention that aim for an environment rich in educational initiatives.

The presence of an educational community made up of professionals, educators, and leaders trained in prevention guarantees an efficient accompaniment and learning process for students. The accompaniment understood as a set of elements that support the integral maturation of the members of the community. Salesian accompaniment is a kind of gestation, birth, growth and consolidation of a personal life project due to "a family environment, the presence of assistance, activities participatory, timely personal word, brief group exhortations, joint celebrations "(GC 23, para. 285). A Salesian accompaniment involves a caring and intentionally educational community where each member is an active and benevolent participant among young people. Each member of the community seeks to facilitate the personal knowledge of the other as a result of contact with the vital environment and the most personal nucleus (thoughts, feelings, desires, fears, dreams) in which the community develops and lives. (Chen & Kuo, 2019)

An intentionally educational community lives a style of educational presence that is not so concerned with defending themselves from constant change, from new languages, from possible fears of taking risks and making mistakes. But instead, it is a community that proposes, stimulates, generates growth, and encourages the person to become what he/she is, what he/she is called to be according to their own life project and the options within their own personal life (CG 23, para. 201; Cian, 2001).

Human limitations (selfish motives) should be reduced by a community of educators aware of a preventive leadership that encourages students to be the best for society and educate from and for the positive. The desire for power is a subtle control. Therefore, the constant presence, the values assumed and proposed, the rectitude of intention and the clarity in the ultimate intention of all educational action are factors that improve a positive impact of any organizational dynamics (Fig. 37).

Figure 37 Learning Community

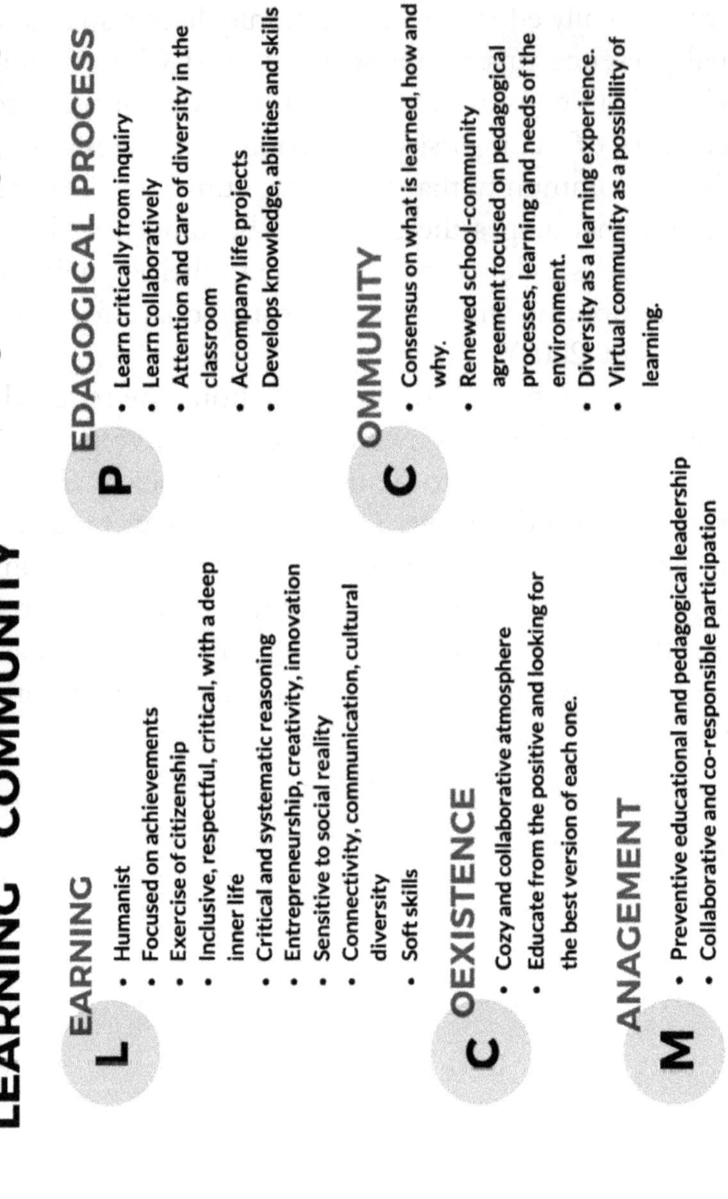

LEARNING COMMUNITY

L EARNING
- Humanist
- Focused on achievements
- Exercise of citizenship
- Inclusive, respectful, critical, with a deep inner life
- Critical and systematic reasoning
- Entrepreneurship, creativity, innovation
- Sensitive to social reality
- Connectivity, communication, cultural diversity
- Soft skills

P EDAGOGICAL PROCESS
- Learn critically from inquiry
- Learn collaboratively
- Attention and care of diversity in the classroom
- Accompany life projects
- Develops knowledge, abilities and skills

C OMMUNITY
- Consensus on what is learned, how and why.
- Renewed school-community agreement focused on pedagogical processes, learning and needs of the environment.
- Diversity as a learning experience.
- Virtual community as a possibility of learning.

C OEXISTENCE
- Cozy and collaborative atmosphere
- Educate from the positive and looking for the best version of each one.

M ANAGEMENT
- Preventive educational and pedagogical leadership
- Collaborative and co-responsible participation
- Continuous assessment
- Salesian Preventive Identity

Educational interaction should be considered as an individual interpersonal relationship and as an intentional community with the desire to facilitate the maturation of the person. This type of interaction is not easy to implement by those who understand the relationship in terms of a role, but it is not difficult for those who experience educational interaction as a "presence-assistance" experienced as vital for the good of the other. This presence-assistance gradually pays attention to others, in communication with the educator, in respect for autonomy and personal growth. An educator assists students with benevolent care and paternal/maternal traits as a conscious assimilation of the necessary family environment that said presence-assistance requires because one wants to be present.

Educational strategies in accompaniment

In the Salesian context, a strategy is a duty for the educator, not only a way to intervene intermittently or when deemed necessary. A preventive leader educator understands and lives these strategies as part of his personal spirit, as a manual of procedures established in the cerebral amygdala. It is a metacognitive competence implanted in the value and decision making system: the Salesian leader decides and acts because prevention is part of his DNA. The educator lives and influences intentionally educational all the time, any situation, anywhere.

Educational strategies are practical interventions open to constant enrichment where analysis, planning, and implementation are strengthened by prevention.

Strategies become spontaneous ways of doing things, and educational intentions enrich any decision that seeks to draw from the deepest part of the self, and with a kind energy that each one possesses, the best version of each person.

Be a constant presence with an active and focused accompaniment

An educational strategy in the Salesian education system is an active and continuous presence of educators who attend both individually and as a community. Such a strategy facilitates the training of any educator as a Preventive Leader, in the formulation and support of personal life projects and organizational projects.

Leadership with this strategy has a greater impact on the process of self-knowledge that allows reaching the depths of each person's most intimate interiority. A Preventive Leader, when confronted with their own motivations, dreams, desires, fears, experiences, etc., can be ready to provide those resources when he/she is accompanying others. Presence as assistance requires that the person accompanying has a responsible use of freedom in the choices that must be taken daily. The only one who knows himself and has self-control is more responsible for their own decisions. Salesian assistance means to be present, to be active, to be attentive in order to achieve a better version of oneself, to guarantee the common good as much as possible.

The presence of the leading educator as an active and determined assistant is an attitude rather than a position (advisor, principal, assistant principal, etc.). This attitude allows him/her to make use of everything he/she has in his/her person and be enriched in collaboration with the rest.

Assistance, assumed as a social skill, is used at any time and on any possible occasion for the transformation of the entire environment, seeking to turn the classroom, the school, the school community into an intentionally familiar, joyous, and educational atmosphere.

Don Bosco proposed the presence of the educator and his unconditional availability as expressions of the educative vocation so, the mind, heart, intelligence, and person is available when the young person needs it, in any educational situation that requires preventive measures. This will lead young people to make more conscious decisions about their life project.

According to Lenti (2008), prevention understood in Don Bosco as an "educational strategy" must:

a) provide young people with the support needed in their personal struggles so that they can face difficulties constructively;
b) aim to limit and encapsulate the risk young people are in so that they can get out of danger, or at least to avoid a situation of greater risk.

The preventive leader educator knows that his presence must be where the students are. An active presence, according to Cian (2001), should be in particular moments and places in which the students have fun and spontaneously manifest themselves doing what they like (maybe during a break between classes, maybe during sports, maybe at an extracurricular activity, etc.). The outcome is that the educator-expert prepares the learners with their friendly presence and positive influence to be willing to do what the students like least (hard work, responsibilities beyond what is stipulated in standards, sustained commitment, and a constant of intelligent and disinterested service).

The Preventive educator´s presence should be focused on clear goals, since its first and most important objective transcends mere assistance to the place and time indicated by role or regulation. The preventive educator who knows and lives his focus presence understands that he is to prepare for life and from life. He educates to elucidate the best in each person.

Active and focused presence means careful attention to all the educators that make up the learning community. Such careful and caring attention is expressed in a series of positive actions, intentionally educational activities, personalized guidance interventions, and continuous and persistent influence from the positive in each person.

The presence of the educator understood this way within the educational context allows us to better understand the expression in the Salesian language used to describe educators as animators. In other words, a person with an intention that seeks to "bring out the best in each person in all aspects, circumstances, and decisions" (GC 23, para. 155).

The educator as animator renounces any form of manipulation or authoritative communication but does not renounce communicating content that seeks the integral good of the other. The means of communication must be used prudently (WhatsApp, Facebook, You-tube, Snapchat, Instagram) but the message and the mean are not rejected, the signs and symbols will be adapted. The educator uses a clear, direct and opportune language in his interventions with simplicity and naturalness since it is the type of language that is usually used in a family.

The preventive leader helps and encourages, using his own experience to raise awareness. The educator draws on the experience gained from their own processes to accompany the students to analyze, interpret, extend, synthesize, and enrich the process of self-knowledge of each student.

Accompaniment now generates greater ethical sensitivity and more respect for the person's processes. An educator who understands and lives preventiveness never imposes his own values, even if he considers them valid. Instead, a Preventive Leader tries to make the individual and the group evaluate the proposed values and facilitate the conditions (preventive environment, family atmosphere, positive experiences) for a free choice that leads them to become the best people to the world, to do the best in the construction of the common good, to think about the most suitable proposals for the specific and historical context (where a service is offered to the community), to motivate in projects of integral promotion bringing people together in the achievement of the educational goals with social impact (rallies, fundraising campaigns, care of common areas, etc.).

A leading educator understood in this way is a person continually updated with advances in the field of personal and group educational learning experience (professional development, human development, psychosocial development, etc.). He/she is a preventive leader who promotes awareness of his/her own value as a person and his/her leadership style, is convinced of what he or she is. Preventive Leaders have clarity in the objectives that they pursue with what they propose and what they know how to do. The Preventive Leaders have experience and certainty in the *hows* since contact with their interiority has given them the reasons for or against doing something. They know that they cannot do everything, have everything, or achieve everything alone; hence the accompanying lead educator also thinks about who to involve and to achieve ultimate educational goals.

The Preventive Leader enjoys healthy and enriching coexistence because he/she understands the positive impact of a place or a person who has gestures of benevolence and educational love.

A preventive educator is one who possesses wisdom because he knows that his motivations are underlying the decision made and acts accordingly. He/she is also the one who lives what he/she preaches trying to energize the motivations of others, whether they are conscious. The educator is preventive due to his great capacity for interpersonal relations-ships and a sense of community, and his/her responsibility for the decisions made as an individual and as a leader in the educational community. According to Doyle (2007), this type of leader considers the organization as an institution of society and community and, therefore, an institution with responsibility towards and for the community.

Be a generator of a pedagogy of possibility

Educational intentionality is an essential part of the pedagogy of possibility (Braido, 2001). This type of pedagogy differs from others by its objectives, rhythms, ways, achievements, and activities. It is a careful pedagogical proposal in the way of bringing a personalized educational approach to both the educator and the one educated. It is a pedagogy of possibility since it tries not to be monochromatic in its proposed learning experiences. The office, the workplace, the playground, the classroom, the auditorium, the field trip, are spaces rich in meaningful educational experiences. They can become intentionally educative atmospheres. It is to be educated from and for life. It is a pedagogy of possibility when the organizational structures are supports, but not obstacles to educate the citizen and the human being in their entirety.

When the spaces and organizational schemes become common ground for intentional planning that links minds, hearts, wills, creativity, concerns, or dreams. The pedagogy of possibility avoids the division of knowledge or the subordination to the proposed curriculum as the only navigation letter.

The pedagogy of possibility is when one considers the complexity that life has within it and all the wealth of possible responses to diverse existential situations that it is intended to accompany with and in the group. Diversity is a possibility of meeting, of dialogue, of mutual enrichment without forgetting the challenges that an environment of diversity brings with it.

Don Bosco (2007) proposes some insights for this pedagogy of possibility from his successful youth experiences called *Companies* (Immaculate, Conference of Saint Vincent de Paul, etc.). Today these youthful experiences of possibility can be identified, evaluated and updated from the Salesian educational experience. Currently the possibilities of educational experiences can be understood as reference and/or membership groups (clubs, associations, societies) that are formed by shared interests, where students find familiarity, closeness, friendship, common hobbies, and activities (skate board, hiking, diving, study groups, cycling, defense of human rights, legal and/or psychological counseling, sports, book club, gamers, etc.).

Spontaneous groups formed by shared interests are an essential and indispensable part of the Salesian educational proposal. They represent a valid instrument for the transfer of experiences, knowledge, competences, social skills, and emotional intelligence through collaboration between students and educators.

These groups are an important tool in establishing a vital convergence between the requirements of a curricular education and a conscious and active enrichment of skills beyond those required in the curriculum. Theater, music, dance, sports, to name a few, are activities that reinforce the values proposed or learned. Work in the midst of disadvantaged communities, literacy, first aid, or legal advice, are some social activities that can be verified for relevance and meaning in the lives of those involved in these community actions (Braido, 2001).

The pedagogy of possibility also proposes a formal education whose humanistic culture should impregnate the whole educative experience. It is a pedagogy that values the plurality of work experiences in the education of future leaders in society with the Salesian preventive imprint. Since theory nurtures practice, and praxis is the space where theory finds its verification.

It is a pedagogy that encourages and trains the individual to use free time in a responsible and creative way, since each person is responsible for their decisions (Bosco, 2007). In this pedagogy, the educator knows the negative experiences in life, the limits in educational proposals, the failures in learning experiences, but he proposes an anthropological optimism that has matured in the experience of goodness present in every human being. The pedagogy of possibility is the reflection of real possibilities facing specific circumstances and contexts. A Preventive Leader is an educator who proposes a pedagogy of possibility which is not naive, nor for the naive (Bosco, 2007).

Social Parameters for a Preventive Leader Educator

The spirit and values of Salesian pedagogy, born from the Don Bosco Preventive System and lived in the *Valdocco's Oratory* enriches nature, activity, and the way of being educated. In the author's opinion, every educational experience must consider three social spheres where the identity of the person is expressed and where the preventive educator shows sensitivity for some to the proper context where he/she is immersed in their educational work: Discernment as a life plan and self-care, culture of encounter and dialogue as essential skills in lifelong learning, and solidarity as a human expression of entrepreneurship.

Be a promoter of discernment

The *first social sphere* for every Preventive Leader is the discernment of reality based on the key question: Why, in this specific context (neighborhood, city, district, area, municipality) must there be a Salesian educational presence? The answer to this question will present the necessary elements to identify the significance of the proposal for that particular context. It will also elucidate the non-negotiable elements of its own identity. It will also allow us to glimpse the possible foci of social impact that the educational presence has for its specific environment. I go so far as to say that the key to answering our question lies in whether or not there exists a need for a presence within the context whose oratory criteria will contribute significantly and with relevant social impact. The reason why this presence should be there is because the Salesian oratory style would better fit there in its four key elements:

1. the first criterion is the type, quality, and purpose of the educational proposal itself (school that educates),
2. the second is the type of interaction and the quality of the organizational culture as an atmosphere that promotes the basic values of socialization (family-friendly home),
3. the third is the importance of leisure and non-curricular activities (playground where friends are made spontaneously) that make the educational proposal go beyond curricular classes or credit courses and interpersonal relationships that only revolve around issues of professionalization,
4. the fourth is the explicit proposal of openness to transcendence, which reinforces the philosophy of life that everyone has, and which seeks to modify itself

with the wise convergent conjugation of an educational environment of strategies, institutional policies, organizational structures, pedagogical priorities, curricular objectives, and educational models (experience of the Church).

A strategic work plan, an institutional project, an organizational chart or institutional identity and policies, all these elements in any educational presence must consider the Oratorian criterion as a starting, and constant reference point without neglecting the appropriate government requirements for each country and for each curriculum recognized by the State. It is not a negotiable matter, and not accidental that the Oratory is the permanent criterion of renewal and educational possibility. The technology in the classroom, the accumulation of activities, the physical spaces renewed and well used, all this is little importance if the oratory is not the criterion of educational quality and service.

The experience or absence of this will determine whether the Salesian educational presence is convenient, necessary, and important for the boys and girls of that place.

Educative processes, experiences, ongoing formation, incentives for educators and administrators, etc., are efforts not aligned to the achievement of the ultimate goal of the entire Salesian proposal if they lose sight of their origin and goal educationally speaking: the Valdocco Oratory embraces in the person of the preventive leader as the iliving form of the Preventive System.

The *second social sphere* of discernment of reality seeks the individual. This sphere considers individual consciousness as the axis of constant and ongoing discernment. The discernment needs a method. The method proposed by Lonergan could be applied. It means:

- be attentive to all the information received from the outside;
- be intelligent in the internal process of learning and understanding;
- be reasonable with the information, feelings, emotions, and motions that are possessed, with the knowledge acquired and the decisions made based on the process itself in its previous phases;
- be responsible for the process of self-awareness and the results that are triggered by it;
- be respectful of yourself and of others with a humble attitude of solidarity and responsibility in being and sustaining one's existence in relation to the existence of the other.

The personal life project should be the *final product* of the intentional educational process since it means responding to the challenge of being the best for the world (CG 23, para. 186).

Discerning personal reality should lead to self-care. Taking care of yourself implies a way of being, an attitude, a way of thinking about the practices of your own subjectivity. Self-care requires ones who is capable of caring for others. However, to reach that level, it is necessary to deliberate on what you want for yourself, what you are looking for, what you project for your future.

To better understand self-care, Hernández (1999) proposes, following Aristotle´s concept of *phronesis*. Hernández says:

> The subject of phronesis addresses his ultimate purposes, true happiness, through an exercise of deliberation, that is, of reasoning or reflection on what is good for himself, the subject who deliberates can

'become someone else' after having deliberated. That is the underlying reason for deliberation: the gradual transformation of oneself (pp. 17-18).

Self-care corresponds to a process of being educated, not in the traditional sense in which someone is going to teach and someone else is the one who learns. Self-care is a specific action that must be carried out by the individual who is given the possibility of expressing his limited word self-centered on himself so that he can abandon the way of life in which he finds himself, and seek a more better human version of himself for the best care of others.

Taking care of yourself is a kind of operation within you because you are the one who knows yourself best and knows what you need to be in harmony. It is an unfinished journey towards interiority, with spiraling, constant and cumulative returns into oneself.

Taking care of yourself allows you to carry out with the help of others, a certain type of internal modifications. These modifications affect the body, soul, thoughts, behaviors or way of being seeking a better knowledge and self-control, and a positive transformation allows you to face life. Discernment provides more tools for a better response to life itself.

Be a promoter of a culture of encounter and dialogue

Since the development of the preventive educator in his leadership requires a pedagogy of possibility, one of the central skills in the educational experience is dialogue. It is understandable that dialogue implies encounter instead of silent acceptance, debate instead of *irenism*, tireless search for truth rather than comfortable assimilation of what is given, relentless moreover struggle before a power that seduces and clouds what is right.

Educational dialogue as a factor of social impact is more than just the communication of a private truth. Therefore, people dialogue for the pleasure of speaking and for the search to reach an agreement for the achievement of a concrete good. Dialogue as educational and as a factor of social impact requires respect and benevolence, closeness and the ability to listen attentively, which is not the same as simply hearing something (Francis, 2013). The interpersonal encounter and the educational dialogue as factors of social impact suppose a subject who is convinced that the other has something important to say (Mucci, 2014).

A comprehensive educative practice should focus on the training of the individual and on the process of the individual itself. The social formation of the individual can be conceived as a process of personal and social skills (critical thinking, collaborative, connectivity, communication, creativity, cultural diversity).

Knowing how to dialogue implies a historical perspective of the individual in whom the present acquires importance by virtue of the past; a perspective that provides data and information to understand his development as a person towards the future. It is something that corresponds more to self-training rather than just to skills.

Self-formation arises more from an internal process and is therefore linked to the ethical and aesthetic senses. Seeks not only professional knowledge, but also what is fundamentally good, the experience of beauty, and the enjoyment of harmony. The experiences of community service, practices of social immersion, missions, and extracurricular activities of social impact are the result of dialogue with the environment and its challenges or needs, always from the peculiar perspective of the preventive educator. The Preventive Leader educates for responsible citizenship, educates for life fully, and educates for the assimilation of a mission in life.

Dialogue and meeting of the educator with other facilitate the fusion of horizons of meaning (Rodríguez, 2016). According to Sala (2009), that which allows the fusion of horizons is "to begin with the analysis of the pre-understanding that places us in the sense of belonging, to go through the memory and to advance from a distance to the appropriation of the shared common horizon" (p. 249). A modification to our way of understanding ourselves is achieved by the mutual enrichment of the encounter with the other with intentionality.

The statement *expansion of the horizon* in Gadamer (2004) is illuminating "Applying this to the thinking mind, we speak of narrowing of the horizon, but also of the possible expansion of the horizon, of the opening of new horizons, and so on" (p. 301). One´s starting point is the horizon of interpretation; as one´s knowledge progresses, one horizon changes to accommodate new data, new ways of seeing and understanding, new patterns of interpretation, new experiences that may be the possibility of continuing education. It is a fusion of horizons when the other person dares to do the same: to modify their point of view from where they interpret. A risk that may be achieved, as Gadamer (2004) says: "A person who has no horizon does not see enough and therefore overvalues what is closest to him [...] having a horizon means not being limited to what is close, but to be able to see beyond that "(p. 301) .

A person who has a horizon, according to Rodríguez (2016), knows the importance of the horizon itself which is limited but not rigid. This horizon moves with the subject as it broadens or modifies it from his own experience and the experience with others. This fusion of horizons is facilitate as a possibility of continuous expansion, openness, and inclusion of the rest, the others, and the Other.

A horizon reveals a limited personal situation but is also an epiphany of the person in the endless journey of the constant and permanent search the elusive meaning of life. Encounter or disagreement, dialogue or non-dialogues, can be epiphanic moments of the person's very being living or coexisting with others. It is an exercise in self-knowledge because ones show oneself to the other, and to myself. However, there is always something to know, something to discover, something to improve.

Vulnerability, the impossibility of knowing everything, having everything, or being able to do everything, of any human being, forces us to accept what Gadamer (2004) explains as "the historical movement of human life consists in the fact that it is never absolutely linked to any point of view, and therefore can never have a truly closed horizon" (p. 303). The horizon is something in which the human being moves and something that moves with the human being. Acquiring a new horizon of meaning is "looking beyond what is at hand not to look the other way but to see it better" (Gadamer, 2004, p. 305).

The open space that Rodríguez (2016) proposes as the unfinished fusion of horizons becomes a place of mediation for dialogue in order to receive, evaluate, and criticize the contributions of others. This expansion of horizons allows the formation of human social life, the planning of an educational community, and the evaluation of life and action of any institution in solidarity with its social environment.

Be supportive in solidarity

A preventive educator who discerns, who dialogues, who cares for himself and others, who is open to the fusion of horizons, knows that he is not autonomous. Every member of an educational community is impelled to show sensitivity to social problems, especially those that blur social justice. *Civil friendship* is interior availability to the demands of the other, an evident expression of philanthropy. Hence, solidarity can be considered as "the ability to see people, very different from "us," included in the category "we" (Rorty, 1991, p. 210).

Solidarity is another aspect that allows the exercise of interdependent communication that arises as a person, as an organization, and as a society in search of the common good, in the open space of the process of merging horizons.

Solidarity, according to Ratzinger (2004), is lived when the human being is aware of mutual responsibility for others, especially those in need. Such awareness can open the gift of the self to a social sphere where one receives what he offers, and where one can always give more than what has been given. That is why an egocentric attitude can never be natural to the human being in its genuine form.

The formation of consciousness of citizenship in solidarity, is manifested in social terms with the active participation in the distribution of goods and situations that revolve or are concerned with human development. Such education in solidarity also implies the effort for a fairer social order where tensions can be better dealt with, and where conflicts can be resolved with less waste of energy and time through dialogue. Projects of solidarity require precision, concreteness and community networking. Such projects look for mature forms of shared social action found in schools. They can strengthen experiences of community, experiences of support for the environment awareness campaigns, experiences of specialized humanitarian aid, and attention to the impoverished. Taking into account that the intention of the foci is solidarity and not the non-binding punctual-assistance and without compromise that goes beyond an action in itself-foreign to the center of a person who claims to be supportive.

The formation of an active and responsible citizenship requires overcoming the superficial self-centered attitudes present in every human group since it requires a clear relationship between solidarity, subsidiarity, justice, and service. It also requires a patient analysis to transform the structures that allow or maintain situations where institutional-type social resources do not guarantee fair access or the distribution of goods or the search for the common good, especially for the least favored.

In turn, in the face of solidarity, a subsidiary action is needed where the participation of the individual impacted by solidarity commit himself to continuous improvement on his own. (GC 23, para. 213)

Solidarity from the perspective of Saint John Paul II (1985) is more than specific emotions or actions. He states that:

> This is not a feeling of vague compassion or superficial anguish at the misfortunes of so many people, both near and far. On the contrary, it is a firm and persistent determination to commit to the common good; that is, the good of all and of each individual, because we are all really responsible for all (para. 38).

The discernment of reality, assuming the moment, and the promotion of a culture of encounter and dialogue orient towards solidarity as a fundamental element for the renewal of educational presences. Solidarity aims to guarantee that everyone has the possibility of carrying out a standard of living life. The creativity looks to the future with confidence and hope are towards intelligent solidarity.

Self-reflection of Chapter V

Checklist: Preventive Leadership Development

In your role as a preventive leader you ...	Y	N
1. You offer cordial and assertive treatment to each person.		
2. You are responsibly committed to the life project of each young person in your environment.		
3. You show empathy for the other as a sign of your love for your neighbor.		
4. You commit to the values of the organization (school, parish, oratory, etc.).		
5. You are a model of the values that you promote.		
6. You do not limit your accompaniment by schedule or role assignment.		
7. You are a living, continuous and kind presence.		
8. You recognize your students for their individuality.		
9. You have a real concern for your students and their individuality.		
10. You have emotional maturity based on the search for the best of the students.		
11. You show a deep readiness to be affectionate.		
12. The loving kindness you show is balanced and harmonious.		
13. You foster and inspire trust with everyone at all times.		
14. You act familiarly with everyone and at all times.		
15. You implement rules in the form of prevention to avoid risky situations.		
16. You seek compliance with the rules through awareness and knowledge.		
17. You facilitate the personal process of self-awareness.		
18. You ask only for what is reasonably possible		

19. You are able to intuit the best in search of the common good.		
20. You make decisions focused on the search for the common good.		
21. You put your personal resources (experience, knowledge, will) at the service of the formation and growth processes of students.		
22. You participate with a paternal/maternal love in the growth of the students.		
23. You understand life as a vocation of service.		
24. You accompany processes that involve all aspects of the human being (physical, social, spiritual, rational).		
25. You create atmospheres of family spirit, joy and confidence.		
26. You promote meeting spaces where freedom and spontaneity are experienced.		
27. You are the embodiment of the Salesian Oratory.		

6. Effects of the Preventive Leadership

Possible factors of leadership development with preventive traits: convergence paradigm[3]

The first factor in play for the achievement of a strong unitary life project as a result of convergence is a method common to all human beings in the process of knowing themselves and their context, a process inherent in the human person, because reflection, meditation, the encounter with oneself, accompanies the human being as it is innate to him. In addition to this, a preventive leader makes decisions either because of his position in the organizational structure or because of his level of influence among others, or because of the real or symbolic power received or concomitant with the position itself. Given the possibility of a reflection different from what is commonly assumed in leadership theories, it is relevant to recover the centrality of the human being and rediscover the importance of a process of self-awareness and self-appropriation in the person in leadership position.

In other words, it is convenient to highlight the importance of a method that allows the educator to situate himself in his being and in his specific doing.

It favors the deep encounter of oneself by answering who

---

[3] It is convenient to refer to chapter VI in Rodriguez, A. (2018). *Education from the Heart. Salesian Leadership in the University*. Navarra - Universidad Salesiana A.C.

he is, what moves him to take a certain action, what factors he must consider and which ones to discard, what sustains or guides his life project, how to link "must be" with "being able to do" in the claim of the common good, and how to discern what is right and what is convenient.

The proposal in Chapter II embodies the need for every leader to be attentive, to be intelligent, to be responsible, to be respectful, and to be a person of and in community. The continuous appropriation of one's interiority requires the convergence of all internal realities (feelings, emotions, desires). It also requires that which while what moves the subject from within it (dreams, projects, hopes, desires) while demanding a way of being authentic in the face of the reality that each person is.

A first factor for an educator concerned with the achievement of his personal life project takes place when he exercises self-knowledge or self-appropriation. This supposes a leadership with less internal conflicts as individuals and a better capacity to articulate, socialize, give direction and channel with shared effort (Avolio and Hannah, 2008). Ashley and Reiter-Palmo (2012) consider that a leading educator "with a high level of self-awareness tends to generate better results than those with low levels of self-awareness" (p. 2). Bolman and Deal (2013) point out that when educators do not have the ability to change their own frameworks of interpretation in a continuous process of awareness, their effectiveness in leadership positions deteriorates dramatically.

The second factor in play for a leading educator is to achieve a strong unitarian life project as a result of convergence. It is also to achieve the educational environment that serves as an atmosphere of interaction and respect between educator-student, educator-educator, educator-principal, educator-family parent, and educator-context. Such a preventive atmosphere is intentionally sought and proposed to promote and favor knowledge, the development of competencies and skills, and the proposal of some learning strategies because it involves what is taught and how it is taught. There are many proposals for educational atmospheres, but the preventive educator is interested in the one that rescues a pedagogy of possibility, a transcendent motivation that is based on deep self-appropriation and integral development.

The social aspect of the person and learning, the real construction of shared knowledge, opens up the possibility of a socio-constructivist scaffolding that, in Vygotsky's perspective, language as a social instrument and the learning community are an atmosphere conducive to learning. Language and the learning community are two elements that motivate the students to learn and the teachers to teach. The convergence of both are a key to success and significant learning in world-class schools (Andere, 2015).

The third factor at stake is benevolence love. Benevolence, reason, interiority, and community of inquiry are key parts of a system that seeks the positive in each person, a system that energizes from the good that one possesses by nature, and a system that seeks the best version of oneself for the world.

Educational strategies, learning environment parameters, preventive conditions are determining factors in the achievement of an educational leader with an enriched DNA: the Salesian DNA. It becomes the way of seeing, thinking, feeling, deciding, and doing among current youth generation (Millennials, Centennials, *Touchscreen*).

The Salesian educator with his/her modified DNA is the lived form of the Preventive System. Where he/she goes there a Salesian Oratory is because he/she takes it as criterion of action and life. Identity and renewal need to be rooted in Don Bosco, and faithful to the youth of today.

In the light of the elements outlined in the preceding sections, Preventive Leadership considers a process of cognitive and emotional internalization as a starting point in the process of internalization. All the elements of the cognitive and decision-making process are considered as condition *sine qua non*. The preventive leader is capable of bringing out the best in people because he/she has gone through the same process with himself, bringing out the most positive version of himself.

A preventive leader carefully considers the moments that make up the personal history of each member of the organization because each life matters, and each story is an irreplaceable narrative of life.

The Grace of Unity

A Preventive Leader who faces complex, global, competitive, unpredictable, volatile, and ambiguous environments with unprecedented transformations in all areas and with scenarios of uncertainty, he/she needs continuous skills development to discern social and situational contexts in which he/she is able to make decisions. A Preventive Leader must understand complex dynamics in decision making processes to determine collective and interpersonal networks of discernment (Fig. 38).

Figure 38 Loop learning

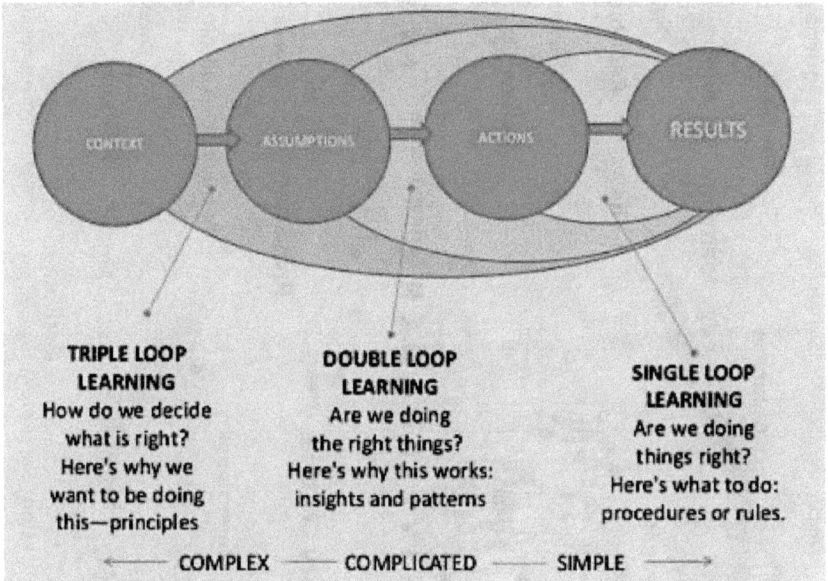

There are two loops for any educator who claims to be a Preventive Leader: the energy loop that nurtures from within (INLO) and the energy loop that nurtures the projection of the future (FLO).

The loops of nutrition from within (INLO) and the one that nurtures the projection of the future (FLO) are two aspects of the same reality. Both crystallize conditions, parameters, criteria, educational strategies, and social parameters that all Preventive Leader must apply in all the circumstances.

The grace of unity cited by Viganó in the 1980s is the inner movement to serve other. It allows a deep experience of fullness. The grace of unity supports a better understanding of the outcomes that any educational effort brings of life: a strong unified and fulfilled project of life. (Fig. 39)

Figure 39 INLO & FLO

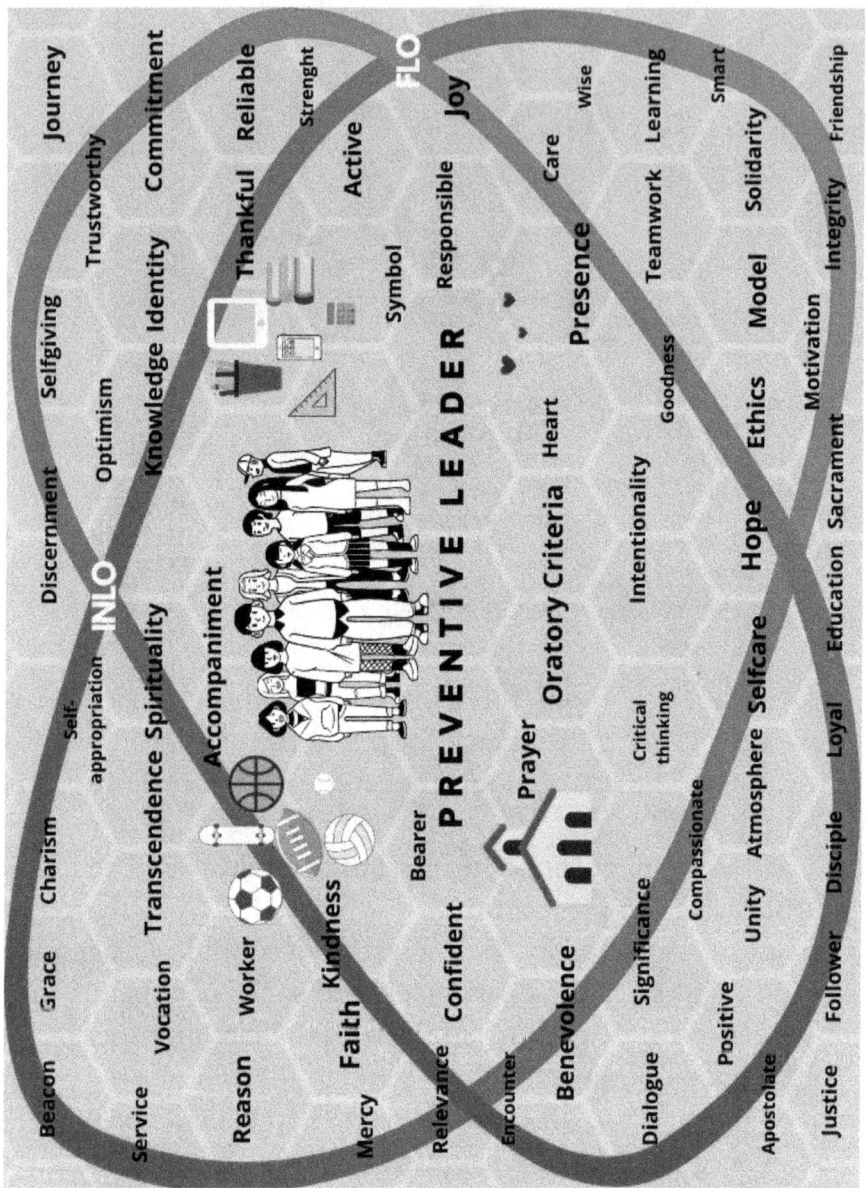

Any theory of leadership or leadership development should be a collaborative reflection of the knowledge that passes from the horizontal way of doing and thinking (competences, abilities, skills) to the vertical way of understanding and developing leadership (self-knowledge, self-awareness, personal motivations, internalized values, transcendence, vocation, dedicated life). This horizontality and verticality suppose the internal-external impulse of self-development. The horizontal-vertical movement seems to be an individual and collective process supported by complex theories(Day and Sin, 2011; Petrie, 2014; White, 2011), the convergence of various leadership theories, and are enriched by the Preventive System in symbiosis with the educator.

This concatenation of loops –INLO-FLO– can be described in terms of the constructive development theory (Fig. 40). The energy supplied to Preventive Leaders allow them to:
- a) Live with organizational principles that guide them growth in a better understanding of themselves and the external world;
- b) Involve the reality of incessant change from one development scheme to another, usually looking at a higher level to which each leader can reasonably aspire;
- c) Promote new challenges in the organizational environment or climate that demand different skills to respond to qualitatively different patterns and criteria by a VUCA and UTRU context and with different generations: Millennials, Centennials, Touch screen (Day, D., Fleenor, Atwater, Sturm & Mckee, 2014; Rodríguez & Rodríguez, 2015).

Figure 40 INLO & FLO as double loop process

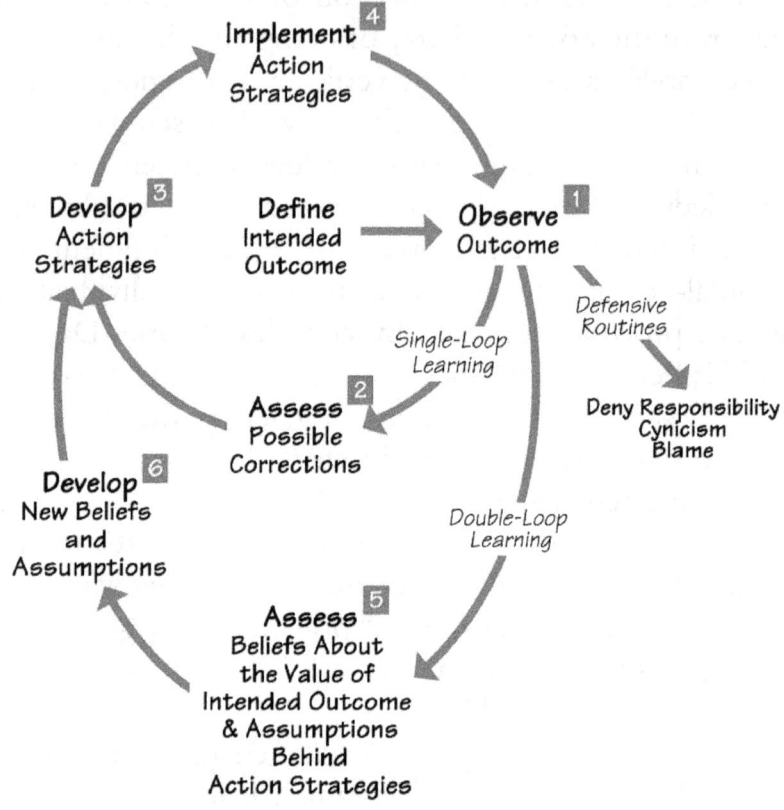

INLO as a framework for the development of the preventive educational leader

Focused on common human processes, this loop can drive Preventive Leaders to develop themselves, their followers, and their organizations.

Avolio and Gardner (2005) observed that authentic leadership development involves "continuous processes by which leaders and followers become self-aware and establish open, transparent, trusting, and genuine relationships" (p. 322).

Michie and Gooty (2005) support this notion of a genuine self in relation to others with their central thesis: positive emotions directed by others (gratitude, appreciation, respect, collaboration, etc.) motivate educational leaders to behave in ways that reflect self-transcendent values (honesty, loyalty, equality, justice, truthfulness, etc.). According to O'Connell (2014), an educator is the individual whose authenticity is built up in the continuous discovery of their own identity and convictions. Such authenticity present is evidence of accompanied.

INLO is considered as a process of internalization. INLO is an unstoppable movement that begins with the natural desire for knowledge in each human being and continues to grow until all aspects of human existence are open to the mystery and to transcendency. According to Lonergan (1992), this desire manifests a series of structural conditions within the individual as a continuous process that is part of the path of human development for each subject is aware of their own consciousness. Part of reality could be intentionally present for individuals. However, the focus for Lonergan is the conscious subject of his own acts at empirical, intellectual, rational, moral, and spiritual level. Previous chapters have analyzed what Lonergan provides with his Generalized Empirical Method by which the knower can reach the interior of the self with consistency in feelings, thoughts, and actions (Sánchez, 2011).

INLO becomes a life proposal that is accompanied methodologically in the process of self-knowledge, self-awareness, and individual and collective self-care. This energy loop, for a Preventive Leader allows him to develop advanced competencies of self-awareness, self-regulation, internalized moral perspective, balanced processing, positive modeling, relational transparency, and humanistic behavior.

Preventive Leader´s identity progress from the individual level, where the self is defined in terms of the uniqueness of others –I am who I am–, through the relational level, where the self is defined in terms of roles and relationships –I am a citizen, a lawyer, a doctor, etc.–, to the collective level, in which the self is defined in terms of group or organizational affiliations –population, nationality, percentage, sample–. (Lord and Hall, 2005)

INLO as a framework for the development of Organizational Preventive Leadership

Leadership is something that most organizations care about and those with educational purposes are no exception. But what is most important is not which leadership theory or model is correct, but how to develop leaders and theories of leadership in the most effective and efficient way possible in Salesian settings. The convergence between Lonergan's method, Vygotsky's socio-constructivism, and the Preventive System seems to be a possible way to achieve this kind of leadership style. The development of the educator as Preventive Leader permeating requires balance between personal internalization and the challenges of social reality (discernment, dialogue, solidarity).

Leadership development becomes a subset of the individual development of one's identity, directly related to the experience of values and the internalization of experiences. Leaders who are able to learn from their experiences tend to participate in higher levels of preventive leadership (Rodríguez, 2015). The Preventive Leader is, using Lonergan's expressions, "a concrete and intelligible totality-unity-identity, characterized by acts of sensitivity, perception, imagination, inquiry, understanding, formulation, reflection […]

and judge[ment]" (Lonergan, 1992, p. 343-344).

Through the appropriation of one's identity, together with the related skills of metacognition, self-regulation, and self-motivation allow a Preventive Leader his own methodological process (Chan, Hannah, & Gardner, 2005; Lord & Hall, 2005). The trajectories and life experiences of leaders and followers become important pieces of leadership development firmly embedded in the spiral of continual development of preventive leadership.

INLO is considered as a comprehensive promotion project that seeks the complete maturation of individuals and groups. In a Preventive Leader, this project focuses on the need to provide positive development through a continuous training process.

The Preventive Leader stimulates his/her abilities through the conditions of prevention, educational benevolence, the use of reason, intentionality, self-awareness, and transcendence. These conditions generate an organic set of convictions, attitudes, actions, methods, and structures that can progressively establish a peculiar form of personal and community action. An intentional educational presence, an educational process, and a positive practice of prevention, blending together are some of the central indicators of the energy loop that nurtures from within –INLO– (Gardner et al., 2005; Viganó, 1978; 1989).

Preventive Leadership is possible in the most varied contexts. It becomes a program for life instead of a plethora of diplomas and credentials (Rodríguez, 2017; Rodríguez and Rodríguez, 2015). INLO involves the maturation of the self and others in the interconnected space between individuals, groups, and organizations (Avolio and Gardner, 2005; Bradbury and Lichtenstein, 2000; Buber, 1970). Preventive Leadership development encompasses the double aspect of prevention: protecting from untimely negative experiences and, at the same time, developing the potential of the individual through positive suggestions sustained in personal life projects (Vecchi, 1995).

FLO for the development of preventive educational leaders

The desire to do good for others and to do it from the fields of education is a starting point for meeting and dialogue. O'Connell (2014) considers plausible a philosophical approach from multiple perspectives aimed at living and leading, balancing active participation with the timely practice of observation, reflection, and detachment.

The humanistic perspective, in its general content, must consider each educator as a Preventive Leader in the formation towards freedom in the search and preservation of what is good. A Preventive Leader with FLO is a builder of benevolence, human love with, a presence to whom life is a gift and a task. A Preventive Leader with FLO is responsible for being professionally competent seeking the formation of a moral conscience and a sense of solidarity with social and political aspects of dialogue.

A Preventive Leader can be an educator who values and defends the dignity of each human being, who merges horizons of justice and social peace in the fight for the promotion of human beings, who values the collaboration with others (reason).

The Preventive Leader with FLO is open to transcendence, to the search for truth, to the meaning of human fraternity, to the value of life, and to the axiological praxis and spirituality (religion).

A Preventive Leader with FLO promotes a generation of an organizational environment permeated by a family spirit, mutual trust, dialogue, joy, and friendship (benevolence, *loving-kindness*).

A Preventive Leader with FLO has a caring and authoritative responsibility that offers vital guidance and teaching, and it requires commitment. FLO is both benevolent love and moral authority that seeks the greater good in the integral promotion of others (Vecchi, 1995). Preventive Leadership involves the art of developing positive leadership by presenting what is good through appropriate immersion experiences, through the participation of those who intend to be preventive leaders. A Preventive Leader with FLO also facilitates attractive challenges, adequate contexts, and accompaniment by a constant and cordial presence (trascendence).

A family environment aims to expand all personal resources illuminating each personality and leading each individual to reformulate the philosophy of their own life and the personal search for transcendence.

FLO is the art facilitating growth among young leaders. This could be done by appealing to their inner freedom, by transforming external conditioning and formalism through self-assessment, and by a gradual self-appropriation (animators, volunteers). FLO is the art of sharing heart with new leaders in their aspirations (empathy, social ability).

Value models is used purposefully by the Preventive Leader to instill a cultural heritage, in which the community of inquiry and learning brings new members into contact. (educational-pastoral community). In this sense, the fusion of horizons is an important tool to open attitudes and actions that creates the interrelation between educator-experts and learners.

Convergency model of Preventive leaders with the constructivism approach realizes that learning cannot, and should not, be considered as an individual activity. Learning must take place in social contexts because leaders "learn from challenging work to solve complex problems
and lead a team, and [consequently] they use this knowledge to foster team communication and improve performance" (Hirst, Mann, Bain, Pirola-Merlo and Richter, 2004, p. 321).

A community where everyone is a learner facilitates an ethical and cultural dimension that balances on the self-referential conscience and allows, at the same time, a common discernment based on trust and mutual respect (Day, 2000). A community of inquiry and learning provides a solid culture that understands progress as an exchange of good things by everyone. Without stifling individual affirmation, diversity provides an opportunity for mutual enrichment. A community of learning and inquiry can nurture a strong culture of personal sense of service. A community of inquiry is open to transcendence, to individual capability of questioning about existence and its ultimate meaning. A community of learning is formed by individuals seeking appropriate answers to the most essential questions about happiness, life or faith.

FLO as frame of reference facilitates the generation of meaning and individual purpose in the face of uncertainty and complexity. FLO allows the development of participation, responsibility, resilience, and adaptability (Drath et al., 2008).

The process of leadership accompaniment requires a continuous application of practical wisdom, discernment, social and interpersonal intelligence, behaviors base on values, and cognitive-emotional sensitivity.

The educator, considered a preventive leader, is invited to personally possess these competences, also, to promote and develop these same skills among the members of the educational community. They propose interventions in the immediate social environment. (Brown, 2012; Day et al., 2014; O'Connell, 2014)

FLO as a framework for the development of Organizational Preventive Leadership

The development of Preventive Leadership implies a desire to be with and among others sharing life, projects, and experiences (Galli and Müller-Stewens, 2012; Rodríguez, 2017). This intentional presence involves a formative matrix of processes rich in complexity and convergence. Organizational Preventive Leadership development highlights the importance of leaders creating positive learning environments and fostering cross-cultural communication (Avolio and Gardner, 2005; Chan, 2005).

A Preventive Leader creates full initial immersion experiences with small-scale trial and error. These experiences facilitate mutual interactions in real time, and co-enrichment in situations with real people that require accompaniment. Some skills required for today's social connection are: collaboration, teamwork, coaching, trust in others, a shared vision, intrinsic cooperative behavior, and fluency in managing multiple scenarios (Fowler, 2006).

O'Connell (2014) proposes the "acceptance, understanding, and incorporation of the needs and identities of everyone, everywhere, with honor and admiration of each person and the unique contributions of each culture and its capabilities" (p. 194). The needs of others is an ethical challenge for a response in solidarity.

The Preventive Leader is called to possess a convinced vision of transcendence as a fundamental element in cultures in the education of each individual.

The leader with benevolent educational love builds an atmosphere of trust, dialogue, and family. He/she accompanies other leaders in the own process of maturity and growth.

FLO leads the leader to discover the seeds of good in his own culture and own personal history. A Preventive Leader with FLO seeks educational strategies to promote positive psychological capacities and a safe environment (Walumbwa et al., 2008). In every organization or group there are difficult moments: sometimes creates by toxic people (Stamateas, 2015). However, in the Salesian Preventive System nobody is lost, no one is hopelessly damaged, no one should be easily replaceable.

Each educator who considers himself a Preventive Leader has the will power to become a better person. Ligon, Hunter, and Mumford (2008) also argue that outstanding leaders rely on past experiences to create meaning in building a personal narrative consistent with one's life story. Every young person, in fact, has within himself the desire to a better, full and happy life. Saint John Bosco used to say "In every child, and even in the most miserable of them there is an element that, if the educator can discover [this element] and stimulate it, [the individual] reacts with generosity." (Vecchi, 1995)

Possible indicators of the development of a Preventive Leader

The Salesian Preventive System is a polyphony of constructs based on values. Some of the standards for Leaders who assume and live the preventive proposal are: trust, commitment, active citizenship, positive psychological capital, sustainable well-being in the workplace, efficiency in what has been done, compassion, passion for authenticity, purpose of full life, value-based behavior, relational connectivity, disciplined, behavioral coherence, self-care, and grateful outlook on life. When O'Connell (2014) outlines the capabilities of 21st-century leaders, he proposes that a purposeful leader shows a commitment to personal mission, passionately lives his personal life project, and seeks beneficial relationships in form of shared roles, delegated work, and service to the community.

Prevention becomes an expression of, an empathetic and cordial, proactive and educational life. Positive modeling is the primary mechanism through which Preventive Leaders develop authentic followers. The results of relationships between preventive leaders and authentic followers include high levels of follower trust in the leader, commitment to continuous improvement, family environment, well-being in the workplace, and a more sustainable life.

Some traits in the action of a Preventive Leader are: leadership as the result of a collective agreement, alignment with a common objective as a result of coordination between expert knowledge and qualified work, and a commitment as a provision to serve collective interests.

A Preventive Leader nurtures and cares for an environment in which others learn to negotiate shared decisions, to consciously participate in mutual influence, and to develop relevant meanings, valuable goals, formative contexts, and binding agreements over time (Rodríguez and Sánchez, 2017; Wassenaar and Pearce, 2012). The world and all aspects of life, become the classroom where learning and teaching take place and the multiple roles that every person assumes and lives become the "curriculum of a full and meaningful life."

Possible indicators of the development of Preventive Leadership

The expansive landscape for a theory and development of Preventive Leadership needs reinvention, innovation and exchange of knowledge with the continuous flow of new information for analysis and assessment. It is a way to build full of challenges and novelties, imbalances between what tradition says and what the current context calls for blurring boundaries between what is done out of habit and what should be done out of significance and relevance.

The proposal of the Preventive Leader is intended to embrace, nurture, and enrich the style of being and doing of any person convinced of the methodology, spirituality, and model that comes from the Salesian Preventive System. The Preventive Leadership approach convincingly embraces the network of preventive principles, criteria, and strategies as a common guide and benchmark for further reflection and current practice.

Self-reflection of Chapter VI

Check List: Preventive Leader

Features of the energy that nurtures from within and of the energy that nurtures the projection of the future	Y	N
1. You have confidence in yourself.		
2. You have confidence in others.		
3. You are an educator intentionally involved.		
4. You are an active citizen.		
5. You are satisfied with your life.		
6. You have a positive psychological capital.		
7. You enjoy sustainable well-being in your workplace.		
8. You are efficient in your work.		
9. You are compassionate.		
10. You like to be authentic.		
11. You have a purpose in your life.		
12. You consider that you are living a full life.		
13. Your behavior is based on values.		
14. You enjoy relationships with other people.		
15. You are consistent between what you think, you say, and you do.		
16. You are disciplined.		
17. You are an educator embracing the INLO and FLO loops.		
18. You take care of yourself.		
19. You are grateful even in difficult moments of life.		
20. You consider yourself a blessed person and therefore live fully.		

Final Thoughts

Today there is a paradoxical phenomenon: a strong sense of individuality, but at the same time, a high risk of fragmentation. On the one hand, the world shrunk and has become a global village (McLuhan, 1964), where information flows through the world saturating it. Today, everyone anywhere can see everything (Barevičiūtè, 2010). But at the same time, this world has never been deeply fragmented. All realities appear as disassembled pieces of a mosaic that individuals no longer know how to reassemble themselves. Today there is great fragmentation of time, space, values and sensitivity. Life is connected "with other parts of the world through the media" (Martens, Dreher and Gaston, 2010, p. 576). Faced with all this, it is appropriate to promote dialogue from a perspective that addresses the fragmentation of personal life, attention, and time. Preventive Leadership as a model, method, and body of guiding principles of an educational leadership proposal is essential for the construction of critical agents and the formative culture throughout life. Preventive Leadership is essential for a society that seeks democracy and development. For this, it is vitally important to develop the leadership potential that educators possess.

Society will always need leaders who are ethical, collaborative, transformative with a strong sense of service, humanism, and prevention. Schools are in a unique position to influence teacher leadership development: the teacher's classroom experience can offer formal and informal experiences for leadership training and praxis.

The managerial work in schools can provide specific curricular and non-curricular training for the formation of positive, transformational, authentic, helpful leaders. Educational models can generate tutoring, modeling, and mentoring opportunities that accompany their leadership experiences (Lavery and Hine, 2013).

The school as an educational entity is present in social life and can be a real possibility of an effective experiment in the face of a discouraging scenario of the educational reality at all levels: students who do not learn, teachers who do not teach, schools that do not motivate, families that do not accompany, etc. In the world in general, the mobility of social classes is largely operated through formal education. This would explain the great demand for high-quality schools and educational institutions with the best official and international accreditation. Furthermore, the schools and specific teachers seem to be a good source of social and political leadership that has not been fully used for greater impact and the construction of the common good. In fact, educative systems are a key element for the economic, cultural, and social development of any society that seeks a better quality of life, competitiveness, and sustained growth (Grimaldo, 2015). But today something is not working well. More money *per capita*, but worse educative results; more years of formal education, but fewer opportunities for well-paid jobs; more technological tools unthinkable in previous generations are now available, but students more and more confused, diluted, and apparently more insignificant. Today the cognitive and learning sciences have promising insights, but it seems that fewer teachers are not willing to be more dedicated in the classroom.

The educational work in the style of Saint John Bosco is a challenge for a Catholic religious force that was born in the courtyards of *Valdocco* in the 19th century, serving children at risk. Today, after more than 150 years serving in more than

130 countries as educators and pastors, it is profitable to consider decisively:

    a) a fidelity to a charism without neglecting to raise quality standards that allow significance and relevance in each social context where it finds the educational location;
    b) the demanding improvement of the learning experiences of learners motivated to learn;
    c) a salesian educational model that elucidates preventive educators leaders motivated to educate;
    d) accompaniment in the formation of leaders whose Salesian preventiveness must be part of their DNA;
    e) the real, pertinent, and verifiable service to citizens in disadvantaged situations that make up future generations and who represent the most valuable portion of society.

Considerations

1. The capacity for self-appropriation and the use of the theoretical framework of Preventive Leadership (conditions, parameters, educational strategies, and social parameters) can facilitate the adaptation and renewal of education in the complex, changing, and volatile challenges that the global leadership faces.
2. Leadership is a complex interaction between people and environments that emerges through social systems. The Preventive Leadership methodology encourages the development of genuine and original decision making mentality, a set of values, and a credible ethical behavior in different contexts.

3. The Preventive Leadership proposal can evolve and adapt as part of the leaders' own cognitive schema as they become more aware and understand the self and the identities and abilities of others. The framework is designed to compel leading educators to develop and act autonomously throughout their lives as all human beings, reflecting and learning from their lives and leadership experiences. Leaders gain authenticity when they act, and they justify their actions on the basis of the meaning system provided by their life stories. Attentiveness, to the method of leadership development and to the set of principles that guide behavior and decisions, allows the educator to consolidate a set of distinctive capacities through which his Preventive Leadership style will be defined. His/her personal leadership development will be completed through a strongly unitary personal life project.

4. It is possible to consider that the richness of the Preventive Leadership can have a strong presence in the most varied of educational contexts because to be a leading educator with a sensitivity for Salesian preventiveness is to educate from the positive and for the positive. Also, the Preventive Leadership seeks to increase, build and take advantage of the healthy energy that every person has. Leadership in the future will be a matter of discovering the positive energy in each person, stimulating the best in each individual, and developing the potential of everyone because this energy is the pledge of hope for the future.

5. The leadership process implies an accompaniment to achieve INLO and FLO. Enriches the leader in the complexity of the social context VUCA and UTRU. The grace of Unity is an ultimate imperative in the process of formation of every leader.

6. A convergence paradigm is proposed as a framework that addresses youth's experience. The development of Preventive Leadership that includes a body of leadership theories also seeks to transcend the obsolete notion that leadership development occurs only through specially designed programs in classrooms or senior management courses. Instead, it is a process that can take place anywhere. Using the two focal loops INLO and FLO as backdrops for ongoing educational work. The leader with *preventive DNA* can participate in the next-generation leaders in real time and in specific locations. The rich Salesian tradition in matters of training leaders turn transform within high social and organizational values and vision.
7. The use of the Preventive Leadership proposal provides bases for all educators to consider themselves leaders and for each one to participate productively in the training process to the leadership of others from whatever front they find themselves. INLO and FLO applied in a convergent way lead any educational leader to develop competencies such as agility for new and disruptive approach to learning self-awareness at deep levels of interiority, sense of the world in a more complex environment, inclusive new solutions to educative challenges, and facing change in complex environments.
8. A Preventive Leader is:
    a. A leader who uses loving-kindness with empathy and who is benevolent to everyone at all times;
    b. A leader who is reasonable in proposals and interventions, in decisions and processes, in his methods and regulations;
    c. A leader who lives an intentionally formative attitude that is always beyond what is assigned

by role or position; a leader who promotes in-depth personal reflection, self-awareness and an environment warmed with familiarity;
d. A leader who discerns according to the Oratorian criterion;
e. A leader who tries to be constantly present among the people, especially the youth generation, with an active and determined presence;
f. A leader who is concerned with the construction of the social good, solidarity and equity in society.

Closing thought

Some people want changes to happen, others dream that changes will happen, only a few make changes happen. It only remains for me to say that: If your actions inspire others to dream more, to learn more, to do more and to be the best for the world, YOU are a preventive leader who is living the passion to educate from the heart.

References

Adams, G., & Diamond, M. (1999). Psychodynamic perspectives on organizations: Identity, politics and change. *American Behavioral Scientist, 43*(2), 221-224.

Al-Huneidi, A., & Schreurs, J. (2012). Constructivism based blended learning in higher education. *International Journal of Emerging Technologies in Learning, 7*(1), 4-9.

Alonso, F., Lopez, G., Manrique, D., & Vines, J. (2005). An instructional model for web- based e-learning education with a blended learning process approach. *British Journal of Educational Technology*, 36(2), 217-235.

Andere, M. E. (2015). *¿Cómo es el aprendizaje en escuelas de clase mundial?* [How is learning in schools World-class?] Tomo I. Finlandia, Flandes, Países Bajos, Suiza, Chile, Estados Unidos, México (Vol. 1). Pearson Educación de México.

----------------. (2017). *Director de Escuela en el siglo XXI ¿Jardinero, pulpo o capitán?* [School Director in the XXI Century. Gardener, octopus or captain?]. Siglo XXI Editores.

Anderson, P. (1999). Perspective: Complexity theory and organization science. *Organization Science, 10*, 216-232.

Antonakis, J. A., & Sivasubramaniam, N. (2003). Context and leadership: An examination of the nine-factor Full-Range Leadership Theory using the Multifactor Leadership Questionnaire. *The Leadership Quarterly, 14*(3), 261-295.

Antonakis, J., Day, D. V., & Schyns, B. (2012). Leadership and individual differences: At the cusp of a renaissance. *Leadership Quarterly, 23*, 643-650.

Aquino, T. (1994). *Summa Theologicae*. BAC.

Aristóteles. (2005). *Ética a Nicómaco*, [Nicomachean Ethics] Libro IX, capítulo V (Vol. 1). (P. Azcaráte, Ed.). Proyecto Filosofía en Español.

Armstrong, D. (2005). *Organization in the mind: Psychoanalysis, group relations, and organizational consultancy*. Karnac Books.

Aronowitz, S., & Giroux, H. (1985). *Education under siege: The conservative, liberal, and radical debate over schooling*. Bergin & Garvey.

Ashkanasy, N. M., & Humphrey, R. H. (2011a). A multi-level view of leadership and emotions: leading with emotional labor . In A. Bryman, D. Collinson, K. Grint, B. Jackson, & M. U.-B. (Eds.), *The Sage Handbook of Leadership*. Sage Publications.

Ashkanasy, N. M., & Humphrey, R. H. (2011b). Current emotion research in organizational behavior. *Emotion Review, 3*, 214-224.

Ashley, G. C., & Reiter-Palmo, R. (2012). Self-awareness and the evolution of leaders: The need for a better measure of self- awareness. *Journal of Behavioral & Applied Management*, 14(1), 2-17.

Astin, A. W., y Astin, H. (2000). *Leadership reconsidered: Engaging higher education in social change*. Kellogg Foundation.

Athanasopoulou, A., & Dopson, S. (2015). *Developing leaders by executive coaching- practice and evidence*. Oxford University Press.

Avolio, B. J. (2005). *Leadership Development in Balance: Made/Born*. Erlbaum.

--------------. (2007). Promoting more integrated strategies for leadership theory-building. *American Psychologist*, 62(1), 25-33.

Avolio, B., Bass, B., & Jung, D. (1995). *Multifactor Leadership Questionnaire (Technical Report). Center for Leadership Studies*. Binghamton University and Garden.

Avolio, B., Kahai, S., & Dodge, G. (2001). E-leadership: implications for theory, research, and practice. *The Leadership Quarterly*, 11, 615-668.

Avolio, B., Reichard, R. J., Hannah, S. T., Walumbwa, F. O., & Chan, A. (2009). A meta- analytic review of leadership impact research: Experimental and quasi-experimental studies. *The Leadership Quarterly*, 20(5), 764-784.

Avolio, B., Walumbwa, F., & Weber, T. (2009). Leadership: Current Theories, Research, and Future Directions. *Annual Review of Psychology*, 60, 421-449.

Avolio, B., & Gardner, W. (2005). Authentic leadership development: Getting to the root of positive forms of leadership. *The Leadership Quarterly*, 16, 315-338.

Avolio, B., & Hannah, S. (2008). Developmental Readiness: Accelerating Leader Development. *Consulting Psychology Journal: Practice and Research*, 60, 331- 347.

Axelrod, S. D. (2012). "Self-awareness": At the interface of executive development and psychoanalytic therapy. *Psychoanalytic Inquiry*, 32(4), 340-357.

Bächtold, M. (2013). What do students "construct" according to constructivism in science education? *Research in Science Education*, 43(6), 2477-2496.
Bandura, A. (1986). *Social foundations of thought and action: A social cognitive theory*. Prentice-Hall, Inc.
Bandura, A. (1988). Self-regulation of motivation and action through goal systems. In G. H. V. Hamilton, & N. H. (Eds.), *Cognitive perspectives on emotion and motivation*. Dordrecht: Martinus Nijhoff.
Barbuto, J. E., & Wheeler, D. (2006). Scale development and construct clarification of servant leadership. *Group & Organization Management*, 31(3), 300-326.
Barevičiūtè, J. (2010). The locality of the "global village." In the aspect of communication: Pro et contra M. McLuhan. *Limes*, 3(2), 184-194.
Barrios, J. M. (2008). Sobre la llamada educación posmoderna [On the So-called Postmodern Education]. *Revista Española de Pedagogía*, 77(241), 527-540.
Bass, B. M. (1991). *Leadership and performance beyond expectations*. Free Press.
Bass, B. M., & Riggio, R. E. (2006). *Transformational Leadership*. Lawrence Erlbaum.
Bass, B. M., & Bass, R. (2008). *The bass handbook of leadership. Theory, research, and managerial applications*. Free Press.
Bauerlein, M. (Ed.). (2011). *The digital divide: Arguments for and against Facebook, Google, texting, and the age of social net-working* (1st ed.). Penguin.
Bauman, Z. (2006a). *Ética Posmoderna* [Postmodern Ethics]. Siglo XXI.
---------------. (2006b). *Vida Líquida* [Liquid Life] (Vol. 143). Paidós.
-------------- . (2008). *Consuming life*. Polity Press.
Bauman, Z., & Bordoni, C. (2016). *Estado de Crisis* [State of Crisis]. Paidós.
Bauman, Z., & Donskis, L. (2015). *Ceguera Moral. La pérdida de sensibilidad en la modernidad líquida* [Moral Blindness. The Loss of Sensitivity in the Liquid Modernity] Paidós.
Bazerman, M., & Chugh, D. (2006). Decisions without Blinders. *Harvard Business Review*, 82(1), 88-97.
Bennis, W. G. (1986). Transformative power and leadership. En T. J. Sergiovanni, & J. Corbally (Eds.), *Leadership and organizational culture* (pp. 64-71). University of Illinois Press.
------------------. (2007). The challenges of leadership in the modern world: An introduction to the special issue. *American Psychologist*, 62(1), 2-5.

----------------. (2012). The crucibles of authentic leadership. In D. V. Day, & J. Antonakis (Eds.), *The nature of leadership* (pp. 543- 556). Sage.

Berson, Y., & Avolio, B. J. (2004). Transformational leadership and the dissemination of organizational goals: A case study of a telecommunication firm. *Leadership Quarterly, 15*, 625-646.

Bertalanffy, L. (1968). *General systems theory: Foundations, development, applications.* George Braziller.

Bion, W. (2003). *Learning from experience.* London: Karnac.

Blake, R., & Mouton, J. (1964). *The Managerial Grid.* Gulf Publishing.

Bolden, R. (2011). Distributed leadership in organizations: A review of theory & research. *International Journal of Management Reviews, 13*, 251-269.

Bolden, R., Gosling, J., Maturano, A., & Dennison, P. (2003). *A review of leadership theory and competency frameworks. Centre for Leadership Studies.* University of Exeter.

Bolden, R., Petrov, G., & Gosling, J. (2008). Tensions in Higher Education Leadership: Towards a Multi-Level Model of Leadership Practice. *Higher Education Quarterly, 62*(4), 358-376.

----------------. (2009). Distributed leadership in higher education rhetoric and reality. *Educational Management Administration & Leadership, 37*, 257-277.

Bolman, L. G., & Deal, T. (2013). *Reframing Organizations: Artistry, choice, and leadership.* John Wiley & Sons Inc.

Bono, J. E., & Ilies, R. (2006). Charisma, positive emotions, and mood contagion. *Leadership Quarterly, 17*, 317-334.

Bosco, G. (1898-1948). *Memorie Biografiche di Don (del Beato... di San) Giovanni Bosco.* (V. 1.-9. (Vol. 1-19). (G.B. Lemoyne, V. 1. A. Amadei, V. 1.-1. E. Ceria, & V. 2. E. Foglio, Eds.) LAS.

----------------. (1955-1959). *Epistolario di san Giovanni Bosco.* (E. Ceria, Ed.). SEI.

----------------. (1988). *Opere edite: prima serie, Libri e opuscoli 1977- 1978* (Vol. 1). LAS.

----------------. (2007). *Memoirs of the Oratory of Saint Francis de Sales from 1815 to 1855.* (Reprinted from Memorie dell'Oratorio di S. Francesco di Sales dal 1815 al 1855. (E. Ceria, Ed., & D. Lyons, Trans.). SEI.

Bradbury, H., & Lichtenstein, B. (2000). Relationality in organizational research: Exploring the space between. *Organization Science, 11*, 551-564.

Braido, P. (2001). *Prevenir, no reprimir. El sistema educativo de Don Bosco* [Prevention not Repression. Educative Method of Don Bosco]. CCS.

------------. (2013). *Prevention not Repression. Don Bosco.* Kristu Jyoti Publications. Educational System.

Braido, P., Da Silva Ferreira, A., Motto, F., & Prellezo, J. M. (Eds.). (1992). *Don Bosco Educatore. Scritti e testimonianze* [Don Bosco Educator. Writings and Testimonies]. LAS.

Brown, D. J. (2012). In the minds of followers: Follower-centric approaches to leadership. In D. V. Day (Ed.), *The nature of leadership* (pp. 331-362). Sage.

Brown, K., & Cole, M. (2001). Cultural historical activity theory and the expansion of opportunities for learning after school. In M. J. Packer, & M. Tappan (Eds.), *Cultural and critical perspectives on human development*. SUNY Press.

Brown, M. E., Treviño, L. K., & Harrison, D. (2005). Ethical leadership: A social learning perspective for construct development and testing. *Organizational Behavior and Human Decision Processes, 97*, 117-134.

Brunner, L., Nutkevitch, A., & Sher, M. (2006). *Group relations conferences. Reviewing and exploring theory, design, role-taking and application.* Karnac.

Bryman, A. (2007). Effective leadership in higher education: A literature review. *Studies in Higher Education, 32*(6), 693-710.

Buber, M. (1970). *I and thou.* (W. Kaufmann, Trans.). Scribner's Sons.

Buchanan, D. A., Addicott, R., Fitzgerald, L., Ferlie, E., & Baeza, J. (2007). Nobody in charge: Distributed change agency in healthcare. *Human Relations, 60*(7), 1065- 1090.

Burns, J. M. (2010). *Leadership.* Harper Perennial Political Classic.

Caraher, L. (2015). *Millennials & Management: The Essential Guide to Making it Work at Work.* Routledge.

Carson, J. B., Tesluk, P., & Marrone, J. (2007). Shared leadership in teams: an investigation of antecedent conditions and performance. *Academy of Management Journal, 50*, 1217-1234.

Chan, A. (2005). Authentic leadership measurement and development: Challenges and suggestions. In W. L. Gardner, B. J. Avolio, & F. O. Walumbwa (Eds.), *Authentic leadership theory and practice: Origins, effects and development* (pp. 227-250). Elsevier.

Chan, A., Hannah, S. T., & Gardner, W. L. (2005). Veritable authentic leadership: Emergence, functioning, and impacts. In W. L. Gardner, B. J. Avolio, & F. O. Walumbwa (Eds.), *Authentic leadership theory and practice: Origins, effects and development* (pp. 3-41). Elsevier.

Chang, Y., & Brickman, P. (2018). When group work doesn´t work: Insights from students. *CBE-Life Sciences Education*, 17(3), 1-17.

Chapman, J., & Aspin, D. (2001). Schools and the Learning Community: Laying the Basis for Learning across the Lifespan. In D. Aspin, M. Chapman, M. Hatton, & Y. Sawano (Eds.), *International Handbook on Lifelong Learning* (Vol. 2, pp. 405- 446). Kluwer Academic Publichers.

Chen, C., & Kuo, C. (2019). *An optimized group formation scheme to promote collaborative problem-based learning.* Computers & Education, doi:10.1016/j.compedu.2019.01.011.

Chiosso, G. (2014, November 19-23). *Problemi aperti e prospettive del Congresso, Bicentenario della nascita di don Bosco. Presentazione nell Congresso Storico Internazionale* [Open Problems and Prospects for The Congress, Bicentenary of the Birth of Don Bosco. Presentation At The International Historical Congress]. Salesianum.

Chu Chih, L., & Ju (Crissa) Chen, I. (2010). Evolution of constructivism. *Contemporary issues in Education Research*, 3(4), 63-66.

Chugh, D., & Bazerman, M. (2007). Bounded Awareness: What you fail to see can hurt you. *Mind & Society*, 6, 1-18.

Chun, J. U., Yammarino, F. J., Dionne, S. D., Sosik, J. S., & Moon, H. K. (2009). Leadership across hierarchical levels: Multiple levels of management and multiple levels of analysis. *Leadership Quarterly, 20*, 689-707.

Cian, L. (2001). *El sistema educativo de Don Bosco. Líneas maestras de su estilo* [Don Bosco's Educational System. Master Lines of His Style]. CCS.

Cilliers, P. (1998). *Complexity and Postmodernism: Understanding Complex Systems*. Routledge.

CIMAC-MESOAMERICA. (2018). *Escuela Salesiana en América* [Salesian Schools in the American Continent].

Cochran-Smith, M. y Villegas, A. (2016). Research on Teaching Preparation. Charting the Landscape of a Sprawling Field. In Gitomer, D. y Bell, C. (Eds.). *Handbook of Research on Teaching.* (pp. 439-547). American Educational Research Association.

Cogliser, C. C., & Schriesheim, C. (2000). Exploring work unit context and leader-member exchange: a multi-level perspective. *Journal of Organizational Behavior*, 21, 487-511.

Cole, M. (1996). *Cultural Psychology: A once and future discipline*. Harvard University Press.

Coll, C. (2001). Constructivismo y educación: la concepción constructivista de la enseñanza y el aprendizaje [Constructivism and education: the constructivist conception of teaching and learning]. In C. Coll, J. Palacios y A. Marchesi (comps.), *Desarrollo psicológico y educación 2. Psicología de la educación escolar* [Psychological Development and Education 2. Psychology of School Education.] (pp. 157- 186). Alianza Editorial.

Colman, A., & Geller, M. H. (1985). *Group relations reader 2*. The A.K. Rice Institute.

Conger, J. A. (2011). Charismatic leadership. In A. Bryman, D. Collinson, K. Grint, B. Jackson, & M. U.-B. (Eds.), *Sage Handbook of Leadership*. Sage Publications.

Cortés Pacheco, C. (2016). La amistad política en santo Tomás de Aquino: entre la justicia y la misericordia [Political Friendship in Saint Thomas Aquinas: Between Justice and Mercy]. *Espíritu*, LXV (151), 101-127.

Coutu, D. L. (2002, May). How resilience works. *Harvard Business Review*, 46-55.

Currie, G., & Lockett, A. (2011). Distributing leadership in health and social care: concertive, conjoint or collective? *International Journal of Management Reviews*, 13(3), 286-300.

Cytrynbaum, S., & Noumair, A. (2004). *Group relations reader: 3*. The A.K. Rice Institute.

Dansereau, F., Alutto, J. A., & Yammarino, F. J. (1984). *Theory testing in organizational behavior: The varient approach*. Prentice-Hall.

Davis, S. H. (2006). Influencing transformative learning for leaders. *School Administrator*, 63(8).

Day, D. V. (2000). Leadership development; a review in context. *The Leadership Quarterly*, 11, 581-614.

Day, D. V., Fleenor, J., Atwater, L., Sturm, R., & McKee, R. (2014). Advances in leader and leadership development: A review of 25 years of research and theory. *The Leadership Quarterly*, 25(1), 63-82.

Day, D. V., Gronn, P., & Salas, E. (2004). Leadership capacity in teams. *The Leadership Quarterly*, 15, 857-880.

Day, D. V., & Sin, H. (2011). Longitudinal tests of an integrative model of leader development: Charting and understanding developmental trajectories. *The Leadership Quarterly*, 22, 545-560.

De Déa Roglio, K., & Light, G. (2009). Executive MBA Programs: The Development of the Reflective Executive. *Academy of Management Learning & Education*, 8(2), 156- 173.

Deaton, A. (2015). *El Gran Escape. Salud, riqueza y los orígenes de la desigualdad* [The Big Escape. Health, Wealth and the Origins of Inequality]. FCE.

Denis, J.-L., Langley, A., & Sergi, V. (2012). Leadership in the plural. *Academy of Management Annals*, 6(1), 211-283.

Derridá, J. (2004). *Eyes of the university*. Stanford University Press.

Derue, D. S., Nahrgang, J. D., Wellman, N., & Humphrey, S. E. (2011). Trait and behavioral theories of leadership: An integration and meta-analytic test of their relative validity. *Personnel Psychology, 4*(1), 7-52.

Dionne, S. D., Yammarino, F., Atwater, L., & James, L. (2002). Neutralizing substitutes for leadership theory: leadership effects and common-source bias. *Journal of Applied Psychology*, 87, 454-464.

Dopson, S., Ferlie, E., McGivern, G., Fischer, M., Ledger, J., Behrens, S., & Wilson, S. (2016). *The impact of leadership and leadership development in higher education: a review of the literature and evidence*. Retrieve from London: Leadership Foundation for Higher Education. (Research and development series): http://wrap.warwick.ac.uk/78847

Doran, M. R. (2008). Discernment and Lonergan´s Fourth Level of Consciousness, *Gregorianum*, 89 (4), 790-802

Douglas, C., Ferris, G., & Perrewe, P. (2005). Leader political skill and authentic leadership. In W. Gardner, B. Avolio, & F. Walumbwa (Eds.), *Authentic leadership theory and practice: origins, effects and development*. Elsevier.

Doyle, J. F. (2007). The case of a servant leader: John F. Donnelly, Sr. In R. Vecchio (Ed.), *Leadership. Understanding the dynamics of power and influence in Organizations* (pp. 416-443). Notre Dame.

Drath, W. (2001). *The Deep Blue Sea: Rethinking the Source of Leadership*. Jossey-Bass & Center for Creative Leadership.

Drath, W. H., McCauley, C. D., Palus, C. J., Velsor, E. V., O'Connor, P. M., & McGuire, J. B. (2008). Direction, alignment, and commitment: Toward a more integrative ontology of leadership. *The Leadership Quarterly*, 19, 635-653.

Driver, R., Asoko, H., Leach, J., Mortimer, E., & Scott, P. (1994). Constructing scientific knowledge in the classroom. *Educational Researcher*, 23(7), 5-12.

Driver, R., Guesne, E., & Tiberghien, A. (Eds.). (1985). *Children's ideas in science*. Open University Press.

Duit, R. (1995). The constructivist view: a fashionable and fruitful paradigm for science education. In L. Steffe, & J. Gale (Eds.), *Constructivism in education* (pp. 271- 285). Erl-baum.

---------. (2003). Conceptual change: a powerful framework for improving science teaching and learning. *International Journal of Science Education*, 25(6), 671-688.

Dunne, T. (2017, September 25). *Internet Encyclopedy of Philosophy. A Peer-Reviewed Academic Resource.* Retrieve from Bernard Lonergan https://www.iep.utm.edu/lonergan/

Dvir, T., & Shamir, B. (2003). Follower developmental characteristics as predicting transformational leadership: a longitudinal field study. *The Leadership Quarterly*, 14, 327-344.

Eagly, A. H., & Karau, S. J. (2002). Role congruity theory of prejudice toward female leaders. *Psychological Review, 109*(3), 573.

Eccles, J. S., & Wigfield, A. (2002). Motivational beliefs, values, and goals. *Annual Review in Psychology* (53), 109-132.

Engeström, Y. (2009). Expansive learning: toward an activity- theoretical reconceptualization. In K. Illeris (Ed.), *Contemporary theories of learning: learning theorists in their own words* (pp. 53-73). Taylor & Francis.

Epitropaki, O., & Martin, R. (2004). Implicit Leadership Theories in Applied Settings: Factor Structure, Generalizability, and Stability Over Time. *The Journal of applied psychology, 89*, 293-310.

Esguerra, R. (2017). Clínica y ciencia con humanitarismo y ética [Clinic and Science With Humanitarianism and Ethics]. *Acta Médica Colombiana*, 42(4), 240-242.

Eurich, T. (2017). *Insight*. New York: Crown Business.

Fairhurst, G. (2009). Considering context in discursive leadership research. *Human Relations*, 62, 1607-1634.

----------------. (2011). *The power of framing*. San Francisco: Jossey- Bass.

Ferlie, E., Fitzgerald, L., McGivern, G., Dopson, S., & Bennett, C. (2013). *Making wicked problems governable? The case of managed health care networks.* Oxford University Press.

Fiedler, F. (1964). A contingency model of leadership effectiveness. In L. Berkowitz (Ed.), *Advances in experimental social psychology*. Academic Press Inc.

Fiedler, F. (1967). *A Theory of Leadership Effectiveness*. McGraw-Hill.

Finamore, R. (2014). *Realismo e Metodo. La riflessione epistemologica di Bernard Lonergan* [Realism and Method. Bernard Lonergan's Epistemological Reflection]. Rome, Italy: Gregorian & Biblical Press.

FinancialFood.es. (30 de enero de 2019). *El 75% de los centennials influye en las decisiones de compras familiares* [75% of Centennials Influence Family Shopping Decisions]. Retrieve from https://www.financialfood.es/default.aspx?where=5&id=1&n=31462

Fischer, M. D., & Sievewright, B. (2014). *Developing the study of Australian leadership: a contextual review of the literature.* University of Melbourne.

Fisher, B., Turner, R., & Morling, P. (2009). Defining and Classifying Ecosystem Services for Decision Making. *Ecological Economics*, 68, 643-653.

Fisher, C. D. (2000). Mood and emotions while working: missing pieces of job satisfaction? *21*, 185-202.

Fitzgerald, L., Ferlie, E., McGivern, G., & Buchanan, D. (2013). Distributed leadership patterns and service improvement: evidence and argument from English healthcare. *The Leadership Quarterly*, 24(1), 227-239.

Flanagan, J. (1997). *Quest for Self-knowledge: An Essay in Lonergan's.* University of Toronto Press.

Fleishman, E. (1951). *Leadership climate and supervisory behavior. A study of the Leadership role of the Foreman in an Industrial situation.* Columbus, Ohio: Personnel Research Board The Ohio State University.

Foster, W. (1986). *Paradigms and promises.* Prometheus. Philosophy.

Fowler, S. M. (2006). Training across cultures: What intercultural trainers bring to diversity training. *International Journal of Intercultural Relations*, 30, 401-411.

Francis. (2013). *Pastoral visit to Cagliari meeting with the Academic and Cultural World address of Holy Father Francis.* Retrieve from qqhttp://w2.vatican.va/content/francesco/en/travels/2013/inside/documents/papa-francesco-cagliari-20130922.html

Freire, P. (1998). *Pedagogy of freedom: Ethics, democracy, and civic courage.* Rowman & Littlefield.

-----------. (2012). *Pedagogy of the oppressed.* Herder & Herder.

Freud, F. (1921). *Group psychology and the analysis of the ego. Complete works of Sigmund Freud.* Hogart.

Fry, L. W. (2003). Toward a theory of Spiritual Leadership. *The Leadership Quarterly*, 14, 693- 727.

Fry, L. W., Vitucci, S., & Cedillo, M. (2005). Spiritual leadership and army transformation: Theory, measurement, and establishing a baseline. *The Leadership Quarterly, 16*, 835-862.

Fullan, M. (2001). *Leading in a Culture of Change.*: John Wiley & Sons.

George, B. (2003). *Authentic Leadership: rediscovering the secrets to creating lasting value.* Jossey-Bass.

Gadamer, H. (2004). *Truth and Method* (2nd Edition ed.). (J. Weinsheimer, & D. G. Marshall, Trans.) Continuum.

Galli, E. B., & Müller-Stewens, G. (2012). How to build social capital with leadership development: Lessons from an explorative case study of a multi-business firm. *The Leadership Quarterly*, 23(1), 176-201.

Gardner, W. L., Avolio, B. J., Luthans, F., May, D. R., & Walumbwa, F. (2005). "Can you see the real me?" A self-based model of authentic leader and follower development. *The Leadership Quarterly*, 16(3), 343-372.

George, B. (2016, July 06). *The Truth About Authentic Leaders.* Retrieved on March, 2020 from Harvard Business School. Working Knowledge: https://hbswk.hbs.edu/item/the-truth-about-authentic-leaders

Gerstner, C. R., & Day, D. (1997). Meta-analytic review of leader-member exchange theory: correlates and construct issues. *Journal of Applied Psychology*, 82, 827- 844.

Gioia, D., Schultz, M., & Corley, K. (2000). Organizational identity, image, and adaptive instability. *Academy of Management Review, 25*, 63-81.

Giroux, H. (2011). Educational visions: What are schools for and what should we be doing in the name of education? In J. L. Kincheloe, & S. Steinberg (ed.), *Thirteen questions* (pp. 295-302). Peter Lang.

Goldsmith, M. (2003). *Global Leadership: The Next Generation.* Financial Times Prentice Hall.

Goleman, D. (1998). *Working with emotional intelligence.* Bantam Books.

----------------. (2015). *¿Cómo ser un líder?* [What makes a leader?]. Ediciones B.

----------------. (2016, November). *What Makes a Leader?* Retrieve from Harvard Business Review: https://hbr.org/2004/01/ what-makes-a-leader

Goleman, D., & Senge, P. (25 de noviembre de 2016). *Triple Focus: Un nuevo acercamiento a la Educación* [Triple Focus: A New Approach to Education]. Ediciones B, S.A. Retrieve from https://www.linkedin.com/pulse/20131125023629-117825785-the-signs-of-a-leader-s-empathy-deficit-disorder

González, N. (20 de abril de 2013). *Los niños de la generación Touch* [Kids from the Touch Generation]. Retrieve from El Observador: https://www.elobservador.com.uy/nota/los- ninos-de-la-generacion-touch-2013420500

Gooty, J., Connelly, S., Griffith, J., & Gupta, A. (2010). Leadership, affect and emotions: a state of the science review. *Leadership Quarterly, 21*, 979-1004.

Graen, G. (1969). Instrumentality theory of work motivation: Some experimental results and suggested modifications. *Journal of Applied Psychology, 53*, (whole no. 2, part 2).

Graen, G. B., & Uhl-Bien, M. (1995). Relationship based approach to leadership development of leader-member exchange (LMX) theory of leadership over 25 years applying a multilevel multidomain perspective. *The Leadership Quarterly,* 6, 219-247.

Graen, G., & Uhl-Bien, M. (1995). Relationship-Based Approach to Leadership: Development of Leader-Member Exchange (LMX) Theory of Leadership over 25 Years: Applying a Multi-Level Multi-Domain Perspective. *Leadership Quarterly, 6*(2), 219-247.

Grant, A. M. (2012). Leading with meaning: Beneficiary con- tact, prosocial impact, and the performance effects of transformational leadership. *Academy of Management Journal,* 55(22), 458-476.

Green, S., Hassan, F., Immelt, J., Marks, M., & Mei-Land, D. (2003). In search of global leaders. *Harvard Business Review,* 81, 38-45.

Greenleaf, R. (1977). *Servant Leadership: A Journey Into the Nature of Legitimate Power and Greatness.* Paulist Press.

——————. (1978). *The Institution as Servant.* The Greenleaf Center.

——————. (1987). *Teacher as Servant: A Parable.* The Greenleaf Center.

——————. (1996). *On Becoming a Servant Leader.* Jossey-Bass.

——————. (1998). *The Power of Servant-Leadership.* Berrett-Koehler Publisher Inc.

——————. (1991). *The Servant as Leader.* Robert Greenleaf Center.

——————. (1998). *The Power of Servant Leaders.* Berrett-Koehler.

——————. (2003). *The Servant-Leader Within.* Paulist Press.

Grimaldo, H. (2015). La responsabilidad social de las Universidades: Implicaciones para América Latina y el Caribe [The Social Responsibility of Universities: Implications for Latin America and the Caribbean]. In H. E. A. (Ed.), *Visiones e iniciativas sobre la responsabilidad social de las universidades en América Latina y el Caribe* (pp. 273-275). San Juan, Puerto Rico: United Nations for Education and Culture Organization.

Grint, K. (2005). Problems, problems, problems: The social construction of leadership. *Human Relations*, 58(11), 1467-1494.
Gronn, P. (2002). Distributed leadership as a unit of analysis. *Leadership Quarterly, 13*, 423-451.
Gupta, A. K., Tesluk, P. E., & Taylor, M. S. (2007). Innovation at and across multiple levels of analysis. *Organization Science, 18*, 885-897.
Hannum, K. M., & Craig, S. (2010). Introduction to special issue on leadership development evaluation. *The Leadership Quarterly*, 21, 581-582.
Harari, Y. N. (12 de Agosto de 2018). *WIRED*. Retrieve from https://www.wired.co.uk/article/yuval-noah-harari-extract-21-lessons-for-the-21st- century
Hargreaves, A., & Fink, D. (2006). *Sustainable Leadership*. Jossey-Bass.
Harter, S. (2002). Authenticity. In R. S. (Eds.), *Handbook of positive psychology (pp. 382-394)*. University Press.
Hartle, R., Baviskar, S., & Smith, R. (2012). A field guide to constructivism in the college science classroom: Four essential criteria and a guide to their usage. *Bioscience*, 38(2), 31-35.
Hartman, J. H., & McCambridge, J. (2011). Optimizing Millennials" communication styles. *Business Communication Quarterly*, 74(1), 22-44.
Harvard Business Review. (13 de January de 2016). *What Really Influences Employee Motivation*. USA.
Hatfield, E., Cacioppo, J. T., & Rapson, R. L. (1994). *Emotional Contagion*. Cambridge University Press.
Hazy, J. (2006). Measuring leadership effectiveness in complex sociotechnical systems. *Emergence: Complexity and Organization, 8*(3), 58-77.
Hazy, J. K., Goldstein, J., & Lichtenstein, B. (2007). Complex systems leadership theory: an introduction. In J. K. Hazy, J. Goldstein, & B. Lichtenstein (Eds.), *Complex Systems Leadership Theory: New Perspectives from Complexity Science on Social and Organizational Effectiveness* (pp. 1-13). ISCE Publisher.
Heifezt, R., Grashow, A., & Linsky, M. (2009). *The Practice of Adaptive Leadership. tools and tactics for changing your Organization and the World*. Harvard Business Press.
Hernández, V. (1999). *La ética a Nicómaco de Aristóteles* [Aristotle's Nicomachean Ethics]. Editorial Alianza.
Hersey, P., & Blanchard, K. (1969). *Management of organizational behavior: Utilizing human resources*. Prentice-Hall.
Hidi, S., & Renninger, K. (2006). The four-phase model of interest development. *Educational Psychologist* (41), 11-127.

Hirst, G., Mann, L., Bain, P., Pirola-Merlo, A., & Richter, A. (2004). Learning to lead: The development and testing of a model of leadership learning. *The Leadership Quarterly*, 15(3), 311-327.

Hoffman, B. J., Woehr, D. J., Maldagen-Youngjohn, R., & Lyons, B. D. (2011). Great man or greatvmyth? A quantitative review of the relationship between individual differences and leader effectiveness. *Journal of Occupational and Organizational Psychology*, 84(2), 347-381.

Hofstede, G. H. (2001). *Culture's Consequences: Comparing Values, Behaviors, Institutions, and Organizations Across Nations.* Sage.

Hoppe, B., & Reinelt, C. (2010). Social network analysis and the evaluation of leadership networks. *The Leadership Quarterly*, 21, 600-619.

House, R. (1977). A theory of charismatic leadership. In J. Hunt, & L. Larson (Eds.), *Leadership: The cutting edge* (pp. 189-207). Southern Illinois University Press.

House, R. J., Hanges, P., Javidan, M., Dorfman, P., & Gupta, V. (2004). *Culture, Leadership, and Organizations: The GLOBE Study of 62 Societies.* Sage.

House, R., & Mitchell, T. (1975). *Path-Goal Thery of Leadership.* Washington University.

Howell, J., & Avolio, B. (1993). Transformational leadership, transactional leadership, locus of control, and support for innovation: Key predictors of consolidated-business-unit performance. *Journal of Applied Psychology*, 78(6), 891-902.

Humphrey, R. H. (2013). *Effective Leadership: Theories, Cases, and Applications.* Los Angeles: SAGE Publications.

Hutchins, E. (1995). *Cognition in the wild.* Cambridge, MA: MIT Press.

Innovación educativa. (5 de octubre de 2018). *Reimagine Education Lab.* Retrieve from https://xavieraragay.com/innovacion_educativa/estamos-cambiando-de-fase-es-hora-de-enfocar-la-trasformacion-profunda-de-la-educacion

Izard, C. E. (1991). *The Psychology of Emotions.* Springer Science & Business Media.

Jaques, E. (1970). *Work, creativity and social justice.* International Universities Press.

Jarvis, C., Gulati, A., McCririck, V., & Simpson, P. (2013). Leadership matters: tensions in evaluating leadership development. *Advances in Developing Human Resources*, 15(1), 27-45.

Jenkins, E. (2000). Constructivism in school science education: powerful model or the most dangerous intellectual tendency? *Science Education*, 9, 599-610.

Johansen, B. (2012). *Leaders make the future. Ten new leadership skills for an uncertain world.* Berrett- Koehler Publisher.

Juan Pablo II. (1985). *Dilecti Amici. Apostolic Letter to the youth of the world on the occasion of International Youth Year.* Retrieve from vatican.va:http://www.vatican.va/holy_father/john_paul_ii/apost_letters/documents/hf_jp- ii_apl_31031985_di- lecti-amici_en.html

----------------. (1988). *Iuvenum Patris. Commemorative Letter to the Successor of Saint John Bosco.* Retrieve from http://www.vatican.va/holy_father/john_paul_ii/letters/1988/documents/hf_jp-ii_let_19880131_ iuvenum-patris_it.html

Judge, T. A., Bono, J. E., Ilies, R., & Gerhardt, M. W. (2002). Personality and leadership: A qualitative and quantitative review. *Journal of Applied Psychology, 87*, 765-780.

Judge, T., & Bono, J. (2000). Five-Factor model of personality and transformational leadership. *Journal of Applied Psychology*, 85(5), 751-765.

Kabat-Zinn, J. (1994). *Wherever you go, there you are: Mindfulness meditation in everyday life.* Hyperion.

Kaifi, B., Nafei, W., Khanfar, N., & Kaifi, M. (2012). A Multi- Generational workforce: Managing and understanding Millennials. *International Journal of Business & Management*, 7(24), 88-93.

Kant, E. (1997). *Critique of Pure Reason.* (P. Guyer, & A. W. Wood, Trans.) CUP.

Katz, R. L. (1974, September/October). Skills of an effective administrator. *Harvard Business Review, 52*(2), 90-102.

Kegan, R., & Lahey, L. (2010). Adult development and organizational leadership. In N. Nohria, & R. Khurana (Eds.), *Handbook of leadership theory and practice: A Harvard Business School Centennial Colloquium* (pp. 769-787). Harvard Business Press.

Keller, R. T. (2006). Transformational leadership, initiating structure, and substitutes for leadership: a longitudinal study of research and development project team performance. *Journal of Applied Psychology*, 91, 202-210.

Kenney, R. A., Schwartz-Kenney, B. M., & Blascovich, J. (1996). Implicit Leadership Theories: Defining leaders described as worthy of influence. *Personality and Social Psychology Bulletin, 22*, 1128-1143.

Kerins, M. R., & Matrangola, D. (2012). Generational spin: How supervisors view the Millennials. *Perspectives on Administration & Supervision*, 22(3), 74-84.

Kezar, A. J., Carducci, R., & Contreras-McGavin, M. (2006). *Rethinking the "L" word in higher education: the revolution in research on leadership.* Jossey-Bass.

King, K. P., & Biro, S. (2000). A transformative learning perspective of continuing sexual identity development in the workplace. *New Directions for Adult and Continuing Education,* 112, 17-27.

Kinnaman, D. (2011). *You lost me: Why young Christians are leaving church, and rethinking faith.* Baker Books.

Klein, M. (1988). *Envy and gratitude and other works 1946-1963.* Hogarth.

Klein, T. J. (2005). Integrative learning and interdisciplinary studies. *Peer Review,* 7(4), 8- 10.

Lane, H. W. (2004). *The Blackwell Handbook of Global Management: A Guide to Managing Complexity.* Wiley- Blackwell.

Lanz, C. C. (2012). Taking care of self and the other in education. *Utopia y Praxis Latinoamericana,* 17(56), 39-46.

Larson, A. (1968). *Eisenhower: The president nobody knew.* Popular Library.

Lavery, S., & Hine, G. (2013). Catholic school principals: Promoting student leadership. *Catholic Education: A Journal of Inquiry & Practice,* 17(1), 41-66.

Lawrence, P., & Lorsch, J. (1967). Differentiation and integration in complex organisations. *Administrative Science Quarterly,* 12(1), 1-47.

Lawrence, W., Bain, A., & Gould, L. (1996). *The fifth basic assumption.* Tavistock.

Leihan, D. (2011, June 19). *Public Opinion Polls: Useless in Our Volatile Society?* Retrieve from [Web log post]: http://www.huffingtonpost.ca/donald-lenihan/public-opinion-polls_b_879785.html

Lenti, A. J. (2011). *Don Bosco: Historia y Carisma* [Don Bosco: History and Charism] (Vol. 2 Expansión: De Valdocco a Roma). (J. J. Bartolomé, & J. G. González, Edits.) CCS.

———. (2007-2008). *Don Bosco. History and Spirit* (Vol. 1-7). LAS.

Lichtenstein, B. B., Uhl-Bien, M., Marion, R., S., A., Orton, J. D., & Schreiber, C. (2006). Complexity leadership theory: An interactive perspective on leading in complex adaptive systems. *Emergence: Complexity and Organization,* 8(4), 2-12.

Liden, R. C., & Maslyn, J. M. (1998). Multidimensionality of leader-member exchange: an empirical assessment through scale development. *Journal of Management* 24, 43-72.

Lavery, S.,& Hine, G. (2013). Catholic school principals: Promoting student leadership. *Catholic Education: A Journal of Inquiry & Practice,* 17(1), 41-66.

Ligon, G. S., Hunter, S. T., & Mumford, M. D. (2008). Development of outstanding leadership: A life narrative approach. *The Leadership Quarterly, 19*(3), 312-334.

Linsky, M., & Heifetz, R. (2002). *Leadership on the Line: Staying Alive through the Dangers of Leading.* Harvard Business School Press.

Lonergan, B. (1967). *Cognitional Structure in Collection: Papers by Bernard Lonergan.* Herder.

---------------. (1973). *Method in Theology.* University of Toronto Press for Lonergan Research Institute of Regis College.

---------------. (1992). In*sight: A Study of Human Understanding* (Vol. 3). (F. E. Crowe, & R. Doran, Eds.) University of Toronto.

López, J. M. (8 de mayo de 2017). *Las redes sociales en números: WhatsApp, Facebook, Instagram y Twitter.* [Social Networks in Numbers: WhatsApp, Facebook, Instagram and Twitter]. Retrieve from https://blogthinkbig.com/las-redes-sociales-en-numeros-whatsapp-facebook- instagram-y-twitter

Lord, R. G., & Maher, K. J. (1993). *Leadership and information processing. Linking perceptions and performance.* Routledge.

Lord, R. G., Day, D. V., Zaccaro, S., & Avolio, B. J. (2017). Leadership in Applied Psychology: Three waves of Theory and Research. *Journal of Applied Psychology, 102*(3), 434-451. http://dx.doi.org/10.1037/apl0000089

Lord, R. G., Foti, R. J., & De Vader, C. L. (1984). A test of leadership categorization theory: Internal structure, information processing, and leadership perceptions. *Organizational Behavior and Human Performance, 34,* 343-378.

Lord, R. G., y Hall, R. J. (2005). Identity, deep structure, and the development of leadership skill. *The Leadership Quarterly* 16, 591-615.

Lowe, K. B., & Gardner, W. (2000). Ten years of the Leadership Quarterly: contributions and challenges for the future. *The Leadership Quarterly,* 11, 459-514.

Luthans, F., & Avolio, B. (2003). Authentic Leadership Development: a positive developmental approach. In K. Cameron, J. Dutton, & R. Q. (Eds.), *Positive Organizational Scholarship: Foundations of a New Discipline* (pp. 241-258). Berre-Koehler Publishers.

Malhotra, A., Majchrzak, A., & Rosen, B. (2007). Leading virtual teams. *Academic Management Perspectives,* 21, 60-70.

Marion, R. (1999). *The Edge of Organization: Chaos and Complexity Theories of Formal Social Organization.* Sage.

Marion, R., & Uhl-Bien, M. (2001). Leadership in complex organizations, *Leadership Quarterly, 12,* 389–418.

Marion, R., & Uhl-Bien, M. (2003). Complexity theory and Al-Qaeda: Examining complex leadership. *Emergence: Complexity Issues in Organizations and Management, 5,* 56-78.

Markham, S. E. (1985). An investigation of the relationship between unemployment and absenteeism — A multi-level approach. *Academy of Management Journal, 28,* 228-234.

Markham, S. E. (1998). Pay-for-performance dilemma revisited: Empirical example of the importance of group effects. *Journal of Applied Psychology, 73,* 172–180.

Markham, S. E. (2010). Leadership, levels of analysis, and déjà vu: Modest proposals for taxonomy and cladistics coupled with replications and visualization. *Leadership Quarterly, 21,* 1121-1143.

Markham, S. E. (2012). The evolution of organizations and leadership from the ancient world to modernity: A multilevel approach to organizational science and leadership. *Leadership Quarterly, 23,* 1134-1151.

Markham, S. E., & McKee, G. H. (1995). Group absence behaviour and standards: A multilevel analysis. *Academy of Management Journal, 38,* 1174–1190.

Martens, P., Dreher, A., & Gaston, N. (2010). Globalisation, the global village and the civil society. *Futures, 42*(6), 574-582.

Martí, A. C., García-Campayo, J., & DeMarzo, M. (Ed.). (2014). *Mindfulness y Ciencia. De la tradición a la modernidad* [Mindfulness and Science. From Tradition to Modernity]. Alianza Editorial.

Masiá, C. J. (2004). *Fragilidad en esperanza* [Fragility in Hope]. Enfoques de Antropología. Bilbao, España: DDB.

Masten, A. S., & Reed, M. J. (2002). Resilience in development. In C. R. Snyder, & S. J. (Eds.), *Handbook of positive psychology* (pp. 74-88). Oxford University Press.

Matthews, M. (2000). Constructivism in science and mathematics education. In D. Phillips (Ed.), *National Society for the Study of Education, 99th Yearbook* (pp. 161-192). University of Chicago Press.

McCleskey, J. A. (2014). Situational, Transformational, and Transactional Leadership and Leadership Development. *Journal of Business Studies Quarterly, 5*(4), 6-9.

McLuhan, M. (1964). T*he Gutenberg Galaxy: The Making of Typographic Man.* University of Toronto Press.

Meindl, J. (1995). The romance of leadership as a follower-centric theory: a social constructionist approach. *The Leadership Quarterly*, 6(3), 329-341.

Mendenhall, M. E. (2001). Introduction: new perspectives on expatriate adjustment and its relationship to global leadership development. In G. K. Stahl (Ed.), *Developing Global Business Leaders: Policies, Processes, and Innovations* (pp. 1-16). Quorum.

Menges, J. I., & Kilduff, M. (2015). Group emotions: cutting the Gordian knots concerning terms, levels of analysis, and processes. *Academic Management Annual*, 9, 845-928.

Menzies, I. (1993). *The functioning of social systems as a defence against anxiety*. Tavistock Institute.

Meyer, A. D., Gaba, V., & Colwell, C. A. (2005). Organizing far from equilibrium: Nonlinear change in organizational fields. *Organization Science*, 16, 456-473.

Meynell, H. (2009). Taking A(nother) look at Lonergan's Method. *New Blackfriars*, 1028, 474-500.

Michie, S., & Gooty, J. (2005). Values, emotions, and authenticity: Will the real leader please stand up? *The Leadership Quarterly*, 16(3), 441-457.

Miller, E. (1993). *From dependency to autonomy: Studies in organization and change*. Free Association.

Miller, M. (2006). Transforming Leadership: What does love have to do with it? *Transformation*, 23(2), 94-106.

Mobley, W. H., Gessner, M., & Arnold, V. (1999). *Advances in Global Leadership*. JAI.

Montero, L., & Gewerc, A. (2018). La profesión docente en la sociedad del conocimiento. Una mirada a través de la revisión de investigaciones de los últimos 10 años [The Teaching Profession in the Knowledge Society. A Look Through the Research Review of the Last 10 Years]. *Revista de Educación a Distancia*, 56(3), 1-22.

Morrison, J., Rha, J., & Helfman, A. (2003). Learning awareness, student engagement, and change: a transformation in leadership development. *Journal of Education for Business*, 79(1), 11-17.

Mucci, G. (2014). L'importanza del dialogo nell'«Evangelii Gaudium» [The importance of Dialogue in the «Evangelii Gaudium»]. *La Civiltà Cattolica*, 165(3936), 600-605.

Mumford, M. D., Zaccaro, S. J., Connelly, M. S., & Marks, M. A. (2000). Leadership skills: Conclusions and future directions. *The Leadership Quarterly, 11*(1), 155-170.

Mumford, M., & Van Doom, J. (2001). The leadership of Pragmatism: Reconsidering Franklin in the Age of Charisma. *The Leadership Quarterly, 12*(1), 279-310.

Mumford, T., Campion, M., & Morgeson, F. (2007). The leadership skills strataplex: Leadership skill requirements across organizational levels. *Leadership Quarterly, 18*, 154-166.

Myers, T. (2005). Developing a Culture of Student Leadership. *Teacher,* 3(1), 26-29.

Neuberger, O. (1990). Führung (ist) symbolisiert. Plädoyer für eine sinnvolle Führungsforschung [Leadership is symbolized (symbolizes). Plea for meaningful leadership research]. In W. G. Wiendieck G, *Führung im Wandel. Neue Perspektiven für Führungsforschung und Führungspraxis (pp. 89-130)*. Ferdinand Enke.

Neuberger, O. (1995). *Führen und Geführt werden [To lead and to be led]*. Ferdinand Enke.

Neuberger, O. (2002). *Führen und führen lassen. Ansätze, Ergebnisse und Kritik der Führungsforschung [To lead and to let lead. Approaches, findings and critique of leadership research]*. Lucius & Lucius,.

Neumann, J., Kellner, K., & Dawson-Shepherd, A. (1997). *Developing organisational consultancy*. Routledge.

Northouse, P. (2019). *Leadership: theory and practice* (10th Edition ed.). Sage Publications.

Nuthall, G. (2000). El razonamiento y el aprendizaje del educando en el aula [The Student's Reasoning and Learning in the Classroom]. In B. J. Biddle, T. Good, & I. Goodson (Eds.), *La enseñanza y los profesores. 2: La enseñanza y sus contextos* [Teaching and Teachers. 2: Teaching and its Contexts] (pp. 19-114). Paidós.

O'Connell, P. (2014). A simplified framework for 21st century leader development. *The Leadership Quarterly*, 25(2), 183-203. doi: 10.1016/j.leaqua.2013.06.001

O'Connor, P. M., & Quinn, L. (2004). Organizational capacity for leadership. In C. D. McCauley, & E. Van Velsor (Eds.), *The Center for Creative Leadership Handbook of Leadership Development* (pp. 417-437). Jossey-Bass.

Offermann, L. R., Kennedy, J. K., & Wirtz, P. W. (1994). Implicit leadership theories: Content, structure and generalizability. *Leadership Quarterly, 5*, 43-58.

Ololube, N. P. Egbezor, D.E., Kpolovie, P. J. & Amaele, S. (2012). Theoretical debates on school effectiveness research: lessons for Third World education development agendas. In N. P. Ololube & P. J. Kpolovie (eds.), *Educational management in developing economies: cases "n" school effectiveness and quality improvement* (pp. 1-18). Lambert Academic Publisher (LAP), Germany.

Orazi, D., Good, L., Robin, M., Van Wanrooy, B., Butar, I., Olsen, J., & Gahan, P. (2014). *Workplace leadership a review of prior research.* The University of Melbourne, Centre for Workplace Leadership.

Parry, K., & Bryman, A. (2006). Leadership in organizations. In S. Clegg, C. Hardy, T. Lawrence & W. Nord (Eds.), *The SAGE Handbook of Organization Studies.* Sage.

Patton, M., & Patton, M. (2002). *Qualitative Research and evaluation methods.*: Sage.

Pearce, C., & Conger, J. (2012). *Shared Leadership: Reframing the Hows and Whys of Leadership.* Sage.

Petrie, N. (2014). *Future trends in Leadership Development.* San Diego, CA: Center for Creative Leadership.

Pfeffer, J. (2015). *Leadership BS: fixing workplaces and careers one truth at a time.* Harper Press.

Philip, T. M., & Garcia, A. (2013). The importance of still teaching the *iGeneration*: New technologies and the centrality of pedagogy. *Harvard Educational Review*, 83(2), 300-319.

Phillips, J. S., & Lord, R. G. (1981). Causal attributions and perceptions of leadership. *Organizational Behavior and Human Performance, 28*, 143-163.

Piaget, J. (1954). *Construction of Reality in the Child.* Basic Books.

-----------. (1971). The Origin of Intelligence in Children. WW Norton & Co.

Pinchao, L. (2016). Hacia una práctica evaluativa que favorezca el aprendizaje y mejore la enseñanza [Towards an Evaluative Practice that Favors Learning and Improves Teaching]. *UNIMAR*, 34(1), 57-69.

Posner, G., Strike, K., Hewson, P., & Gertzog, W. (1982). Accommodation of a scientific conception: toward a theory of conceptual change. *Science Education*, 66(2), 211- 227.

Ratzinger, J. (2004). *Caminos de Jesucristo* [Ways of Jesus Christ]. Cristiandad.

—————. (1 de marzo de 2008). *Mensaje del Santo Padre Benedicto XVI a Don Pascual Chávez, Rector Mayor de los Salesianos de Don Bosco con motivo del XXVI Capítulo General de la Sociedad de San Francisco de Sales.* [Message of the Holy Father Benedict XVI to Don Pascual Chávez, Rector Major of the Salesians of Don Bosco on the occasion of the XXVI General Chapter of the Society of Saint Francis de Sales]. Retrieve from https://w2.vatican.va/content/benedict-xvi/es/letters/2008/documents/hf_ben-xvi_let_20080301_capitolo-salesani.html

Reave, L. (2005). Spiritual values and practices related to leadership effectiveness. *The Leadership Quarterly, 16*, 655-687.

Ricoeur, P. (2004). *Finitud y culpabilidad* [Finitude and Guilt]. Trotta.

Roberts, R. (Julio, 2018). *12 Principles of Modern Military Leadership.* Retrieve from https://www.army.mil/article/208766/12_principles_of_modern_military_leadershi p_part_1

Rodríguez, A. (2007). *Fragilidad en Esperanza. La Vulnerabilidad. Experiencia Humana: Posible Relectura de Sentido* [Fragility in Hope. Vulnerability. Human Experience: Possible Rereading of Meaning] [Master Thesis]. Universidad Iberoamericana.

—————. (2014, September). *Liderazgo preventivo en la Universidad* [Preventive Leadership in the University]. Presentación en el VI Congreso Iberoamericano de Pedagogía, Santiago de Chile, Chile. Retrieve from: http://ediciones.ucsh.cl/ojs/index.php?journal=congresodepedagogia&page=artcle&op=view&path%5B%5D=431&path%5B%5D=317

—————. (2015). Liderazgo Preventivo en la Universidad. Una experiencia plausible [Preventive Leadership in the University. A Plausible Experience]. *Alteridad, 10*(1), 58-85. doi: 10.17163/alt.v10n1.2015.05

—————. (2016). Education as Fusion of horizons. *Vitam, 2*(2), 5-22.

—————. (2017, Oct-Dic). Vulnerables sin salir de casa. *Metapolítica, 21*(99), 35-39.

—————. (2018). *Educating from the Heart. Salesian Leadership in the University.* Ediciones Navarra – Universidad Salesiana A.C.

—————. (2018). *Liderazgo Preventivo en la Universidad* [Preventive Leadership in the University]. Ediciones Navarro.

—————. (2020, Abril 16). Educar en tiempo de virus [Educating in Virues Time]. *Revista EDURAMA, 9*, 28-30.

Rodríguez, A., & Rodríguez, Y. (2015). Metaphors for today's leadership: VUCA world, millennial and "Cloud Leaders." *Journal of Management Development, 34*(7), 854-866.

Rodríguez, A. & Sánchez Tapia, S.G. (2020). *Ser Preventivos con 15 acciones* [Be Preventive with 15 Wrokshops]. IMGRA.

Rodríguez, A., & Sanchez, F. (2017). Liderazgo Humanista y Educación. Un acercamiento a Lonergan y Vygotsky [Humanist Leadership and Education. An Approach to Lonergan and Vygostsky]. *Salesianum*, 79(1), 155-174.

Rorty, R. (1991). *Contingencia, ironía y solidaridad* [Contingency, Irony and Solidarity]. Paidós.

Sala, F. (2009). Ciudadanía hermenéutica (un enfoque que rebasa el multiculturalismo de la aldea global en la sociedad del conocimiento) [Hermeneutical Citizenship (An Approach that goes Beyond the Multiculturalism of the Global Village in the Knowledge Society)]. *Andamios*, 6(11), 235-255.

Salesianos de Don Bosco. (1971-1972). *Capitolo Generale Speciale 20. Nouve Constituzione* [Special General Chapter 20. New Constitutions]. LAS.

------------. (1996). *Proyecto de Vida de los Salesianos de Don Bosco* [Project of Life of the Salesians of Don Bosco]. LAS.

------------. (1990). *Capitolo Generale 23. Educazione a la fede.* [General Chapter 23. Education on Faith]. LAS

------------. (2009). *Constitutions of the Society of Saint Francis de Sales.* Kristu Jyoti Publications.

------------. (2016). *Reference Frame of the Salesian Youth Ministry.* LAS.

Salomon, G. (2001). No hay distribución sin la cognición de los individuos. Un enfoque interactivo dinámico [There is No Distribution Without the Cognition of Individuals. A Dynamic Interactive Approach]. In G. Salomon (Ed.), *Cogniciones distribuidas. Consideraciones psicológicas y educativas* [Distributed Cognitions. Psychological and Educational Considerations] (pp. 153-184). Amorrortu.

Sánchez, F. (2011). "La noción de conciencia" propuesta por Bernand Lonergan en Insight ["The Notion of Conscience" Proposed by Bernard Lonergan in Insight]. *Pensar y Educar*, 4, 113-125.

Scandura, T. A., & Lankau, M. J. (1996). Developing diverse leaders: A leader–member exchange approach. *The Leadership Quarterly*, 7(2), 243-263.

Schoeberlein, D. (2015). *Mindfulness para enseñar y aprender. Estrategias prácticas para maestros y educadores* [Mindfulness to Teach and Learn. Practical Strategies for Teachers and Educators] (A. Pareja, Trad.). Gaia Ediciones.

Schoorman, D., Mayer, R., & Davis, J. H. (2007). An integrative model of organizatiomal trust: past, present and future. *Academy of Management Review*, 32(2), 344-354.

Schriesheim, C. A., Castro, S., & Cogliser, C. C. (1999). Leader-member exchange (LMX) research: a comprehensive review of theory, measurement, and data-analytic practices. *Leadership Quarterly, 10*, 63-113.

Shamir, B. (2007). From passive recipients to active co-producers: followers' roles in the leadership process. In B. Shamir, R. Pillai, M. Bligh, & M. Uhl-Bien (Eds.). *Follower-Centered Perspectives on Leadership: A Tribute to the Memory of James R. Meindl* (pp. IX-XXXIX). Inform. Age

Shamir, B., & Eilam, G. (2005). "What's your story?" A life- stories approach to authentic leadership development. *The Leadership Quarterly*, 16(3), 395-417.

Shields, C. M. (2009). Leveling the playing field in racialised contexts: Leaders speaking out about difficult issues. *International Journal of Educational Administration*, 37(3), 55-70.

Smircich, L., & Morgan, G. (1982). Leadership: the management of meaning, *Journal of Applied Behavioral Science*, 18(3), 257-273.

Snyder, C. R., Irving, L., & Anderson, J. R. (1991). Hope and health: Measuring the will and the ways. In C. R. Snyder, & D. R. (Eds.), *Handbook of social and clinical psychology: The health perspective (pp. 285-305)*. Elmsford, NY: Pergamon Press.

Snyder, C. R., Rand, K. L., & Sigmon, D. R. (2002). Hope theory: A member of the positive psychology family. In C. R. Snyder, & S. J. (Eds.), *Handbook of positive psychology (p. 257–276)*. Oxford University Press.

Soares, M. M., Jacobs, K., Wegge, J., Jungmann, F., Liebermann, S., Shemla, M., & Schmidt, K. (2012). What makes age diverse teams effective? Results from a six- year research program. *Work*, 41, 5145-5151.

Sosik, J. J., Godshalk, V. M., & Yammarino, F. J. (2004). Transformational leadership, learning goal orientation, and expectations for career success in mentor–protege' relationships: A multiple levels of analysis perspective. *Leadership Quarterly, 15*, 241-261.

Spahr, P. (2018, May 08). *STU Online*. Retrieved from http://online.stu.edu/transactional-leadership/

Spears, L. C. (2004). The understanding and practice of servant leadership. In L. C. Spears, & M. Lawrence (Eds.). *Practicing Servant-Leadership: Succeeding Through Trust, Bravery, and Forgiveness* (pp. 167-200), Jossey-Bass.

Spendlove, M. (2007). Competencies for effective leadership in higher education. *International Journal of Educational Management*, 21(5), 407-417.

Spillane, J. (2006). *Distributed Leadership*. Jossey-Bass.

Stajkovic, A., & Luthans, F. (1998). Self-Efficacy and Work-Related Performance: A Meta-Analysis. *Psychological Bulletin, 124*(2), 240-261.

Stamateas, B. (2015). *Más gente tóxica. Cómo son los que te hacen mal para sentirse bien* [More Toxic People. How Are Those Who Hurt You, To Feel Good]. Ediciones B.

Starr, J. P. (March 21, 2019). *Can we keep SEL on Course?* Retrieve on March 2019 from Phi Delta Kappan. The Professional Journal for Educators: https://www.kappanonline.org/category/col-starr/

Stein, J. (2013). The New Greatest Generation. Why Millennials Will Save Us All. *Time*, 181(19), 26-34.

Stella, P. (1973). Don Bosco e le trasformazioni sociali e religiosa del suo tempo [Don Bosco And the Social and Religious Transformations of his Time]. In Vol. *La famiglia salesiana riflette sulla sua vocazione nella Chiesa di oggi*, IV. Torino- Leumann, Elle Di Ci.

Stentz, J., Clark, V., & Matkin, G. (2012). Applying mixed methods to leadership research: a review of current practices. *The Leadership Quarterly*, 1(1), 1-11.

Stogdill, R. M. (1950). Leadership, membership and organization. *Psychological Bulletin, 47*(1), 1-14.

Storey, J. (2004). *Leadership in organizations -current issues and key trends*. Routledge.

Sweeney, R. (2012, May). *Millennial Behaviors and Higher Education Focus Group Results. How are Millennials different from previous generations at the same age?* [PowerPoint]. Retrieve from http://library1.njit.edu/staff-folders/sweeney/

Sy, T., Côté, S., & Saavedra, R. (2005). The contagious leader: impact of the leader's mood on the mood of group members, group affective tone, and group processes. *Journal of Applied Psychology, 90*, 295-305.

Taylor, E. W. (2006). The challenge of teaching for change. *New Directions for Adult and Continuing Education*, 112, 91-95.

Tee, E. Y. (2015). The emotional link: leadership and the role of implicit and explicit emotional contagion processes across multiple organizational levels. *The Leadership Quarterly 26*(4), 654-670.

Tosi, H. L., Misangyi, V. F., Fanelli, A., Waldman, D. A., & Yammarino, F. J. (2004). CEO charisma, compensation; and firm performance. *Leadership Quarterly, 15*, 405-420.

Turquet, P. (1974). Leadership: The individual and the group. In J. H. Gibbard, & L. W. (Eds.), *Analysis of groups* (pp. 349-371). Jossey-Bass.

Twenge, J. M. (2013). Teaching generation me. *Teaching of Psychology*, 40(1), 66-69. doi:10.1177/0098628312465870

Tyson, L., Venville, G., Harrison, A., & Treagust, D. (1997). A multidimensional framework for interpreting conceptual change events in the classroom. *Science Education*, 8(14), 387-404.

Uhl-Bien, M., Marion, R., & McKelvey, B. (2007). Complexity leadership theory: Shifting leadership from the industrial age to the knowledge era. *The Leadership Quarterly, 18*(4), 298-318.

Uhl-Bien, M. (2006). Relational leadership theory: exploring the social processes of leadership and organizing. *The Leadership Quarterly*, 17, 654-676.

Useem, M. (2007, March 22). *Spotlight*. Retrieved from: https://www.researchgate.net/profile/Michael_Useem/publication/47677352_Four_lessons_in_adaptive_leadership/links/0046352442c576b64c000000/Four-lessons-in-adaptive-leadership.pdf

Van Dyne, L., & Ang, S. (2006). Getting more than you expect: global leader initiative to span structural holes and reputational effectiveness. In W. Mobley, & E. Weldon (Eds.), *Advances in Global Leadership* (pp. 101-122). Elsevier.

Van Vugt, M., & Ahuja, A. (2012). *Naturally selected: The evolutionary science of leadership*. HarperCollins.

Vallejos, S. (15 de febrero de 2019). *Página 12* [Page 12]. Retrieve from https://www.pagina12.com.ar/175205-el-mundo-segun-los-centennials

Vallín, P. (July 29, 2018). `Centennilas´, la salvación del mundo ['Centennials', The Salvation of the World]. *Magazine edigital*. Retrieve from: http://www.magazinedigital.com/historias/reportajes/centennials-salvacion-mundo

Vargas Llosa, M. (2012). *La civilización del espectáculo* [The Civilization of the Spectacle]. Editorial Alfaguara.

Vecchi, J. E. (1992, May). *El Sistema Preventivo. 100 años de la presencia Salesiana en México* [The Preventive System. 100 Years of the Salesian Presence in Mexico]. México, México: [Conferencia].

---------------. (1995, October/December). Indications for a process of growth in Salesian Spirituality. Some key points in the teaching of Fr. Egidio Viganó. *Acts of the General Council of the Salesian Society of St John Bosco*, 354(76). Editrice S.D.B.

---------------. (1997a). *For you I study...(C 14) Satisfactory Preparation of the Confreres and the quality of our educative work.* 361(77). Editrice S.D.B.

---------------. (1997b). *Nuove poverta, missione salesiana e significativita* [New Poverty, Salesian Mission and Significance]. Atti dal Concilio Generale, 359(77). Editrice S.D.B.

Vidal, R. (2017, August-September). ¿Cuáles son los principales retos de la educación superior en México? [What are the Main Challenges For Higher Education In Mexico?] *El mundo de la Educación*, 1(1), págs. 14-15.

Viganó, E. (1978, July/December). Salesian educational project. *Acts of the General Council of the Salesian Society of St John Bosco*, 290(59). Editrice S.D.B.

-------------. (1988, April/June). The Letter "Juvenum Patris" of his Holiness John Paul II. *Acts of the General Council of the Salesian Society of St John Bosco*, 325(69). Editrice S.D.B.

-------------. (1991, July/September). New education. *Acts of the General Council of the Salesian Society of St John Bosco*, 337(72). Editrice S.D.B.

-------------. (1989, January/March). The Pope speaks to us of Don Bosco. *Acts of the General Council of the Salesian Society of St John Bosco*, 328(70). Editrice S.D.B.

-------------. (1993, April/June). Educating to the faith in the school. *Acts of the General Council of the Salesian Society of St John Bosco*, 344 (74). Editrice S.D.B.

Villa, J. R., Howell, J., Dorfman, P., & Daniel, D. (2003). Problems with detecting moderators in leadership research using moderated multiple regression. *The Leadership Quarterly*, 14, 3-23.

Von Glasersfeld, E. (1998). Cognition, construction of knowledge and teaching. In M. Matthews (Ed.), *Constructivism in science education: a philosophical examination* (pp. 11-30). Kluwer Academy Publishers.

-----------------------. (2013). *Radical constructivism: a way of knowing and learning.* The Falmer Press.

Vygotsky, L. S. (1978). *Mind in society: the development of higher psychological processes.* (M. Cole, V. Steiner, E. Souberman, Eds., M. Cole, V. Steiner, & E. Souberman, Trans.) Harvard University Press.

——————————. (1986). *Thought and language.* Cambridge, MIT Press.

——————————. (1987). *The collected works of L.S. Vygotsky: Problems of general psychology* (Vol. 1). Plenum Press.

Waldman, D. A., Yammarino, F. J., & Avolio, B. J. (1990). A multiple level investigation of personnel ratings. *Personnel Psychology, 43*, 811-835.

Walumbwa, F. O., Avolio, B., Gardner, W. L., Wernsing, T. S., & Peterson, S. J. (2008). Authentic leadership: Development and validation of a theory-based measure. *Journal of Management,* 34(1), 89-126.

Wartofsky, M. W. (1979). *Models. Representation and the Scientific Understanding* (Boston Studies in the Philosophy and History of Science). Springer.

Wassenaar, C. L., & Pearce, C. L. (2012). The nature of shared leadership. In D. V. Day, y J. Antonakis (Eds.), *The nature of leadership* (pp. 363-389). Sage.

Watson, J. M., & Strayer, D. (2010). Supertaskers: Profiles in extraordinary multi- taking ability. *Psychonomic Bulletin & Review,* 17, 479-485.

Weick, K., & Roberts, K. (1993). Collective mind in organizations: Heedful interrelating on flight decks. *Administrative Science Quarterly, 38*(3), 357-381.

Werhane, P., Hartman, L., Moberg, D., Englehardt, E., Pritchard, M., & Parmar, B. (2011). Social constructivism, mental models, and problems of obedience. *Journal of Business Ethics,* 100(1), 103-108. doi:10.1007/s10551-011-0767-3

White, R. F. (2011). Toward an integrated theory of leadership. *Politics and the Life Sciences,* 30(11), 116-121.

Wright, D. (1999, Autumn). Fundamentals. *Independence,* 25-26.

Xiao, Y., Seagull, F., Mackenzie, C., Klein, K., & Ziegert, J. (2008). Adaptation of team communication patterns. Exploring the effects of leadership at a distance: task urgency, and shared team experience. In S. Weisband (Ed.), *Leadership at a Distance: Research in Technologically - Supported Work* (pp. 71- 96). Erlbaum.

Yammarino, F. J., & Dubinsky, A. J. (1990). Salesperson performance and managerially controllable factors: An investigation of individual and work group effects. *Journal of Management,* 16, 87-106.

Yukl, G. (1999). An evaluation of conceptual weaknesses in transformational and charismatic leadership theories. *The Leadership Quarterly, 10*, 285-305.

Yukl, G. A. (2006). *Leadership in Organizations.* Pearson/Prentice Hall.

Zaccaro, S. (2007). Trait-based perspectives of leadership. *American Psychologist, 62*(1), 6-16.

Zaccaro, S. J., Mumford, M. D., Connelly, M. S., Marks, M. A., & Gilbert, J. A. (2000). Assessment of leader problem-solving capabilities. *The Leadership Quarterly, 11*(1), 37-64.

Zaccaro, S. J., & Bader, P. (2003). E-leadership and the challenges of leading E-teams: minimizing the bad and maximizing the good. *Organizational Dynamics*, 31, 377- 387.

Zaccaro, S., Kemp, C., & Bader, P. (2004). *Leader traits and attributes.* Sage Publications.

Zigurs, I. (2003). Leadership in virtual teams: oxymoron or opportunity? *Organizational Dynamics*, 31, 339-351.

www.ingramcontent.com/pod-product-compliance
Lightning Source LLC
Chambersburg PA
CBHW071700160426
43195CB00012B/1529